Principles and Service
of Automotive Air Conditioning

Billy C. Langley

Reston Publishing Company, Inc.
A Prentice-Hall Company
Reston, Virginia

Library of Congress Cataloging in Publication Data

Langley, Billy C.
    Principles and service of automotive air conditioning.

    Includes index.
    1. Automobiles—Air conditioning.   2. Automobiles—
Air conditioning—Maintenance and repair. I. Title.
TL271.5.L36 1984   629.2'77   83-16134
ISBN 0-8359-5638-5
ISBN 0-8359-5615-6 (pbk.)

© 1984 by Reston Publishing Company, Inc.
A Prentice-Hall Company
Reston, Virginia 22090

10 9 8 7 6 5 4 3 2 1

Printed in the United States of America

Contents

11 AUTOMOTIVE HEATING SYSTEMS   233

Preface

Principles and Service of Automotive Air Conditioning is intended to be used as a curriculum guide, a textbook, a course for independent study, or a reference manual. It covers the practical fundamentals and recommended service and safety procedures used in industry. It serves as a comprehensive textbook for the beginning student and a valuable reference for the experienced service technician.

The text consists of 11 chapters, each covering a specific area of this exciting and rewarding industry. Each chapter begins with an introduction to that particular phase and advances through recommended service operations where applicable. Safety procedures are integrated into the text. Review questions that cover the minimum amount of material with which the reader should be familiar conclude each chapter.

Principles and Service of Automotive Air Conditioning provides not only the necessary theory for the student and service technician alike, but examples to help reinforce that theory as well. Operating instructions from various manufacturers who provide service and/or maintenance are incorporated wherever practical.

The first three chapters of the book are devoted to the basic principles of matter, heat and temperature, and work and force, followed by a chapter on refrigerants and lubricants. The next three chapters cover operation of automotive air conditioning systems, types of control systems, and descriptions of control system components. Specific procedures for system maintenance and service, diagnosis and trouble-shooting, and component repair and replacement are provided in the next three chapters. A chapter on automotive heating systems concludes the book.

Everyone knows what air conditioning can do for us; however, very few understand how or why it works. An air-conditioner operates very much like a refrigerator; therefore, we must know the basics of refrigeration in order to understand how an air-conditioning unit functions.

Everyone knows that a boiling tea kettle is hot and that a refrigerator is cold. Beyond this, most people become confused. Actually, there is no such thing as cold; there is merely the absence of heat, just as darkness is the absence of light. To make things cold, we simply remove some of the heat. Thus, cold is a relative term. The purpose of a refrigerator, or an air-conditioning unit, is to remove the unwanted heat from the substance we are attempting to cool.

REFRIGERATION

Refrigeration may be defined as a process of removing heat from an enclosed space or material and maintaining that space or material at a temperature below its surroundings. As heat is removed, a space or material becomes colder than its surroundings. The more heat that is removed from an enclosed area, the colder an object inside becomes. A cold object contains less heat than a warmer object of the same material and weight.

Refrigeration is the process used to cool perishable foods and vegetables so that they remain edible for a longer period of time. It is also used in air-conditioning work to cool the air and remove some of the moisture, to make the inside of a space more comfortable, or to aid in a given industrial process.

In practice, refrigeration is accomplished by the circulation of a fluid known as the *refrigerant.* The refrigerant is circulated through the system by a com-

— 1 —

Physical Properties of Matter

pressor, which increases the pressure on the vaporous refrigerant and causes it to flow to the condenser (see Figure 1-1). In the condenser, the refrigerant is cooled and liquified. It then flows to the flow-control device, where the flow is metered and the pressure is reduced. The refrigerant then flows into the evaporator, where it boils, by picking up heat from the space being cooled, and changes to a vapor. The compressor then draws the refrigerant vapor from the evaporator, and the cycle is started again.

It should be evident from this brief and simplified explanation that you need a basic knowledge of physics and mechanical principles to be successful in this industry on any level. Therefore, we will introduce the following theories to provide a more solid foundation upon which to build your career.

COMMON ELEMENTS

There are more than 100 known basic elements. Of these, 92 are natural ele-

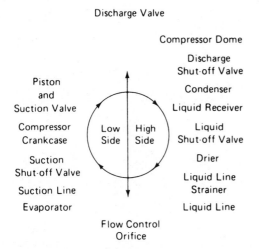

Discharge Valve

Compressor Dome

Discharge
Shut-off Valve

Piston
and
Suction Valve

Condenser

Liquid Receiver

Compressor
Crankcase

Low
Side

High
Side

Liquid
Shut-off Valve

Suction
Shut-off Valve

Drier

Suction Line

Liquid Line
Strainer

Evaporator

Liquid Line

Flow Control
Orifice

FIGURE 1-1.   High and low side diagram.

ments; the rest are synthetic. Everything in nature is made up of these basic elements. In most cases, more than one element is combined to make a substance. The following are some of the most common of these elements.

Aluminum, Cadmium, Chromium, Copper, Iron, Tin, Tungsten, and Zinc. These elements are known as metals and are generally used by themselves. However, a few are sometimes found in compounds or mixtures, called alloys. These elements normally exist as solids.

Calcium, Potassium, Silicon, Sodium, and Sulfur. These elements generally exist in solid form. They are found in many materials and almost always in chemical combination with other elements.

Carbon. This is the principal element found in coal, gasoline, natural gas, oil, and paper. It is also found in many gases, such as carbon dioxide, methyl chloride, and the fluorocarbon refrigerants used in air-conditioning and refrigeration units. Carbon exists as a solid at atmospheric pressures and temperatures.

Nitrogen. Air is made up of several gases. The gas nitrogen constitutes about 78% of the air in the atmosphere. Nitrogen is very important for the proper growth and life of plants.

Oxygen. About 21% of the air is oxygen. It is a gas and is essential to all animal and human life. Because oxygen is an active element, it combines readily with most other elements to form oxides or more complex chemicals.

Hydrogen. This element is found in many compounds. It is especially important in acids, fuels, and oils. It is rarely found alone in nature. Hydrogen is an extremely light gas; when it is burned, water is formed. Burning is the process of properly combining oxygen and hydrogen.

ATOMS

Each element in nature is made up of billions of tiny particles known as atoms. An atom is the smallest particle of which an element is made and which still maintains the characteristics of that element. It is so small that it cannot be seen even with a powerful microscope. For our purposes, an atom is considered to be invisible and unchangeable. It cannot be divided by ordinary means. Atoms of all elements are different; that is, iron is composed of iron atoms and hydrogen is composed of hydrogen atoms.

MOLECULES

The molecule is the next larger particle of a material. It consists of one or more atoms. When a molecule contains atoms of only one kind, it is said to be a molecule of that element. Usually a molecule of an element contains only one atom. However, it can contain several atoms of the same kind. For example, a molecule of iron contains only one iron atom, while a molecule of sulphur usually contains eight sulphur atoms. A small piece of any element consists of billions of molecules. Each of these consists of one or more atoms of that element.

CHEMICAL COMPOUNDS

The molecule of a chemical compound consists of two or more atoms of different elements. This combining of different elements causes the material to become entirely different. The new material does not resemble either of the elements that make it up. For example, an atom of water contains two atoms of hydrogen and one atom of oxygen.

The refrigerants used in air-conditioning and refrigeration units are examples of chemical compounds.

Example 1: A molecule of Refrigerant-12, a colorless gas, consists of one carbon atom, two chlorine atoms, and two fluorine atoms.

Example 2: A molecule of Refrigerant-22 consists of one carbon atom, one hydrogen atom, and two fluorine atoms.

Many of the substances used in our daily living are considered to be compounds. Some of these substances are table salt, baking soda, and calcium chloride.

Molecular Motion. As we have learned, all matter is made up of small particles called molecules. These molecules may exist in three states: solids, liquids, and gases. Each molecule can be broken down into atoms.

In this chapter we will study the theory of molecular movement and action as it is involved in air-conditioning and refrigeration work. A molecule is the smallest particle into which a compound can be reduced before it is broken down into its original elements; for instance, water is made up of two elements, hydrogen and oxygen. The movement or vibration of molecules determines the amount of heat present in a given body. This heat is caused by the friction of the molecules as they rub against each other. The attraction of molecules to one another is reduced as the temperature increases. When a substance is cooled to absolute zero, all molecular motion stops. At this temperature the substance contains no heat.

All molecules vary in weight, shape, and size. They tend to cling together to form a substance. The substance, therefore, will assume the character of the combining molecules. Because these particles are capable of moving around, the substance formed will be, to a degree, dependent on the space between them. The molecules in a solid have less space between them than either in a liquid or a gas. A liquid has more space between the molecules than a solid and less than a gas. A gas has more space between the molecules than either a solid or a liquid. Any particular substance can be made to exist in any of these three forms, depending on the temperature and pressure.

SOLIDS

When a substance is in the solid state, it may be defined as having the ability to retain its shape when supported (see Figure 1-2). All its molecules are identical in size and shape and maintain their relative positions. The molecules in all substances are constantly vibrating. The speed of this vibrating motion depends on the substance's temperature. A higher temperature causes a more rapid vibration.

The earth's gravity acts more strongly on solids than on gases or liquids. There-

FIGURE 1-2.   A solid retains its shape.

fore, a solid must be supported or it will fall in a vertical direction. The force that supports a solid is always in the upward direction (see Figure 1-3). When the solid substance is no longer moving, its weight and the supporting force are said to be in equilibrium.

LIQUIDS

When a substance is in the liquid state, it may be defined as having the ability to assume the shape of the container (see Figure 1-4). The force exerted by the liquid is in the outward or downward direction. The nearer the bottom of the container, the stronger the force. This changing force is due to the weight of the substance and the earth's magnetic force.

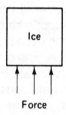

Force

FIGURE 1-3.   Force acting on a solid.

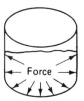

FIGURE 1-4. Force of liquid on a container.

The molecules in a liquid are constantly vibrating, as they are in a solid. However, the vibration is greater because the liquid molecules have less attraction to one another. The speed of molecular vibration is dependent upon the substance temperature; the greater the temperature, the greater the vibration. As liquid molecules become warmer, they take up more space, become lighter, and move toward the top of the liquid, where the force is less. Some of the molecules will break through the liquid surface and escape into the atmosphere. This is called *evaporation*.

GASES

When a substance is in the gaseous state, it may be defined as having the ability to dissipate or escape if not confined in a sealed container (see Figure 1-5). The molecules in a gaseous substance have little attraction for one another or for other substances. Therefore, they are free to move quite violently. Gaseous molecules travel in a straight line, bouncing off one another and the walls of the container in the process.

CHANGE OF STATE

There are three states of matter: solid, liquid, and gas. With the addition or

removal of a sufficient amount of heat, a substance may be caused to change its state. For example, the three states of water are ice, water, and steam. When a specific amount of heat is added to ice, it will eventually change to water, and then into steam. When a specific amount of heat is removed from steam, it will change into water, and then into ice.

DENSITY

Density may be defined as the weight per unit volume of a substance and is ordinarily taken as the *weight per cubic foot.*

Under ordinary circumstances, most substances expand when heated and contract when cooled. However, a few liquids vary from this rule.

Example: When water is cooled, it contracts until the temperature is lowered to 39°F. At this temperature, the water starts to expand. Therefore, the water is at its greatest density at this temperature. As the temperature is lowered to the freezing temperature, the water expands further and ice is formed at 32°F. Because of this, the density of ice is less than that of water.

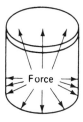

FIGURE 1-5. Force of a gas on a container.

REVIEW QUESTIONS

1. In what three states does matter exist?

2. In what direction is the force exerted by a gas?

3. What causes a change of state of a substance?

4. Define refrigeration.

5. What are the principal elements in air?

6. Define an atom.

7. How many atoms does a molecule of an element contain?

8. Define a molecule of a chemical compound.

9. What determines the amount of heat present in a given body?

10. Name the three states of matter.

All substances in nature contain some heat. Theoretically, the lowest possible temperature that can be reached is 459 degrees Fahrenheit (°F) below zero. Because we are not able to remove all the heat from a substance, we must think in terms of heat transfer from one object to another when we talk about controlling the temperature of that object.

HEAT

Two words that are familiar to everyone are "heat" and "cold." Everyone knows that a boiling tea kettle is hot and that ice is cold. However, most people do not understand the meaning of cold. Actually, there is no such thing as cold. "Cold" is a relative term indicating an absence of heat. When we say something is cold, we are saying that there is an absence of heat, just as darkness is the absence of light. Therefore, to make something cold, heat must be removed. This is the purpose of air conditioning and refrigeration.

Heat Movement. Heat is measured by what it does to certain substances. If a container of water is placed on a stove and the burner is lighted, heat will be applied to the water (see Figure 2-1). As heat is applied to the container, the mercury column in the thermometer will rise, indicating that the water is changing temperature as heat is added by the flame.

The application of heat to a substance, in addition to causing an increase in temperature, may also cause a change of state of that substance; that is, it may change from a solid to a liquid or from a liquid to a gas.

There is a difference between the meaning of the words *heat* and *temperature*. Heat is a measure of quantity, while temperature is a measure of de-

—— 2 ——

Heat
and Temperature

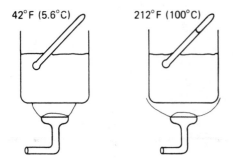

FIGURE 2-1.   Sensible heat.

gree or intensity of heat. Therefore, the terms heat and temperature should not be confused. Two bodies may have the same temperature, yet because of the difference in their volume and heat-absorbing capacity, their heat content may be entirely different. For example, a quart and a gallon of water may be at the same temperature, but the gallon will contain four times as much heat as the quart (see Figure 2-2).

British Thermal Unit. The unit used for measuring heat quantity is the Btu (British thermal unit). A Btu is defined as the

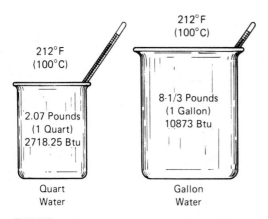

FIGURE 2-2.   Heat content of different quantities.

amount of heat required to raise the temperature of one pound of pure water 1°F. The Btu measures the quantity of heat and has nothing to do with the intensity or degree of heat. The number of Btu's gives the amount of heat in a substance, while degrees Fahrenheit gives the intensity or strength.

Heat Intensity (Temperature). The strength or intensity of heat is measured by a thermometer and is indicated by degrees Fahrenheit or Celsius. Fahrenheit and Celsius are the most commonly used thermometer scales. The scales are divided into degrees and are read as °F or °C. Figure 2-3 shows the relationship between the two thermometers. On the Fahrenheit scale, absolute zero occurs at –460°; on the Celsius scale absolute zero is at –278.3°.

It should be noted that there is a considerable difference in temperature between any certain number of degrees on the two different scales. It is sometimes necessary to change one type of temperature measurement to the other. On the Fahrenheit scale, there are 180° between the freezing and boiling points, while on the Celsius scale there are only 100° between these two points. Notice also that on the Fahrenheit scale 32° is the freezing point and 212° is the boiling point of water. On the Celsius scale the freezing point of water is 0°, while the boiling point is 100°. Therefore, the Celsius degree is 1.8 times larger than the Fahrenheit degree. In converting Celsius degrees to Fahrenheit degrees, multiply the number of degrees Celsius by 1.8 and then add 32. The 32 is added because the Fahrenheit zero degree is 32° below the freezing point of water, which is the same as zero degrees on the Celsius scale.

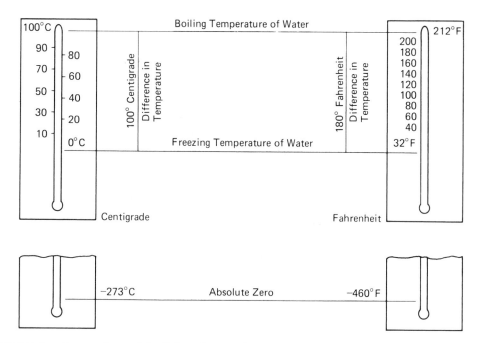

FIGURE 2-3.   Comparison of the Fahrenheit and Centigrade thermometer scales.

Heat Flow. It is important to know that heat always flows from a warmer object to a colder object, much the same as water always flows downhill. The rate of heat flow depends on the temperature difference between the two objects. For example, consider two objects lying side by side in an insulated box. One of the objects weighs 1 lb and has a temperature of 400°F, while the second object weighs 1000 lb and has a temperature of 390°F. The heat content of the larger object will be far greater than that of the smaller object. However, because the temperatures are different, heat will flow from the smaller object to the larger object until their temperatures are the same.

The three ways that heat travels are (1) conduction, (2) convection, and (3) radiation.

Conduction is the flow of heat through an object or between two touching objects (see Figure 2-4). This is a very efficient method of transferring heat because very little heat is lost in the

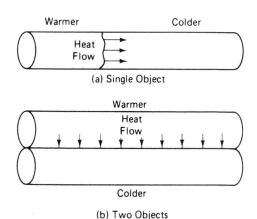

FIGURE 2-4.   Heat transfer by conduction.

process. If you have ever heated one end of a piece of metal and then touched the other end with your bare hand, you felt the heat that had been conducted from the heated end of the metal.

Convection is the flow of heat by use of a fluid, either gas or liquid. The fluids most commonly used with this method are air and water. The heated fluids expand and become less dense and rise, while the cooler fluids contract and become more dense and fall, thus creating a continuous movement of the fluid. Another example of convection is the warm-air heating furnace. Air is heated in the furnace and blown into a room to heat the objects in the room by convection (see Figure 2-5).

Radiation is the transfer of heat by wave motion. These waves can be light waves or radio-frequency waves. The form of radiation with which we are most familiar is that from the sun's rays. When heat is transferred by radiation, the air between the objects is not heated, as can be noticed when a person steps from the shade into the direct sunlight. The air temperature is about the same in either place; however, the person feels warmer in the sunlight (see Figure 2-6). This is because of the heat being transferred by

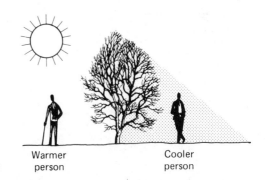

Warmer   Cooler
person   person

FIGURE 2-6.   Heat transfer by radiation.

the rays of the sun. There is little radiation at low temperatures and at small temperature differences. Therefore, heat transferred by radiation is of little importance in actual refrigeration applications. However, if the refrigerated space is located in the direct rays of the sun, the cabinet will absorb radiated heat. This heat absorption from direct sun rays can be a major factor in the calculation of the heat load of the refrigerated space.

The heat will travel in a combination of these processes in a normal refrigeration application. The ability of a piece of refrigeration equipment to transfer heat is known as the overall rate of heat transfer. As we learned earlier, heat transfer cannot take place without a temperature difference. Different materials have different abilities to conduct heat. Metal is a good conductor of heat, while asbestos is a poor one, which means it is a good insulator.

The factors that affect the rate of heat flow are (1) temperature difference, (2) amount of surface area, and (3) type of material the heat must pass through.

Example 1: The greater the temperature difference is, the greater the flow of heat (see Figure 2-7). The heat flow in the rod

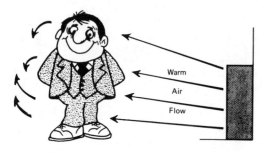

Warm
Air
Flow

FIGURE 2-5.   Heat transfer by convection.

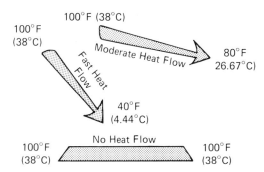

FIGURE 2-7. Temperature difference and heat flow example.

with 100°F on one end and 40°F on the other end will be much faster than the rod having 100°F on one end and 80°F on the opposite end. Also notice that when both ends of the rod are the same temperature, there is no flow of heat.

Example 2: The greater the amount of surface area exposed to the different temperatures, the greater will be the flow of heat (see Figure 2-8). The heat flow will be much greater in the glass with the crushed ice than in the glass containing the larger ice cubes. The crushed ice will melt faster than the cubes, and the cooling rate will also be faster.

Example 3: A material having a high resistance to heat flow will reduce the flow much more than a material having little or no resistance to heat flow. A building that has fiberglass or rock-wool insulation between the joists and rafters will allow much less heat to travel through the structure than a building having only sheathing and sheet rock on the framing (see Figure 2-9).

Specific Heat. The amount of heat required to raise the temperature of 1 lb of any substance 1°F is known as the specific

heat of that substance. Specific heat is also the ratio between the quantity of heat required to change the temperature of a substance 1°F and the amount of heat required to change an equal amount of water 1°F.

From the definition of a Btu given earlier, it can be seen that the specific heat of water must be 1 Btu per pound. The specific heat values of some of the more popular foods are given in Table 2-1. Note that after foods are frozen their specific heat values drop considerably. It may be assumed that the specific heat is a little more than one-half of what it was before the foods were frozen.

Example: The specific heat of water is 1 Btu per pound. The specific heat of ice is 0.504 Btu per pound, thus requiring only 0.504 Btu to change the temperature of 1 lb of ice 1°F.

Sensible Heat. The heat that can be added to or removed from a substance resulting in a change in temperature but no change of state is known as *sensible heat.* The word "sensible" as applied to heat refers to that heat which can be sensed, or measured with a thermometer.

FIGURE 2-8. Amount of cooling surface area example.

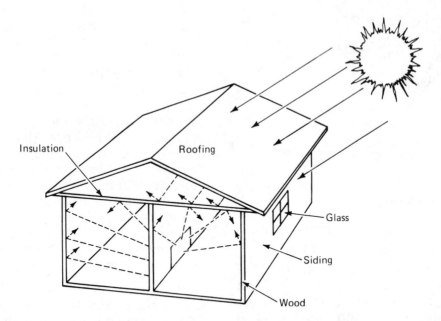

FIGURE 2-9.   Types of material heat must pass through example.

Example: When the temperature of water is raised from 42°F to 212°F, there is a change in temperature of 170°F. This change in temperature is sensible heat. It can be measured with a thermometer (see Figure 2-10).

Latent Heat. The heat that is added to or removed from a substance resulting in a change of state but no change in temperature is known as *latent heat.* Latent heat is sometimes called *hidden* heat. There are four types of latent heat: (1) latent heat of fusion, (2) latent heat of condensation, (3) latent heat of vaporization, and (4) latent heat of sublimation.

TABLE 2-1.   Specific Heat of Foods

Food	Specific Heat (Unfrozen)		Specific Heat (Frozen)	
	BTU	Cal.	BTU	Cal.
Veal	0.70	176.4	0.39	98.28
Beef	0.68	171.36	0.38	95.76
Pork	0.57	143.64	0.30	75.6
Fish	0.82	206.64	0.43	108.36
Poultry	0.80	201.6	0.42	105.84
Eggs	0.76	191.52	0.40	100.8
Butter	0.55	138.6	0.33	83.16
Cheese	0.64	161.28	0.37	93.24
Whole milk	0.92	231.84	0.47	118.44

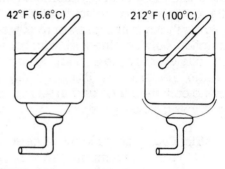

FIGURE 2-10.   Sensible heat.

Latent heat of fusion is the amount of heat that must be added to a solid to change it to a liquid at a constant temperature. Latent heat of fusion is also equal to the heat that must be removed from a liquid to change it to a solid at a constant temperature. An example of latent heat of fusion is the changing of water to ice or ice to water.

Latent heat of condensation is the amount of heat that must be removed from a vapor to change it to a liquid at a constant temperature. An example of latent heat of condensation is the collecting of moisture on the outside of a cold glass.

Latent heat of vaporization is the amount of heat that must be added to a liquid to change it to a vapor at a constant temperature and a constant pressure. An example of latent heat of vaporization is the changing of water into steam.

Latent heat of sublimation is the amount of heat that must be added to a substance to change it from a solid to a

vapor, with no evidence of going through the liquid state. This process is not possible in all substances. The most common example of this is dry ice. The latent heat of sublimation is equal to the sum of the latent heat of fusion and the latent heat of vaporization.

Figure 2-11 illustrates what happens when 1 lb of ice is heated from 0° to 220°F and then cooled back to 0°F. The arrows in the figure indicate that the process is reversible; that is, the water may be changed to steam by adding heat, or the steam may be condensed back into water by removing heat.

Let us follow the process starting in the lower-left corner. The first step in the process shows that when ice is heated from 0° to 32°F, 16 Btu of heat is absorbed by the ice. These Btu's represent sensible heat because they did not change the state of the ice.

When 144 more Btu's are added to the ice, the temperature is still 32°F, but the ice has all melted. Since the ice has changed to water, that is, from a solid to a liquid, a change of state has taken place. The 144 Btu's required to make this

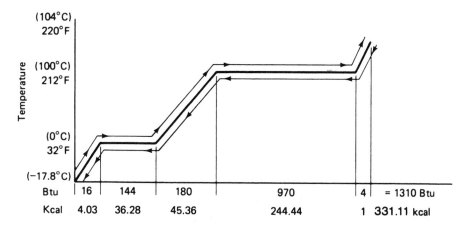

FIGURE 2-11. Relationship of heat and temperature when changing ice to steam.

change of state represent latent heat of fusion.

When 180 Btu's more are added to the water, the temperature of the water is caused to rise to 212°F, which is the boiling point of water at sea level and atmospheric pressure. Since the 180 Btu's changed the temperature but did not change the state of the water, it is termed sensible heat.

When 970 Btu's more are added to the water at 212°F, it has changed into steam at 212°F. Since there is no change in temperature, but a change of state, from liquid to vapor, these 970 Btu's represent latent heat of vaporization.

When 4 Btu's more are added to the steam at 212°F, the temperature is raised from 212° to 220°F. Since this heat resulted in a change in temperature but no change of state, it is termed sensible heat.

If the arrow is followed backward, it can be easily seen that this process is reversible. Exactly the same amount of heat must be given up by the substance as was absorbed by it.

Heat of Compression. Heat of compression occurs when a vapor is compressed mechanically, as in an air-conditioning compressor. As the gas is compressed, the temperature rises. There is practically no increase in the total amount of heat in the gas; only the amount of heat caused by the friction in the compressor is added to the gas. The temperature is raised because the gas molecules are forced closer together; this causes more friction among them, which in turn causes the increase in temperature.

In practice, the low-temperature, low-pressure refrigerant gas is drawn from the evaporator in the refrigeration system to the compressor, where its volume is reduced and its temperature increased to a point above the temperature of the cooling medium (air or water) for the condenser. The heat will be removed from the gas by the cooling medium (air or water), causing a change of state to occur. The gas will be changed to a liquid.

Superheat. Superheat is the heat added to a vapor after the vapor is no longer in contact with its liquid.

Example: When enough heat is added to a liquid to cause all the liquid to vaporize, any additional heat added to the vapor is termed superheat (see Figure 2-12).

Critical Temperature. The critical temperature is the highest temperature at which a vapor may be liquified, regardless of how much pressure is applied to it. In refrigeration and air-conditioning applications, the condensing temperature must be kept below this temperature. If the critical temperature is reached in the condenser, the refrigeration process will stop.

Saturation Temperature. The saturation temperature is a condition of both pressure and temperature at which both liquid and vapor can exist in the same container simultaneously. A saturated liquid or vapor is at its boiling temperature. The saturation temperature increases with an increase in pressure and decreases with a decrease in pressure.

ENTHALPY

The calculations necessary for some air-conditioning and refrigeration estimating involve the use of enthalpy, or total

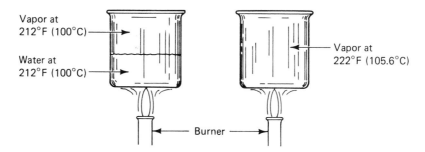

Vapor at
212°F (100°C)

Water at
212°F (100°C)

Vapor at
222°F (105.6°C)

Burner

FIGURE 2-12. Explanation of superheat.

heat contained within the body, including both sensible and latent heat. It is measured in Btu per lb of that substance. In theory, enthalpy is measured from absolute zero of the particular scale being used: −460°F or −273°C. However, the large figures involved when absolute zero is used as a reference point have caused other reference points to be set. Therefore, the zero reference point for water is 32°F and for refrigerants it is −40°F. Once the zero reference point is established for a substance, any enthalpy above that point is positive and any below that point is negative.

PRESSURE

The refrigerant process inside a refrigeration system is very important because it determines the evaporating and condensing temperature of the refrigerant. All liquids have a definite boiling temperature for each pressure. If the pressure over a liquid is increased, the boiling temperature is also increased. If the pressure over a liquid is lowered, the boiling temperature will also be lowered. This is one of the basic principles used in refrigeration work. There are three pressures that are dealt with constantly in

working on these systems: (1) atmospheric, (2) gauge, and (3) absolute.

Atmospheric Pressure. The pressure exerted on the earth by the atmosphere above us is called atmospheric pressure. At any given point, this atmospheric pressure is relatively constant except during changes caused by the weather. As a basic reference for comparison, the atmospheric pressure at sea level has been universally accepted as being 14.7 psi (pounds per square inch). This pressure is equal to the pressure exerted by a column of mercury (Hg) 29.92 inches high (see Figure 2-13).

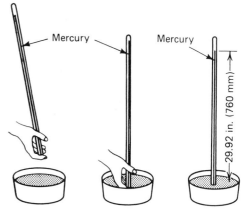

Mercury

Mercury

29.92 in. (760 mm)

FIGURE 2-13. Mercury column supported by atmospheric pressure.

The depth of the atmosphere is less at altitudes above sea level; therefore, the atmospheric pressure is less on a mountain. For example, at a 5,000-ft elevation, the atmospheric pressure is only 12.2 psi.

Gauge Pressure. The reading obtained from a gauge not connected to a source of pressure is known as gauge pressure. This pressure is commonly referred to as 0 psig (pounds per square inch gauge). Pressures below 0 psig are negative gauge readings and are commonly referred to as inches of vacuum, or inches of mercury (Hg). Refrigeration compound low side gauges are calibrated in inches of mercury for readings below atmospheric pressure (see Figure 2-14). Since 14.7 psi is equal to 29.92 in. of mercury, 1 psi is equal to 2 in. of mercury. 29.92/14.7 = 2.03 of mercury. It should be remembered that gauge pressures are

FIGURE 2-14. Refrigeration compound gauge. *Courtesy of Marshalltown Instruments.*

only relative to absolute pressures (see Table 2-2).

Absolute Pressure. The pressure measured from a perfect vacuum is called

TABLE 2.2. Comparison of Atmospheric and Absolute Pressures at Varying Altitudes

Altitude (ft)	PSIA	Pressure in Inches HG	Boiling Point of Water (°F)	Refrigerant Boiling Points (°F)		
				R-12	R-22	R-502
0	14.7	29.92	212°F	−22	−41	−50
1000	14.2	28.85	210	−23	−43	−51
2000	13.7	27.82	208	−25	−44	−53
3000	13.2	26.81	206	−26	−45	−54
4000	12.7	25.84	205	−28	−47	−56
5000	12.2	24.89	203	−29	−48	−57
m	kg/cm²	cm/Hg	°C		°C	
0	1.03	75.9	100	−30	−40.5	−45.6
304	.998	73.2	99	−30.5	−41.7	−46
608	.96	70.6	97.44	−31.7	−42.2	−47
912	.93	68.1	96.3	−32.2	−42.8	−47.8
1216	.89	65.6	95.8	−33.3	−43.9	−48.9
1520	.857	63.2	94.7	−33.9	−44.4	−49.5

absolute pressure. The atmospheric pressure and absolute pressure are the same. Atmospheric pressure is 14.7 psia. Absolute pressure is normally expressed in terms of pounds per square inch absolute (psia). Absolute pressure is equal to gauge pressure plus atmospheric pressure. To find absolute pressure, add 14.7 to the pressure gauge reading.

Example: Find the absolute pressure related to a gauge pressure of 10 psig. 10 + 14.7 = 24.7 psia.

Critical Pressure. The critical pressure of a liquid is the pressure at or above which the liquid will remain a liquid. With this pressure applied, the liquid cannot be changed to a vapor by adding heat.

Pressure Measurement. The measurement of low pressure requires a unit of measurement smaller than the pound or the inch of mercury. The micron is commonly used for measuring these low pressures. A micron is a metric measurement of length and is used in measuring the vacuum in a refrigeration system. It is considered as being absolute pressure and is measured with a micron (see Figure 2-15).

One micron is equal to 1/1000 of a millimeter (mm). There are 25.4 mm in 1 in. Therefore, 1 micron is equal to 1/25,400 in. A refrigeration system that has been evacuated to 500 microns would have an absolute pressure of 0.02 in. of mercury (Hg). At standard conditions, this would be equal to a vacuum reading of 29.90 in. Hg, which is impossible to read on a refrigeration compound gauge.

Laws Affecting Pressure. The effect of temperature on the pressure of gases is of great importance in the refrigeration

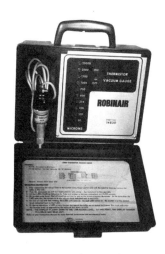

FIGURE 2-15. **Thermistor vacuum gauge.** *Courtesy of Robinair Div., Kent-Moore Corp.*

industry and must be thoroughly understood for an adequate knowledge of how a refrigeration system operates. Several laws deal with the effects of temperature on the pressure of a gas within a confined space: (1) Boyle's law, (2) Charles's law, (3) Dalton's law of partial pressures, (4) Pascal's law, and (5) the general gas law.

Boyle's Law. With the temperature constant, the volume of gas is inversely proportional to its absolute pressure. In practical applications, this can be proved by use of a cylinder with a properly fitted piston (see Figure 2-16a). When simultaneous pressure and volume readings are taken as the gas is being slowly compressed within the cylinder so that no temperature increase will be experienced, a decrease in volume is always accompanied by an increase in pressure (see Figure 2-16b).

Charles's Law. With the pressure constant, the volume of a gas is directly proportional to its absolute temperature.

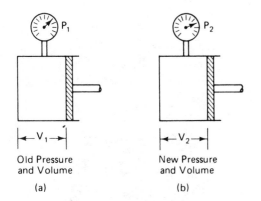

FIGURE 2-16. Application of Boyle's Law.

In practical applications, this can be proved by use of a cylinder with a properly fitted piston (see Figure 2-17a). In this example, the cylinder is fitted with a sliding piston. The cylinder is full of gas at atmospheric pressure. Heat is applied to the cylinder, causing the temperature to rise. Because the piston is easily moved, the volume of gas increases but the pressure remains constant at atmospheric pressure (see Figure 2-17b). On the other hand, if the gas is cooled, the volume of gas will become smaller (see Figure 2-17c). If it were possible to cool the gas to absolute zero, $-460°F$, the volume would be zero because there would be no molecular motion at this temperature.

Dalton's Law of Partial Pressures. Gases occupying a common volume each fill that volume and behave as if the other gases were not present. This law, along with the combination of Charles's law and Boyle's law, forms the basis for deriving the psychrometric properties of air.

A practical application of Dalton's law can be stated thus: The total pressure in a cylinder of compressed air, which is a mixture of oxygen, nitrogen, water vapor, and carbon dioxide, is found by adding together the pressures exerted by each of the individual gases.

Pascal's Law. The pressure applied upon a confined fluid is transmitted equally in all directions. A practical application of Pascal's law is shown with a cylinder of liquid and a properly fitted piston in Figure 2-18. The piston has a cross-sectional area of 1 in.^{2} With 100-psig pressure applied to the piston, the pressure gauges show that the pressure exerted in all directions is equal. This is the basic principle used in most hydraulic and pneumatic systems.

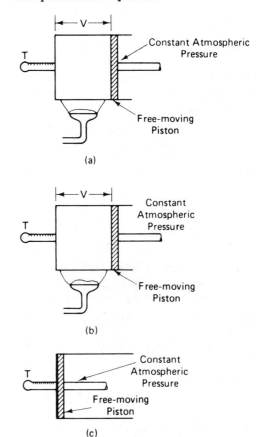

FIGURE 2-17. Application of Charles's Law.

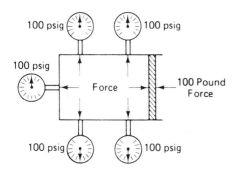

FIGURE 2-18. Application of Pascal's Law.

General Gas Law. This law combines Boyle's law and Charles's law of gases. The general gas law may be used to study changes in the conditions of a gas as long as absolute temperature and absolute pressure are used. Gauge pressure cannot be used. This law is used in calculating the psychrometric properties of air in air-conditioning work.

PRESSURE–TEMPERATURE RELATIONSHIPS

These relationships are of vital importance in the design and servicing of air-conditioning and refrigeration equipment. The temperature at which a liquid will boil is dependent on the pressure applied to it, and the pressure at which it will boil is dependent on its temperature. From this it can be seen that for each pressure exerted on a liquid there is also a definite temperature at which it will boil (provided an uncontaminated liquid is being measured).

In practice, because a liquid will react in the same manner each time it is subjected to a given set of conditions, pressure provides us with a convenient means of controlling the temperature

inside a refrigerated space. When an evaporator is part of a refrigeration system that is isolated from the atmosphere, pressure that is equal to the boiling pressure of the liquid at the desired cooling temperature can be applied to the inside of the evaporator. The liquid will boil at that temperature, and as long as heat is being absorbed by the liquid, refrigeration is being accomplished.

This is also a reversible process. When the pressure over a gas is increased enough to cause the temperature of the gas to be higher than the surrounding medium, heat will be given up and condensation of the gas will occur. This is the principle used in the operation of a refrigeration system condenser.

COOLING

Cooling is merely the removal of heat from a substance. It can be accomplished in several ways; however, we will discuss only the evaporation and expansion methods at this time.

Evaporation. Evaporation is the process that causes water to disappear when it is left in an open container. The evaporation of water depends on two things—temperature and humidity (moisture in air). When water is left in an open container in the summertime, it evaporates rapidly because of the high temperature. If the temperature drops, the rate of evaporation will decrease. If the temperature goes up, the rate of evaporation will increase. Even at temperatures of −40°F, evaporation takes place.

If the air is saturated with moisture (high humidity), it will absorb additional moisture very slowly. If the air is dry (low humidity), it will absorb moisture very rapidly. During a hot spell, when the air is muggy or humid, evaporation of the perspiration from the human body is slow because the saturated air absorbs moisture very slowly.

When water evaporates, a sufficient amount of heat will be absorbed in order to supply the latent heat of vaporization. This heat is absorbed from the water itself or from any object (or air) in contact with the water. The cold, clammy feeling experienced by a person wearing a wet bathing suit is caused by evaporation of the water and absorption of heat from the material of the suit and from the skin of the person.

Expansion. Expansion is the process that causes a cooling effect by compressing a vapor, then rapidly reducing the pressure on the vapor. When a gas is compressed, heat is generated in an amount equivalent to the amount of work done in compressing the gas. A bicycle pump, for example, becomes hot during use because of the heat developed as the air is compressed into the tire. The greater the compression is, the higher the temperature of the compressed air.

The cooling action that occurs when compressed air is allowed to expand is just the reverse of the compression effect. After a long ride over hot roads, the air in the automobile tire becomes very hot and the pressure within the tire is increased. If the valve stem were opened and the hot air allowed to escape, the air would become cool as it was released because of the rapid expansion of the air and resulting reduction in pressure. Some early refrigeration systems used this principle. The air was compressed and then cooled by being passed through a water-cooled coil. The water was used to absorb and carry heat away from the compressed air.

When the air was allowed to expand, the temperature dropped in relation to the amount of heat that was removed by the water while it was in the compressed state. The same principle is used in modern refrigeration compression–expansion systems. However, a refrigerant has replaced the air.

There are three steps involved in the compression–expansion refrigeration cycle:

1. Air or gas is compressed to a high pressure by the compressor.
2. The heat produced by compression is removed by the condenser.
3. The air or gas is expanded, causing a reduction in temperature through the absorption of heat by the air or gas in the evaporator refrigeration is accomplished.

HUMIDITY

Humidity is the general term describing the moisture content of the air; it can be expressed in two ways, as absolute humidity and as relative humidity. Humidity also can be defined as the water vapor within a given space.

The actual amount of moisture, or water vapor, that air can hold depends on the pressure and temperature of the air. As the temperature is lowered, it is able to hold less moisture. Conversely, as the temperature is increased, the amount of moisture it can hold at a given temperature is also increased. This amount of moisture is usually expressed as a percentage figure and is in direct relation to the amount of moisture that the air can absorb at that temperature.

Example: When a given quantity of air at a given temperature is said to have a relative humidity of 50%, this means it is holding only half as much water vapor as it possibly could under those same conditions.

Absolute Humidity. Absolute humidity is generally expressed in grains of water vapor per pound of dry air, or as pounds of water vapor per pound of dry air. It is all the moisture present in a given quantity of dry air.

Example: When 10 lb of air contains 20 grains of water vapor, the absolute humidity is 20 grains. Note that no mention has been made of the temperature, pressure, or percentage of water vapor present; only the actual amount present has been mentioned.

Relative Humidity. Relative humidity is an indication of the amount of moisture, in percentage form, actually present in the air compared to the maximum amount that the air could hold under the same conditions. When air contains all the moisture it can hold at any given temperature, it is saturated. When this condition occurs, the relative humidity is 100%. If the air contains only half the moisture it can hold at a given temperature, the relative humidity is then 50%.

When air is at the saturation point (100% relative humidity) and the temperature is lowered further, a certain amount of moisture will be produced in the form of water droplets. These droplets appear as ice on the evaporator of a refrigerator or as condensation in an air conditioner. A more common example is the water droplets that form on the outside of a glass containing a cold drink (see Figure 2-19). As the air surrounding

the glass comes in contact with the cold surface, the temperature of the air in contact with the glass is reduced sufficiently to cause condensation. This condensation is in the form of water droplets.

Effects of Humidification. Humidification has a tremendous effect on the operation of air conditioning and refrigeration installations. In an air-conditioned building, when the relative humidity is low, the structure will dry out and cracking will appear. Also, the occupants of the building will feel cold, and excessive drafts will be noticed. On the other hand, if the relative humidity is high, the occupants will feel warm and clammy. Condensation may appear on the windows during the winter months, causing the structure to rot and mildew.

In refrigeration applications, when the relative humidity is too low, food will have a tendency to dry out and become useless. If the relative humidity is too high, however, the formation of mold will occur and cause the food to spoil.

DEHYDRATION

Dehydration, also known as *evacuation,* is the removal of air, moisture, and noncondensables from a refrigeration system. A great amount of time and money have been spent on researching the effects of heat and noncondensables

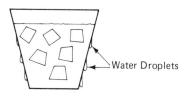

FIGURE 2-19.   Air at 100% relative humidity.

in a refrigeration system. Even now, many of the effects are still a mystery. We do know that their presence in a refrigeration system can result in many forms of damage, such as sludging, corrosion, oil breakdown, carbon formations, and copper plating. These contaminants usually cause compressor failure.

The purposes of dehydration are to protect the refrigeration system as much as possible from contaminants and to cause it to operate as efficiently as possible with a minimum amount of equipment failure.

The methods of dehydration are many and varied. It is the process used to remove water, or water vapor, from inside a closed system. It causes any water present to change to a vapor, which can be pumped from the system more easily. As stated earlier, two methods used to cause a liquid to boil are lowering the pressure exerted on it and applying heat to the liquid. Some of the ways to eliminate moisture from a refrigeration system by the boiling process are as follows:

1. Move the system to a higher elevation, where the ambient temperature is high enough to boil the water at the existing pressure.

2. Apply heat to the system, causing the moisture to boil.

3. Use a vacuum pump to lower the pressure inside the refrigeration system so that the ambient temperature will boil the moisture.

In practice, the first two choices are impractical. Therefore, the vacuum pump method is the most desirable means of removing moisture from a system. To accomplish effective dehydration, the refrigeration system must be evacuated to at least 500 microns. (*Note:* One micron is equal to 1/25,400 of an inch on a ruler.)

NONCONDENSABLES

These consist of any gases, usually air, in a refrigeration system, that cannot be condensed at the temperature and pressure at which the refrigerant will condense; to condense the vapor, therefore, a higher head pressure will be required. The higher head pressure reduces the efficiency of the system. Also, the air takes up space normally occupied by the refrigerant, further reducing the efficiency of the system.

REVIEW QUESTIONS

1. How is heat measured?

2. What are the three methods of heat transfer?

3. Define sensible heat.

4. Define latent heat.

5. Define specific heat.

6. How is temperature measured?

7. What is the unit of measurement used to measure heat?

8. What is atmospheric pressure at sea level?

9. If the pressure is reduced over a liquid, what will happen to its boiling temperature?

10. When does the heat of compression occur?

When cooling an automobile or moving the automobile down the road, we must perform some work. We must use some energy in applying the force required to accomplish these tasks. Then we need some means of measuring what we have done so that we can determine the amount of energy used in accomplishing these tasks. Because of these facts, a basic knowledge of the elements involved in work and force should be attained.

ENERGY

Energy may be defined as the capacity to do work; it may be in the form of heat energy, electrical energy, or mechanical energy. Energy cannot be destroyed. It may, however, be converted from one form to another.

Example: Electrical energy may be converted into mechanical energy (an electric motor) or it may be converted into heat energy (an electric heating element on a stove).

In practice, the heat that we remove by mechanical means from a product in a refrigerator constitutes a load on the machine that we use to remove this heat. Understanding this principle requires some understanding of elementary physics.

FORCE

Force is defined as that which tends to, or actually does, produce motion. Force may be exerted in any direction. In the simple definition of force, direction is not considered. The common unit by which force is measured is the pound.

MOTION

Motion is the movement or constantly changing position or the speed of move-

———— 3 ————

Work and Force

ment per unit of time. Velocity measurements are expressed in feet per minute (ft/min) or foot-second (ft/s).

WORK

Work is the force applied, multiplied by the distance through which this force acts. The unit of work is the foot-pound (ft-lb). A foot-pound is the work done by a force of one pound through a distance of one foot.

POWER

Power is the time rate of doing work. It is work done divided by the time required to do the work. This gives us the amount of work done in a certain amount of time. For example, say a weight of 600 lb has been moved through a distance of 10 ft in 10 min. This problem is the same regardless of the direction of the applied force, whether it is applied horizontally or vertically; nor does it matter whether the resistance is caused by friction, gravity, or gas pressure as in the electric refrigeration compressor.

HORSEPOWER (hp)

In calculation, the foot-pound is too small a unit for ordinary work. Therefore, a larger unit called horsepower (hp) is used. One hp is equal to 33,000 ft-lb/min. Notice that time is involved in calculating horsepower.

MECHANICAL EQUIVALENT OF HEAT

The mechanical equivalent of heat is the amount of heat produced by the expenditure of a given amount of mechanical energy. This has been determined by accurate scientific experiments. If the heat energy represented by 1 Btu could be changed to mechanical energy without energy loss, it would represent 778 ft-lb of work. Thus, we have established a definite relationship between the Btu and the foot-pound. This relationship is represented thus: 1 Btu of energy is equivalent to 778 ft-lb; 1 ft-lb of mechanical energy is equivalent to 1/778 Btu or 0.00128 Btu. To obtain the heat equivalent in Btu from any number of foot-pounds, divide by 778.

━━━━ REVIEW QUESTIONS ━━━━

1. Define energy.
2. Can energy be destroyed?
3. Define motion.
4. How is power determined?
5. Define work.
6. To what is one horsepower equal?
7. Define mechanical equivalent of heat.
8. To what is 1 Btu of energy equivalent?
9. Define force.
10. What is the common unit of measurement for force?

The vapors or liquids used in refrigeration systems are known as *refrigerants*. For practical purposes, a refrigerant is a fluid that absorbs heat by evaporating at a low temperature and pressure and gives up that heat by condensing at a higher temperature and pressure. The evaporation of the refrigerant within the evaporator extracts heat from the surrounding objects. The various parts of the refrigeration system compress and condense the refrigerant so that it can be used over and over again. Even though there are many different types of refrigerants, only R-12 will be discussed here.

REFRIGERANT 12

R-12 Dichlorodifluoromethane (CCl_2F_2) is a refrigerant exclusively used in automotive air-conditioning systems. It has a boiling point of $-21.6°F$ at atmospheric pressure. Therefore, it exists as a vapor at ordinary room temperatures and atmospheric pressure. R-12 will liquify under a pressure of 76 psi at 75°F (see Table 4-1).

R-12 has very little odor; in large concentrations a faint, sweet odor may be detected, however. Its critical temperature is 233.6°F. It is a colorless gas and liquid. It is nontoxic, nonflammable, and nonirritating; it is noncorrosive to any of the ordinary metals even in the presence of water. It is stable under all conditions and temperatures normally encountered in refrigeration. R-12 liquid will dissolve lubricating oil in all proportions; the oil in return will absorb refrigerant vapor. There is no separation or oil blanket formed in the evaporator to interfere with proper vaporization.

R-12 is only slightly soluble in water. It is this characteristic that prevents corrosion of metals in the presence of water. Leaks may be detected with a halide torch, an electronic leak detector, or a

4

Refrigerants and Lubricants

TABLE 4-1.   R-12 Refrigerant Standard Ton Characteristics

Evaporator pressure at 5°F, psia	26.483
Condenser pressure at 86°F, psia	108.04
Compression ratio (86°F/5°F)	4.08
Latent heat of vaporization at 5°F, Btu/lb	68.204
Net refrigerating effect, Btu/lb	50.035
Refrigerant circulated per ton of refrigeration, lb/min	3.9972
Saturated liquid volume at 86°F, ft^3/lb	0.012396
Liquid circulated per ton of refrigeration, in^3/min	85.621
Saturated vapor density at 5°F, lb/ft^3	0.68588
Saturated vapor density at 86°F, lb/ft^3	2.6556
Compressor displacement per ton of refrigeration, ft^3/min	5.8279
Refrigeration per cubic foot of compressor displacement, Btu	34.318
Heat of compression, Btu/lb	10.636
Temperature of compressor discharge, °F	100.84
Coefficient of performance	4.704
Horsepower per ton	1.0023

Courtesy of Freon Products Division, E. I. Du Pont de
Nemours & Co., Inc.

soap bubble solution. The halide torch imparts a blue-green tinge to the flame in the presence of R-12. The cylinder color code for R-12 is white.

REFRIGERANT–OIL RELATIONSHIPS

When reciprocating compressors are used, oil and refrigerants mix continuously. Oils used in refrigeration compressors are soluble in liquid refrigerants and at room temperatures will mix completely. *Miscibility* is the term used to express the ability of liquid refrigerant to mix with oil.

Any oil that is circulating in a refrigeration system is exposed to both very high and very low temperatures. Because of the critical nature of lubrication under these conditions and the damage that can be done to the system by wax or other impurities that may be in the oil, only highly refined oils specifically prepared for refrigeration systems can be used.

In general, naphathanic oils are more soluble in refrigerants than paraffinic oils. Separation of the oil and refrigerant into separate layers can take place with either type of oil; however, naphathanic oils separate at somewhat lower temperatures. This separation does not necessarily affect the lubricating properties of the oil, but it could cause problems in properly supplying the oil to the working parts.

Because oil must pass through the compressor cylinders to provide lubrication to the moving parts, a small amount of oil is always circulating with the refrigerant. Oil and refrigerant vapor do not mix readily. Therefore, oil can be properly circulated through the system only if the refrigerant vapor velocities are kept high enough to sweep the oil along the piping. If the velocities are not kept high enough, the oil will tend to lie on the bottom of the refrigeration tubing, which will decrease the heat transfer and possibly cause a shortage of oil in the compressor. As the refrigerant evaporating temperatures become lower, the oil separation becomes more critical. The velocity of the oil increases with a decrease in temperature. Therefore, the proper design of refrigerant piping is necessary for proper oil return.

A basic characteristic of a refrigerant and oil mixture inside a sealed system is that oil attracts liquid refrigerant. This liquid refrigerant will vaporize and migrate through the system to the compressor crankcase, even though no pressure differential exists to cause the movement. When the refrigerant reaches the compressor crankcase, it will condense back into a liquid. This refrigerant migration will continue until the compressor oil is saturated with liquid refrigerant.

The excess of liquid refrigerant in the compressor crankcase will result in a violent foaming and boiling action of the oil, on compressor start-up, and may cause all the oil to leave the compressor crankcase, resulting in problems. Therefore, some provisions must be made to prevent the accumulation of excess liquid refrigerant in the compressor crankcase, such as running the compressor approximately 5 minutes each week.

REFRIGERANT TABLES

To accurately determine the operating performance of a refrigeration system, very precise and accurate information is required concerning the various proper-ties of refrigerants at any pressure and temperature that may be considered. Refrigerant manufacturers have calculated and compiled this data in the form of tables listing the thermodynamic properties of each refrigerant.

An excerpt from an R-12 saturation table, which lists five major saturation properties of this refrigerant, is shown in Table 4-2. Pressure, volume, and density have been discussed previously.

Enthalpy is a term used in thermodynamics to describe the total heat content of a substance. In a discussion of refrigerants, enthalpy is expressed in terms of Btu per pound of refrigerant. An arbitrary base for saturated liquid at −40°F has been accepted as the standard zero value. More simply stated, the enthalpy of any liquid refrigerant is zero at −40°F. Liquid refrigerant below that temperature is considered to have a negative enthalpy, while at all temperatures above −40°F the refrigerant has a positive enthalpy value.

The difference in enthalpy values in different parts of the refrigeration system is commonly used to rate the performance of the refrigeration unit. If the heat content per pound of a refrigerant entering and leaving a cooling coil can be determined, and the flow rate of the refrigerant is known, the cooling capabilities of that coil can be calculated.

Entropy is best described as a mathematical ratio used in thermodynamics (see Table 4-2). Thermodynamic principles are used in the solving of complex refrigeration problems, but are seldom used in commercial refrigeration and air-conditioning applications. Therefore, a discussion of thermodynamics is not pertinent in this text.

TABLE 4-2. Saturation properties—temperature table of R-12*
Courtesy of Freon Products Div., E.I. DuPont de Numours & Co., Inc.

TEMP. °F	PRESSURE		VOLUME cu ft/lb		DENSITY lb/cu ft		ENTHALPY Btu/lb			ENTROPY Btu/(lb)(°R)		TEMP. °F
	PSIA	PSIG	LIQUID v_f	VAPOR v_g	LIQUID $1/v_f$	VAPOR $1/v_g$	LIQUID h_f	LATENT h_{fg}	VAPOR h_g	LIQUID s_f	VAPOR s_g	
−40	9.3076	10.9709*	0.010564	3.8750	94.661	0.25806	0	72.913	72.913	0	0.17373	−40
−39	9.5530	10.4712*	0.010575	3.7823	94.565	0.26439	0.2107	72.812	73.023	0.000500	0.17357	−39
−38	9.8035	9.9611*	0.010586	3.6922	94.469	0.27084	0.4215	72.712	73.134	0.001000	0.17343	−38
−37	10.059	9.441*	0.010596	3.6047	94.372	0.27741	0.6324	72.611	73.243	0.001498	0.17328	−37
−36	10.320	8.909*	0.010607	3.5198	94.275	0.28411	0.8434	72.511	73.354	0.001995	0.17313	−36
−35	10.586	8.367*	0.010618	3.4373	94.178	0.29093	1.0546	72.409	73.464	0.002492	0.17299	−35
−34	10.858	7.814*	0.010629	3.3571	94.081	0.29788	1.2659	72.309	73.575	0.002988	0.17285	−34
−33	11.135	7.250*	0.010640	3.2792	93.983	0.30495	1.4772	72.208	73.685	0.003482	0.17271	−33
−32	11.417	6.675*	0.010651	3.2035	93.886	0.31216	1.6887	72.106	73.795	0.003976	0.17257	−32
−31	11.706	6.088*	0.010662	3.1300	93.788	0.31949	1.9003	72.004	73.904	0.004469	0.17243	−31
−30	11.999	5.490*	0.010674	3.0585	93.690	0.32696	2.1120	71.903	74.015	0.004961	0.17229	−30
−29	12.299	4.880*	0.010685	2.9890	93.592	0.33457	2.3239	71.801	74.125	0.005452	0.17216	−29
−28	12.604	4.259*	0.010696	2.9214	93.493	0.34231	2.5358	71.698	74.234	0.005942	0.17203	−28
−27	12.916	3.625*	0.010707	2.8556	93.395	0.35018	2.7479	71.596	74.344	0.006431	0.17189	−27
−26	13.233	2.979*	0.010719	2.7917	93.296	0.35820	2.9601	71.494	74.454	0.006919	0.17177	−26
−25	13.556	2.320*	0.010730	2.7295	93.197	0.36636	3.1724	71.391	74.563	0.007407	0.17164	−25
−24	13.886	1.649*	0.010741	2.6691	93.098	0.37466	3.3848	71.288	74.673	0.007894	0.17151	−24
−23	14.222	0.966*	0.010753	2.6102	92.999	0.38311	3.5973	71.185	74.782	0.008379	0.17139	−23
−22	14.564	0.270*	0.010764	2.5529	92.899	0.39171	3.8100	71.081	74.891	0.008864	0.17126	−22
−21	14.912	0.216	0.010776	2.4972	92.799	0.40045	4.0228	70.978	75.001	0.009348	0.17114	−21
−20	15.267	0.571	0.010788	2.4429	92.699	0.40934	4.2357	70.874	75.110	0.009831	0.17102	−20
−19	15.628	0.932	0.010799	2.3901	92.599	0.41839	4.4487	70.770	75.219	0.010314	0.17090	−19
−18	15.996	1.300	0.010811	2.3387	92.499	0.42758	4.6618	70.666	75.328	0.010795	0.17078	−18
−17	16.371	1.675	0.010823	2.2886	92.399	0.43694	4.8751	70.561	75.436	0.011276	0.17066	−17
−16	16.753	2.057	0.010834	2.2399	92.298	0.44645	5.0885	70.456	75.545	0.011755	0.17055	−16
−15	17.141	2.445	0.010846	2.1924	92.197	0.45612	5.3020	70.352	75.654	0.012234	0.17043	−15
−14	17.536	2.840	0.010858	2.1461	92.096	0.46595	5.5157	70.246	75.762	0.012712	0.17032	−14
−13	17.939	3.243	0.010870	2.1011	91.995	0.47595	5.7295	70.141	75.871	0.013190	0.17021	−13
−12	18.348	3.652	0.010882	2.0572	91.893	0.48611	5.9434	70.036	75.979	0.013666	0.17010	−12
−11	18.765	4.069	0.010894	2.0144	91.791	0.49643	6.1574	69.930	76.087	0.014142	0.16999	−11
−10	19.189	4.493	0.010906	1.9727	91.689	0.50693	6.3716	69.824	76.196	0.014617	0.16989	−10
− 9	19.621	4.925	0.010919	1.9320	91.587	0.51759	6.5859	69.718	76.304	0.015091	0.16978	− 9
− 8	20.059	5.363	0.010931	1.8924	91.485	0.52843	6.8003	69.611	76.411	0.015564	0.16967	− 8
− 7	20.506	5.810	0.010943	1.8538	91.382	0.53944	7.0149	69.505	76.520	0.016037	0.16957	− 7
− 6	20.960	6.264	0.010955	1.8161	91.280	0.55063	7.2296	69.397	76.627	0.016508	0.16947	− 6
− 5	21.422	6.726	0.010968	1.7794	91.177	0.56199	7.4444	69.291	76.735	0.016979	0.16937	− 5
− 4	21.891	7.195	0.010980	1.7436	91.074	0.57354	7.6594	69.183	76.842	0.017449	0.16927	− 4
− 3	22.369	7.673	0.010993	1.7086	90.970	0.58526	7.8745	69.075	76.950	0.017919	0.16917	− 3
− 2	22.854	8.158	0.011005	1.6745	90.867	0.59718	8.0898	68.967	77.057	0.018388	0.16907	− 2
− 1	23.348	8.652	0.011018	1.6413	90.763	0.60927	8.3052	68.859	77.164	0.018855	0.16897	− 1
0	23.849	9.153	0.011030	1.6089	90.659	0.62156	8.5207	68.750	77.271	0.019323	0.16888	0
1	24.359	9.663	0.011043	1.5772	90.554	0.63404	8.7364	68.642	77.378	0.019789	0.16878	1
2	24.878	10.182	0.011056	1.5463	90.450	0.64670	8.9522	68.533	77.485	0.020255	0.16869	2
3	25.404	10.708	0.011069	1.5161	90.345	0.65957	9.1682	68.424	77.592	0.020719	0.16860	3
4	25.939	11.243	0.011082	1.4867	90.240	0.67263	9.3843	68.314	77.698	0.021184	0.16851	4
5	26.483	11.787	0.011094	1.4580	90.135	0.68588	9.6005	68.204	77.805	0.021647	0.16842	5
6	27.036	12.340	0.011107	1.4299	90.030	0.69934	9.8169	68.094	77.911	0.022110	0.16833	6
7	27.597	12.901	0.011121	1.4025	89.924	0.71300	10.033	67.984	78.017	0.022572	0.16824	7
8	28.167	13.471	0.011134	1.3758	89.818	0.72687	10.250	67.873	78.123	0.023033	0.16815	8
9	28.747	14.051	0.011147	1.3496	89.712	0.74094	10.467	67.762	78.229	0.023494	0.16807	9
10	29.335	14.639	0.011160	1.3241	89.606	0.75523	10.684	67.651	78.335	0.023954	0.16798	10
11	29.932	15.236	0.011173	1.2992	89.499	0.76972	10.901	67.539	78.440	0.024413	0.16790	11
12	30.539	15.843	0.011187	1.2748	89.392	0.78443	11.118	67.428	78.546	0.024871	0.16782	12
13	31.155	16.459	0.011200	1.2510	89.285	0.79935	11.336	67.315	78.651	0.025329	0.16774	13
14	31.780	17.084	0.011214	1.2278	89.178	0.81449	11.554	67.203	78.757	0.025786	0.16765	14
15	32.415	17.719	0.011227	1.2050	89.070	0.82986	11.771	67.090	78.861	0.026243	0.16758	15

* Inches of mercury below one atmosphere

POCKET PRESSURE–TEMPERATURE CHARTS

Small pocket-sized tables that list the saturation temperatures and pressures of common refrigerants are available from expansion valve manufacturers, refrigerant manufacturers, and supply stores (see Table 4-3). These charts are a ready reference and an invaluable tool for the service technician. They are used to check the performance of a refrigeration system. The suction and discharge pressures can be readily checked by using gauges. These pressures indicate the evaporating and condensing pressures and temperatures of the refrigerant.

HANDLING OF REFRIGERANT CYLINDERS

The pressure created by a liquid refrigerant in a sealed container is equal to its saturation pressure at that liquid temperature as long as there is space above the liquid for vapor. However, if the refrigerant cylinder is overfilled, or if the cylinder is gradually and uniformly overheated, the liquid refrigerant will expand until the cylinder becomes full of liquid. When this occurs, hydrostatic pressure builds up rapidly, producing pressures well above the saturation pressures. Figure 4-1 illustrates the pressure–temperature relationship of a liquid refrigerant before and after the cylinder becomes full of the expanded liquid under gradual and uniform overheating. The true pressure–temperature relationship exists up to the point where expansion room is no longer available in the cylinder.

The extremely dangerous pressures that can result under such circumstances can cause the rupture of the refrigerant

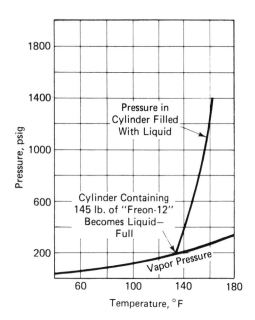

FIGURE 4-1. Hydrostatic pressure with R-12.
Courtesy of Copeland Corp.

cylinder (see Figure 4-2). Under uniform heating conditions, the cylinder in Figure 4-2 ruptured at approximately 1300 psi. If, however, heat is applied with a welding torch, the area of the cylinder wall where the heat is applied may be weakened and the danger of rupture increased. In a controlled test, a cylinder such as the one shown in Figure 4-2 flew over 40 ft in the air upon rupture, a dramatic demonstration showing the danger of overheating refrigerant cylinders.

The Interstate Commerce Commission's regulations prescribe that a liquified vapor container shall not be full of liquid when heated to 131°F. If cylinders are filled in compliance with this regulation, liquid refrigerant may completely fill the cylinder because of the expansion of the liquid at temperatures above 131°F. Fusible metal plugs are designed to protect

TABLE 4-3. Condensed pressure—temperature chart

Courtesy Freon Products, E.I. DuPont de Numours Co., Inc.

Vapor Pressure, Psig

°F.	"Freon-113"	"Freon-114"	"Freon-13"	R-500**
−50		27.2*	57.0	
−48		27.0*	60.0	
−46		26.8*	63.0	
−44		26.6*	66.2	
−42		26.3*	69.4	
−40		26.1*	72.7	7.9*
−38		25.9*	76.2	6.7*
−36		25.6*	79.7	5.4*
−34		25.3*	83.3	4.2*
−32		25.0*	87.1	2.8*
−30	29.3*	24.7*	90.9	1.4*
−28	29.3*	24.4*	94.9	0.0
−26	29.2*	24.0*	98.9	0.8
−24	29.2*	23.7*	103.0	1.5
−22	29.1*	23.3*	107.3	2.3
−20	29.1*	22.9*	111.7	3.1
−18	29.0*	22.5*	116.2	4.0
−16	28.9*	22.1*	120.8	4.9
−14	28.9*	21.6*	125.7	5.8
−12	28.8*	21.1*	130.5	6.8
−10	28.7*	20.6*	135.4	7.8
−8	28.6*	20.1*	140.5	8.8
−6	28.5*	19.6*	145.7	9.9
−4	28.4*	19.0*	151.1	11.0
−2	28.3*	18.4*	156.5	12.1
0	28.2*	17.8*	162.2	13.3
2	28.1*	17.2*	167.9	14.5
4	28.0*	16.5*	173.7	15.7
6	27.9*	15.8*	179.8	17.0
8	27.7*	15.1*	185.9	18.4
10	27.6*	14.3*	192.2	19.8
12	27.5*	13.5*	198.6	21.2
14	27.3*	12.7*	205.2	22.7
16	27.1*	11.9*	211.9	24.2
18	27.0*	11.0*	218.8	25.7
20	26.8*	10.1*	225.8	27.3
22	26.6*	9.1*	233.0	29.0
24	26.4*	8.1*	240.3	30.7
26	26.2*	7.1*	247.8	32.5
28	26.0*	6.1*	255.5	34.3
30	25.8*	5.0*	263.3	36.1
32	25.6*	3.9*	271.3	38.0
34	25.3*	2.7*	279.5	40.0
36	25.1*	1.5*	287.8	42.0
38	24.8*	0.2*	296.3	44.1
40	24.5*	0.5	305.0	46.2
42	24.2*	1.2	313.9	48.4
44	23.9*	1.9	322.9	50.7
46	23.6*	2.6	332.2	53.0
48	23.3*	3.3	341.6	55.4
50	22.9*	4.0	351.2	57.8
52	22.6*	4.8	361.1	60.3
54	22.2*	5.6	371.1	62.9
56	21.8*	6.4	381.3	65.5
58	21.4*	7.3	391.7	68.2
60	21.0*	8.1	402.4	71.0
62	20.6*	9.0	413.3	73.8
64	20.1*	9.9	424.2	76.7
66	19.7*	10.9	435.6	79.7
68	19.2*	11.9	447.0	82.8
70	18.7*	12.9	458.8	85.8
72	18.2*	13.9	470.7	89.0
74	17.6*	15.0	482.9	92.3
76	17.1*	16.1	495.3	95.6
78	16.5*	17.2	508.1	99.0
80	15.9*	18.3	521.0	102.5
82	15.3*	19.5	534.1	106.1
84	14.6*	20.7	547.5	109.7
86	13.9*	22.0	ABOVE CRITICAL TEMPERATURE	113.4
88	13.2*	23.3		117.3
90	12.5*	24.6		121.2
92	11.8*	25.9		125.1
94	11.0*	27.3		129.2
96	10.2*	28.7		133.3
98	9.4*	30.2		137.6
100	8.6*	31.7		141.9
102	7.7*	33.2		146.3
104	6.8*	34.8		150.9
106	5.9*	36.4		155.4
108	4.9*	38.0		160.1
110	4.0*	39.7		164.9
112	3.0*	41.4		169.8
114	1.9*	43.2		174.8
116	0.8*	45.0		179.9
118	0.1	46.9		185.0
120	0.7	48.7		190.3
122	1.3	50.7		195.7
124	1.9	52.7		201.2
126	2.5	54.7		206.7
128	3.1	56.7		212.4
130	3.7	58.8		218.2
132	4.4	61.0		224.1
134	5.1	63.2		230.1
136	5.8	65.5		236.3
138	6.5	67.7		242.5
140	7.2	70.1		248.8
142	8.0	72.5		
144	8.8	74.9		
146	9.6	77.4		
148	10.4	80.0		
150	11.2	82.6		
152	12.1	85.2		
154	13.0	87.9		
156	13.9	90.7		
158	14.8	93.5		
160	15.7	96.4		

*Inches mercury below one atmosphere.
**Patented by Carrier Corporation.

Vapor Pressure, Psig

°F.	"Freon-11"	"Freon-12"	"Freon-502"	"Freon-22"
−50		15.4*	0.0	6.0*
−48		14.6*	0.8	4.7*
−46		13.8*	1.6	3.3*
−44		12.9*	2.5	1.8*
−42		11.9*	3.4	0.3*
−40	28.4*	11.0*	4.3	0.6
−38	28.3*	10.0*	5.2	1.4
−36	28.2*	8.9*	6.2	2.3
−34	28.1*	7.8*	7.2	3.2
−32	28.0*	6.7*	8.3	4.1
−30	27.8*	5.5*	9.4	5.0
−28	27.7*	4.3*	10.5	6.0
−26	27.5*	3.0*	11.7	7.0
−24	27.4*	1.6*	12.9	8.1
−22	27.2*	0.3*	14.2	9.2
−20	27.0*	0.6	15.5	10.3
−18	26.9*	1.3	16.9	11.5
−16	26.7*	2.1	18.3	12.7
−14	26.5*	2.8	19.7	13.9
−12	26.2*	3.7	20.2	15.2
−10	26.0*	4.5	22.8	16.6
−8	25.8*	5.4	24.4	18.0
−6	25.5*	6.3	26.0	19.4
−4	25.3*	7.2	27.7	20.9
−2	25.0*	8.2	29.4	22.5
0	24.7*	9.2	31.2	24.1
2	24.4*	10.2	33.1	25.7
4	24.1*	11.2	35.0	27.4
6	23.8*	12.3	37.0	29.2
8	23.5*	13.5	39.0	31.0
10	23.1*	14.6	41.1	32.9
12	22.7*	15.8	43.2	34.9
14	22.3*	17.1	45.4	36.9
16	21.9*	18.4	47.7	39.0
18	21.5*	19.7	50.1	41.1
20	21.1*	21.0	52.4	43.3
22	20.6*	22.4	54.9	45.5
24	20.2*	23.9	57.4	47.9
26	19.7*	25.4	60.0	50.2
28	19.1*	26.9	62.7	52.7
30	18.6*	28.5	65.4	55.2
32	18.1*	30.1	68.2	57.8
34	17.5*	31.7	71.1	60.5
36	16.9*	33.4	74.1	63.3
38	16.3*	35.2	77.1	66.1
40	15.6*	37.0	80.2	69.0
42	14.9*	38.8	83.4	72.0
44	14.2*	40.7	86.6	75.0
46	13.5*	42.7	90.0	78.2
48	12.8*	44.7	93.4	81.4
50	12.0*	46.7	96.9	84.7
52	11.2*	48.8	100.5	88.1
54	10.4*	51.0	104.1	91.5
56	9.5*	53.2	107.9	95.1
58	8.7*	55.4	111.7	98.8
60	7.7*	57.7	115.6	102.5
62	6.8*	60.1	119.6	106.3
64	5.8*	62.5	123.7	110.2
66	4.8*	65.0	127.9	114.2
68	3.7*	67.6	132.2	118.3
70	2.6*	70.2	136.6	122.5
72	1.5*	72.9	141.1	126.8
74	0.4*	75.6	145.6	131.2
76	0.4	78.4	150.3	135.7
78	1.0	81.3	155.1	140.3
80	1.6	84.2	159.9	145.0
82	2.2	87.2	164.9	149.8
84	2.9	90.2	170.0	154.7
86	3.6	93.3	175.1	159.8
88	4.3	96.5	180.4	164.9
90	5.0	99.8	185.8	170.1
92	5.7	103.1	191.3	175.4
94	6.5	106.5	196.9	180.9
96	7.3	110.0	202.6	186.5
98	8.1	113.5	208.4	192.1
100	8.9	117.2	214.4	197.9
102	9.8	120.9	220.4	203.8
104	10.6	124.6	226.6	209.9
106	11.5	128.5	232.9	216.0
108	12.5	132.4	239.3	222.3
110	13.4	136.4	245.8	228.7
112	14.4	140.5	252.5	235.2
114	15.3	144.7	259.2	241.9
116	16.4	148.9	266.1	248.7
118	17.4	153.2	273.1	255.6
120	18.5	157.7	280.3	262.6
122	19.6	162.2	287.6	269.7
124	20.7	166.7	295.0	277.0
126	21.9	171.4	302.5	284.4
128	23.0	176.2	310.2	291.8
130	24.3	181.0	318.0	299.3
132	25.5	185.9	326.0	307.1
134	26.8	191.0	334.1	315.2
136	28.1	196.1	342.3	323.6
138	29.4	201.3	350.7	332.3
140	30.8	206.6	359.2	341.3
142	32.2	212.0	367.8	350.3
144	33.7	217.5	376.7	359.4
146	35.1	223.1	385.6	368.6
148	36.6	228.8	394.7	377.9
150	38.2	234.6	404.0	387.2
152	39.7	240.5	413.4	396.6
154	41.3	246.5	423.0	406.1
156	43.0	252.6	432.7	415.6
158	44.6	258.8	442.6	425.1
160	46.3	265.1	452.6	434.6

*Inches mercury below one atmosphere.

FIGURE 4-2. Ruptured refrigerant cylinder.
Courtesy of Copeland Corp.

the refrigerant cylinder in case of fire. However, they will not protect the cylinder from a gradual uniform overheating. Fusible plugs begin to soften at 156°F, but the hydrostatic pressure created at this temperature far exceeds the cylinder test pressure.

The following safety rules should always be followed when handling compressed vapor cylinders.

1. Never heat a cylinder above 125°F.

2. Never store refrigerant cylinders in direct sunlight.

3. Never apply flame directly to a cylinder.

4. Never place an electric resistance heater in direct contact with a refrigerant cylinder.

5. Do not drop, dent, or otherwise abuse cylinders.

6. When refilling small refrigerant cylinders, never exceed the weight stamped on them.

7. Always keep the valve cap and head cap in place when the cylinder is not in use.

8. Always open all cylinder valves slowly.

9. Secure all cylinders in an upright position to a stationary object with a strap when they are not mounted in a suitable stand.

Many of the more common refrigerants do not have a disagreeable odor; it might, therefore, be possible to work in an area where there is a considerable amount of refrigerant vapor. Many refrigerants are heavier than air and will replace the air within the room. This is dangerous, because a person must have at least 19.1% oxygen in the air breathed; otherwise, unconsciousness may occur.

1. Be sure that the room is thoroughly ventilated before repairing a refrigerant leak.

2. Check the type of refrigerant before charging the system with refrigerant.

3. Be sure to wear goggles when discharging or charging a system.

4. Be sure to keep liquid refrigerant out of your eyes. If liquid refrigerant should get into your eyes, flush them gently with tap water, and see a physician immediately.

5. Do not breathe the refrigerant vapor from a system that has a burned compressor.

6. Keep burned refrigerant off the skin to prevent acid burns.

7. Never apply an open flame to a refrigerant cylinder; an explosion and serious personal injury could result.

8. Always protect refrigerants from being contaminated with moisture, air, or other substances.

9. Do not allow oil from a burned compressor to touch your skin; it is acidic and may burn.

10. If liquid refrigerant comes in contact with your skin, flush the skin with water and treat the affected area for frost bite.

LUBRICANTS

The common fluorocarbon refrigerants in use today are miscible with the lubricating oil in amounts depending on viscosity, temperature, suction pressure, and so on. In a properly designed refrigeration system, the oil is absorbed into the refrigerant and will travel through the system with it. The lubricating oil should be a staight-run refined mineral oil, free from moisture, sediment, acid, soap, or any substance that is not derived from petroleum. The use of such compounds as ethylene glycol, glycerine, or castor oil is not recommended because these substances are all hygroscopic; that is, they all absorb moisture and become gummy. They also may produce a sticky sludge in the compressor crankcase when the system is idle or when the oil becomes heated. The lubricating oil must be thoroughly dehydrated to avoid the freezing of moisture in the refrigerant flow-control device and to prevent possible emulsification of the oil and the formation of sludge.

BASIC REFRIGERATION SYSTEM

The basic components of a refrigeration system are compressor, condenser, flow-control device, connecting tubing, and the refrigerant (see Figure 4-3). The compressor is sometimes called the heart of the system. It causes the refrigerant to circulate through the system. In operation, the refrigerant is pushed by the compressor to the condenser, where both sensible and latent heat are removed, causing the refrigerant to become a liquid. The liquid refrigerant then goes to the flow control device, where the pressure is reduced, allowing the refrigerant to expand and absorb heat from the refrigerated cabinet. This low-pressure, heat-laden refrigerant vapor is then drawn to the compressor, where the cycle is repeated. The refrigerant system will be discussed in greater detail in later chapters.

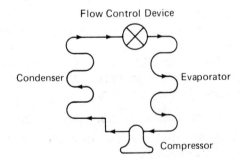

FIGURE 4-3. **Basic refrigeration system.**

━━━━━━━━━━━━━━━━━━━━━━━━━━━━ **REVIEW QUESTIONS** ━━━━━━━━━━━━━━

1. In what state does most refrigerants exist at atmospheric pressure and temperature?

2. How will an increase in pressure on a liquid refrigerant affect its boiling point?

3. On what does the condensing pressure depend?

4. Why is the vaporizing pressure of a refrigerant important?

5. What happens if air gets into a refrigeration system?

6. Why is a small amount of oil always circulating with the refrigerant through the system?

7. Why must moisture be kept out of refrigeration oil?

8. What are the six important parts of a refrigeration system?

9. Define the word refrigerant.

10. What does R-12 smell like?

Automotive air-conditioning systems are devices designed to take heat from inside the automobile and put it outside. All the principles of heat transfer that were discussed in the previous chapter are used in this heat-removal process. These systems are divided into a high-pressure side and a low-pressure side, normally referred to as high side and low side (see Figure 5-1). All the components on the right side of the diagram are in the high side and operate under a high refrigerant pressure; those on the left side are in the low side of the system and operate under a low refrigerant pressure.

BASIC AIR-CONDITIONING SYSTEM

When we consider an air-conditioning system, we find a finned coil through which the air to be cooled passes. This coil is known as the *evaporator* (see Figure 5-2). The refrigerant, which we studied in Chapter 4, is changed to a vapor in the evaporator by absorbing heat and boiling. This heat-laden refrigerant vapor is piped to the outside of the car, and the heat is carried away with it.

Now that the vapor is out of the evaporator, all we need to do is remove the heat from it to use it over again. Since the refrigerant expanded in absorbing the heat, removal of this heat will allow the vapor to be condensed, or changed, back into a liquid.

Because liquid refrigerant boils at temperatures below freezing, the vapors leaving the evaporator feel very cold. We cannot, however, expect to remove heat from these cold vapors with air that is between 70° and 100°F.

However, we can compress the heat-laden vapor into a smaller space and concentrate the heat it contains. In this

5

Operation of Automotive Air-Conditioning Systems

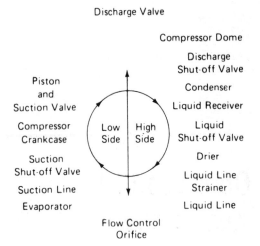

FIGURE 5-1. **High and low side diagram.**

FIGURE 5-3. **Compressor.** *Courtesy of AC Delco/General Motors Corp.*

manner the vapor can be made hotter without any additional heat. It can then be cooled and condensed in the warmer outside air.

This concentration of heat is the responsibility of the compressor (see Figure 5-3). It is not intended that the compressor be used for just circulating

the refrigerant through the system. There are two reasons for its exerting pressure on the refrigerant: (1) Pressure makes the vapor hot enough so that it can be cooled in the warm outside air, and (2) the higher pressure allows a condensing point at the temperature of the surrounding air so that the vapor will condense.

The refrigerant being discharged by the compressor is still a hot vapor and is ready to give up its heat to the outside air. Thus, the refrigerant is passed through a radiatorlike device called a *condenser* (see Figure 5-4). The condenser is really a very simple device. It has no moving

FIGURE 5-2. **Evaporator.** *Courtesy of AC Delco/General Motors Corp.*

FIGURE 5-4. **Condenser.** *Courtesy of AC Delco/General Motors Corp.*

parts. In the condenser, the refrigerant gives up its heat to the outside air and is cooled to the condensation temperature and pressure and then condensed back into a liquid. The liquid collects in a pool in the bottom of the condenser, where it is further cooled and stored until it is needed in the evaporator. The cooling medium (air) for the condenser is passed through the coil by the radiator fan and the ram air as the car travels down the road.

The cooler, liquified refrigerant is now sent to the evaporator, where the refrigeration cycle is started all over again. In the evaporator the pressure and temperature of the refrigerant are reduced to match the temperature of the air flowing over the evaporator coil.

CYCLING CLUTCH SYSTEMS

In all cycling clutch systems, the compressor is operated intermittently by use of the clutch. Operation is controlled by a thermostatic switch that engages and disengages the clutch in response to the temperature inside the automobile. The sensing element of the thermostat is located in the outlet air of the evaporator. When the temperature inside the automobile rises, the switch closes, completing an electrical circuit to the clutch causing it to engage. As the evaporator outlet temperature drops to a predetermined temperature, the thermostatic switch opens the electrical circuit, stopping the compressor operation. The compressor will remain off until the thermostat demands more cooling, at which time the above process is repeated. It is from this intermittent operation of the compressor that the name cycling clutch is derived. The thermostat

is calibrated to allow the coldest possible air temperature out of the evaporator without freezing of the condensate on the evaporator surface.

EVAPORATOR PRESSURE CONTROL VALVE SYSTEMS

In this type of system the compressor operates continuously when the dash controls are in the cooling position. The evaporator outlet air temperature is automatically controlled by an evaporator pressure control valve such as the suction throttling valve, (STV), pilot operated absolute (POA), or evaporator pressure regulator (EPR). These valves throttle the flow of refrigerant through the evaporator as required to maintain a minimum evaporator pressure and temperature, thereby preventing freezing of condensate on the evaporator surface. This type of valve also maintains the maximum evaporator pressure.

REFRIGERANT PRESSURE AND FLOW

The purpose of the compressor is to cause a high pressure on the refrigerant. However, if there is nothing for the compressor to pump against, there will be no pressure buildup. The compressor would merely be circulating the refrigerant through the system.

We cannot however, block the flow of refrigerant through the system entirely. All that is necessary is to put pressure on the refrigerant vapor so that it will condense at normal temperatures and pressures. This must be done sometime after the refrigerant has left the evaporator and before it returns again as a liquid. If the pressure were as high in the evaporator as it is in the condenser, there would be no cooling and the air-conditioning unit would be useless.

CONTROLLING REFRIGERANT PRESSURE AND FLOW

The purpose of the refrigerant flow-control device is to control the pressure and flow of refrigerant through the system. There are several different types of flow-control devices. They all do the same job but in a different way.

The *float valve* is probably the most simple flow-control device; therefore, we will use it to get an idea of how these devices control the flow and pressure of the refrigerant (see Figure 5-5). This valve consists merely of a float that rides on the surface of the liquid refrigerant. As the liquid refrigerant boils off into a vapor, the liquid level drops to a lower level, allowing the float to also fall. The float is connected to the valve by means of a linkage system. As the float is lowered, the valve is opened, allowing more liquid refrigerant into the evaporator. The new liquid refrigerant raises the

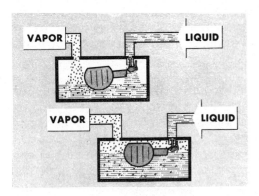

FIGURE 5-5.   Float type flow valve. *Courtesy of AC Delco/General Motors Corp.*

liquid level, raising the float, which in turn closes off the valve and stops the input of liquid refrigerant.

The float valve as described here is fully open or closed during operation. However, in practice it is a modulating device in that it is seldom fully open or fully closed during the operating cycle, thus allowing for a stabilized operating condition in the system.

SYSTEM COMPONENTS

All air-conditioning systems contain the same basic components, such as compressor, condenser, flow-control device, evaporator, connecting tubing, and the refrigerant. However, there are several different kinds of each of these components that we will discuss in detail throughout this text. Each type must be understood in order to effect efficient and economical service.

COMPRESSOR

Automotive air-conditioning compressors are of the reciprocating type. In operation, when the piston is moved downward, refrigerant vapor is drawn into the cylinder; this is the *suction stroke*. As the piston moves upward, the refrigerant vapor is compressed and forced out of the cylinder; this is the *compression stroke*. The flow of refrigerant vapor is controlled by two reed valves in the compressor head and attached to a valve plate. The suction reed controls the refrigerant flow into the compressor, and the discharge reed controls the flow out of the compressor (see Figure 5-6).

The compressor for an automotive air-conditioning unit is mounted under

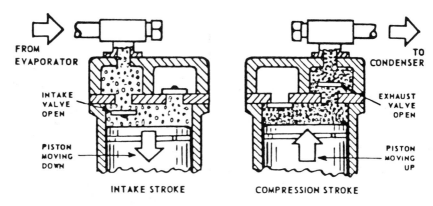

FIGURE 5-6. Compressor operation.

the hood in the engine compartment. The purpose of the compressor is to pull the low-pressure, low-temperature refrigerant vapor from the evaporator and compress it into a high-pressure, high-temperature refrigerant vapor. This compressing action causes the refrigerant to have a higher temperature than the surrounding air, thus enabling the condenser to condense the vapor back into a liquid. The second purpose of the compressor is to cause the refrigerant to circulate through the system.

The compressor is belt driven by the engine crankshaft by use of a clutch pulley assembly. Compressor lubrication is delivered by an oil pump, which is driven by the rotating motion of the compressor crankshaft, except on Tecumseh and York compressors. The pistons moving up and down in the cylinder draw the refrigerant vapor from the evaporator into the suction cavity on the intake stroke (see Figure 5-7). On the compression stroke the vapor is compressed into the discharge cavity and flows out the discharge valve and into the discharge line.

When a cycling clutch system is used, the compressor should start and stop at frequent intervals. Under high load conditions, however, the compressor may operate most of the time. When *evaporator pressure control valve* systems are employed, the compressor operates all the time the dash controls are in the cooling position.

NOTE: Compressors are designed to pump refrigerant vapor only. Pumping liquid refrigerant or oil with a refrigeration compressor will probably cause damage to the valve reeds, pistons, and the cylinders.

Compressor Clutches. All modern automotive air-conditioning systems are equipped with magnetic clutches mounted on the compressor crankshaft. Operation of the compressor is controlled through the clutch by the dash controls. There are two general designs of clutches: (1) rotating coil and (2) stationary coil.

Rotating Coil. On this type, the coil is mounted inside the pulley and rotates with it. A stationary brush assembly and

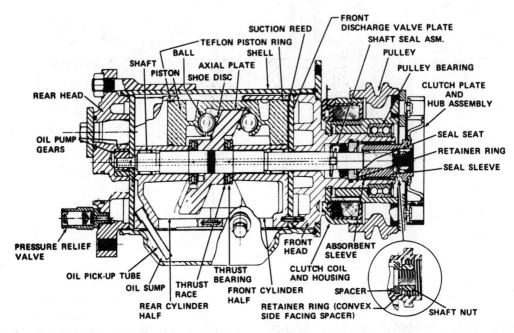

FIGURE 5-7. GM 6-cylinder compressor—internal. *Courtesy of AC Delco/General Motors Corp.*

rotating slip rings, which are part of the coil assembly, are used to make the electrical connections to the coil.

Stationary Coil. On this type, the coil is mounted on the compressor end and the electrical connections are made directly to the coil leads (see Figure 5-8).

The clutch assembly permits the compressor to be engaged or disengaged as required by the dash controls inside the car. On units where the compressor is required to operate continuously, the compressor clutch is controlled by a simple on and off switch. On compressor cycling units, the clutch is controlled by a thermostatic switch located in the passenger compartment. Some units employ an ambient switch to prevent operation of the compressor during extremely cold weather.

TYPES OF COMPRESSORS

In this discussion of compressors, we will cover the General Motors (A6) 6-cylinder, the General Motors (A4) 4-cylinder, the Chrysler, and the Tecumseh and York compressors. The Sankyo and Nippendenso compressors are variations of the GM compressors and will be covered in detail later.

General Motors (A6) 6-Cylinder Compressor.
The General Motors 6-cylinder compressor is of basic double action piston type (see Figure 5-9).

Three horizontal double-acting pistons make up the 6-cylinder compressor. The pistons operate in a 1.5-in. bore and have a 1.25-in. stroke. The axial plate pressed to the shaft drives the pistons. The

ROTATING COIL COMPRESSOR CLUTCH

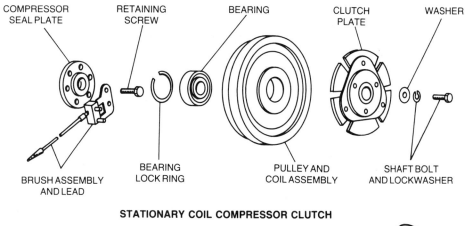

COMPRESSOR SEAL PLATE — RETAINING SCREW — BEARING — CLUTCH PLATE — WASHER

BRUSH ASSEMBLY AND LEAD — BEARING LOCK RING — PULLEY AND COIL ASSEMBLY — SHAFT BOLT AND LOCKWASHER

STATIONARY COIL COMPRESSOR CLUTCH

HUB AND SHOE ASSEMBLY — CLUTCH BEARING — LEAD WIRE — HUB SNAP RING

PULLEY ASSEMBLY — BEARING SNAP RING — CLUTCH FIELD ASSEMBLY

FIGURE 5-8. Stationary and rotating coil compressor clutches.

FIGURE 5-9. GM 6-cylinder compressor–external. *Courtesy of AC Delco / General Motors Corp.*

shaft is driven through a magnetic clutch and pulley (explained earlier). An oil pump mounted on the rear of the compressor picks up oil from the bottom (*sump*) of the compressor and lubricates the bearings and other internal parts of the compressor. Reed-type valves at each end of the compressor open or close to control the flow of refrigerant. Two gastight passages interconnect the chambers of the front and rear heads so that there is one common suction port and one common discharge port. This compressor is used mainly on many

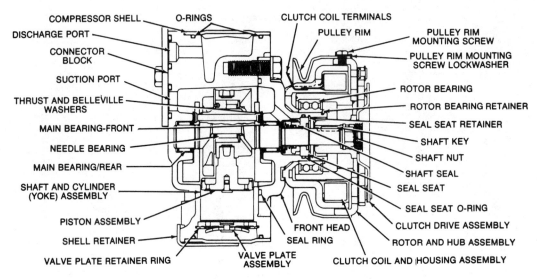

FIGURE 5-10. **GM 4-cylinder compressor–internal.** *Courtesy of AC Delco / General Motors Corp.*

applications other than General Motors built vehicles.

General Motors (R4) 4-Cylinder Compressor. This basic compressor mechanism is a modified Scotch yoke design with 4 cylinders located radially in the same plane (see Figure 5-10). Opposing pistons are pressed into a yoke, which rides upon a slider block located on the shaft eccentric. Rotation of the shaft provides a reciprocating motion with no connecting rods. The mechanism is completely balanced with counterweights. Needle bearings are used for both the shaft journals and the shaft eccentric. Pistons and yokes, along with the main cylinder housing and front cover, provide a lightweight unit (see Figure 5-11). Teflon piston rings are used to provide both a gas compression seal and a piston-to-bore bearing surface. The compressor outer shell is a simple steel band, which encloses a large angular discharge muffler space.

Two O-rings provide a seal between the compressor shell and the compressor cylinder. A rubber seal ring seals the front head to the cylinder assembly, and

FIGURE 5-11. **GM 4-cylinder compressor–external.** *Courtesy of AC Delco / General Motors Corp.*

the shaft seal assembly provides a front head to shaft seal.

Refrigerant flowing into the crankcase from the connector block at the rear is drawn through the reeds attached to the piston top during the suction stroke, and is discharged through the discharge valve plate, which is held in place at the top of the cylinder by a snap ring. The discharge gas flows out of the compressor muffler cavity through the connector block at the rear.

Chrysler Compressor. The Chrysler Air-Temp compressor is a 2-cylinder reciprocating piston Vee-type unit (see Figure 5-12). The high- and low-side service fittings are located between the cylinders on the front and rear of the compressor, respectively, and the intake and discharge passageways are found within the casting. The compressor has a rotary-type oil pump located under the rear cover to provide the compressor lubrication.

This compressor uses an EPR valve that is located in a compressor casting

FIGURE 5-13. Early and late model EPR valves. *Courtesy of AC Delco/General Motors Corp.*

cavity under the low side or suction line fitting (see Figure 5-13). The function of the EPR is to control the evaporator outlet temperature and prevent freezing of the evaporator core.

Tecumseh and York Compressors. The Tecumseh and York compressors are found on many Ford Motor Company and American Motors Corporation vehicles (see Figure 5-14). They are also used in many field installation packages.

These compressors are primarily the same except for the fabrication material. The Tecumseh compressor is made of cast iron, whereas the York is made of forged aluminum. Neither has an oil pump; they are lubricated by a positive lubrication system instead, which uses the differential pressure between the suction intake and the crankcase, plus

FIGURE 5-12. Chrysler compressor. *Courtesy of AC Delco/General Motors Corp.*

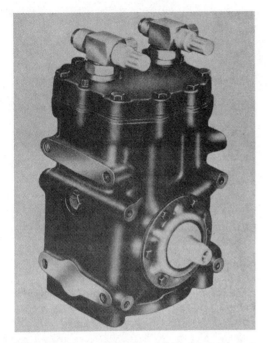

FIGURE 5-14. Typical Tecumseh or York compressor. *Courtesy of AC Delco/General Motors Corp.*

centrifugal force, as a means of circulating oil to and from the sump.

The most noticeable variation between these two compressors is the difference in the cylinder head inlet and outlet ports. Earlier models were designed to accommodate flange-type service fittings. Later models utilize either Roto-Lock or O-ring fittings.

MUFFLER

Most air-conditioning systems today use a discharge muffler (see Figure 5-15). The muffler is located in the discharge line between the compressor and the condenser (see Figure 5-16). The purpose of the muffler is to reduce the characteristic pumping noises created by the

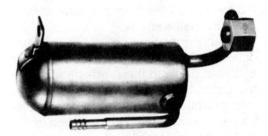

FIGURE 5-15. Muffler. *Courtesy of AC Delco/General Motors Corp.*

compressor. It also acts to reduce the noise transfer through the car body to the passenger compartment when wrapped with a soft sheet of rubber insulation. This insulation is not used on all models.

Mufflers should be installed with the inlet connection at the top and the outlet connection at the bottom. This is to reduce the amount of oil that could be trapped in the muffler.

CONDENSER

The condenser is a refrigerant tube coil mounted in a series of thin cooling fins to provide a maximum amount of heat

DISCHARGE MUFFLER

FIGURE 5-16. Discharge muffler location. *Courtesy of AC Delco/General Motors Corp.*

FIGURE 5-17. Condenser. *Courtesy of AC Delco/General Motors Corp.*

transfer in a minimum amount of space (see Figure 5-17). The condenser is mounted directly in front of the radiator, where it receives the full flow of ram air from the movement of the car going down the road and from the radiator fan (see Figure 5-18).

The purpose of the condenser is to condense or liquify the gaseous refrigerant coming from the compressor. To accomplish this task, the refrigerant must give up its heat to the surrounding air. The condenser receives this hot, high-pressure refrigerant into the condenser inlet at the top, and as the hot vapors pass down through the tubing, the heat is transferred from the refrigerant to the cooler outside air. The air passing through

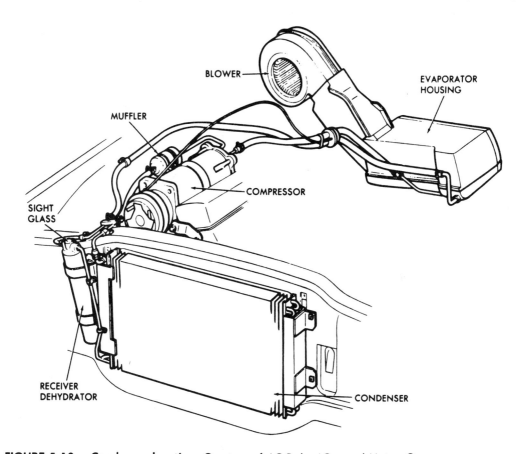

FIGURE 5-18. Condenser location. *Courtesy of AC Delco/General Motors Corp.*

the condenser fins causes a large amount of heat to be transferred. As the refrigerant is cooled, it changes to a warm, high-pressure liquid, which then flows out of the bottom of the condenser, through the tubing, and into the receiver-dehydrator.

RECEIVER-HYDRATOR

The receiver-dehydrator (sometimes called the receiver-drier) acts as a storage tank for the liquid refrigerant coming from the condenser. The refrigerant flows into the upper portion of the receiver tank, which contains a bag of desiccant (a *desiccant* is a material that absorbs moisture) (see Figure 5-19).

The refrigerant, upon flowing through an opening in the bottom of the receiver, is filtered through a mesh screen that is attached to a baffle. The desiccant will

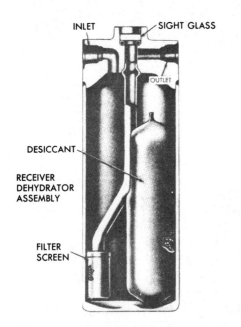

FIGURE 5-19. Receiver-dehydrator assembly. *Courtesy of AC Delco / General Motors Corp.*

absorb any moisture that might be present. Moisture can enter the system during installation or service procedures. These features of the receiver-dehydrator prevent obstruction to the valves or damage to the compressor assembly.

On some receiver-dehydrators, a sight glass is mounted at the top of the assembly or in the liquid line through which a solid column of liquid refrigerant might flow. The purpose of the sight glass is to indicate whether there is enough refrigerant in the system. No bubbles indicate that the system is either completely full or completely empty of refrigerant. Bubbles indicate that the system is low on refrigerant, in which case the leak must be found and repaired and the system recharged with refrigerant.

FLOW-CONTROL DEVICES

The purpose of the flow-control device is to meter the amount of refrigerant going into the evaporator. On some installations this control reacts to the refrigerant pressure in the evaporator, and in other installations it reacts to the temperature; and occasionally this control reacts to both the pressure and temperature. There are several different types of these controls, and we will discuss the most recent types in this text.

To understand how the flow-control device does its job, we need a detailed explanation of the process. Figure 5-20 shows what happens to the refrigerant as it passes through the flow-control device and into the evaporator.

All the area to the left of line 2 represents the refrigerant in the liquid state. The area between lines 1 and 2 represents a vapor-liquid mixture. The

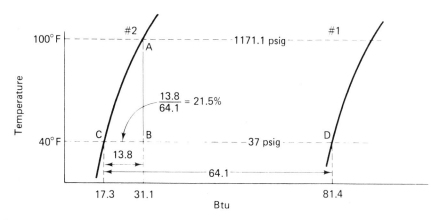

FIGURE 5-20.   Operation of flow control device.

area to the right of line 1 represents the refrigerant in the vapor state.

For this illustration, liquid refrigerant 12 enters the flow-control device at point A under a condition of 117.1 psi and 100°F. As it passes through the flow-control device, the pressure on the refrigerant drops to 37 psi and a temperature of 40°F. This is represented by point B. At point D, a mixture of vapor and liquid exists. This vapor has been formed by some of the liquid being evaporated in order to remove sensible heat from the remaining liquid to cool it down to 40°F. This evaporated refrigerant is called *flash gas.*

Figure 5-20 also shows how the percentage (21.5%) of flash gas is obtained. As line 2 is the saturated liquid line, at C all the refrigerant is in the liquid state at a temperature of 40°F. At this condition, each pound of refrigerant would contain 17.3 Btu. As line 1 is the saturated vapor line, at D all the refrigerant is in the saturated vapor state at a temperature of 40°F. At this point, the refrigerant would contain 81.4 Btu/lb.

For all practical purposes, it can be said that there is no loss or gain in the total heat of the refrigerant as it passes through the flow-control device. Therefore, since 1 lb of liquid refrigerant 12 contains 31.1 Btu as it enters the flow-control device at point A, it will also contain 31.1 Btu as it leaves the flow-control device.

The total heat that 1 lb of refrigerant 12 could absorb between points C and D is 64.1 Btu. As shown in Figure 5-20, the 13.8 Btu represented by the line CD has been used in cooling the remaining liquid refrigerant from 100° to 40°F. The figure shows that 13.8 divided by 64.1 equals 21.5%. Therefore, 21.5% of the liquid has been evaporated or changed into flash gas.

Actually, there is a slight loss in the heat of the refrigerant because of the heat picked up from the valve and refrigerant lines to the evaporator, distributor, and so on. But the amount lost is too insignificant to be considered.

Flash gas may be caused by many factors in the refrigeration system. Figure

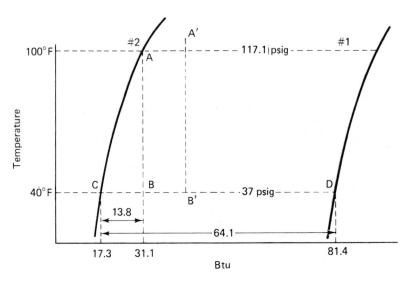

FIGURE 5-21.   Flash gas.

5-21 is the same as Figure 5-20 except that the line A¹B¹ has been added. This line shows the effect of an increased compression ratio on flash gas. Assuming the low-side pressure will remain the same, the compression ratio has been increased by an increase in the head pressure.

The line CB represents the amount of flash gas in Figure 5-20. The line CB¹ represents the new quantity of flash gas with a higher compression ratio. This is one very important reason why the compression ratio should be kept as low as possible.

With the theory of the metering device, the full cycle of compression, condensation, expansion, and evaporation has been explained. Figure 5-22 shows the entire cycle imposed on a temperature–Btu chart. As in the previous figures, all the area to the left of line 2 represents the refrigerant in the liquid state; all the area between lines 2 and 1 represents a vapor–liquid mixture; and all the area to

the right of line 1 represents the refrigerant in the vaporous state.

For a brief review of the cycle, assume point A of Figure 5-22 to be the suction vapor entering the compressor. From point A to point B, the vapor is compressed in the compressor. Notice that not only does the temperature increase, but there is an increase in the heat content of the vapor. This increase is the result of the actual work done to compress the vapor; it is called the *heat of compression*. From point B to B_1, the superheat of the vapor is removed and it is cooled to the saturated vapor line or condensing temperature. From point B_1 to point B_2, the vapor is condensed. From point B_2 to point C, the condensed liquid is subcooled in the condenser. This heat, which is removed from the system, is known as the *heat of rejection*.

From point C to point D, the liquid passes through the flow-control device. Although there is a change in temperature that corresponds to the pressure and

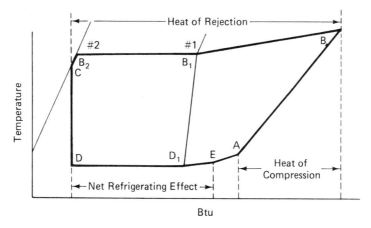

FIGURE 5-22.   Refrigeration cycle.

a partial change of state, the amount of heat in the refrigerant remains the same.

The remaining part of the cycle is heat absorption. From point D to point D_1, the absorption is accomplished entirely by the evaporation of the refrigerant. This is latent heat, since it results in a change of state of the refrigerant. From point D_1 to point E, the heat absorption results in superheating of the refrigerant vapor before it leaves the evaporator at point E. This quantity of heat, which is absorbed from point D to point E, is known as the *net refrigerating effect* and is the actual work done by the refrigeration system. From point E to point A, a small amount of heat is absorbed into the suction line, resulting in additional superheat to the refrigerant.

This cycle is the basis for all compression systems. If it is understood, a complete analysis can be made of any compression–refrigeration system.

Thermostatic Expansion Valves (TXV).
Thermostatic expansion valves were used on earlier automobile models to control the flow of refrigerant into the

evaporator (see Figure 5-23). An orifice in the valve regulates the refrigerant flow into the evaporator. This flow rate is modulated as required by a needletype plunger and seat which varies the orifice opening.

Function. The thermostatic expansion valve is a precision device designed to meter the flow of refrigerant into the

FIGURE 5-23.   Thermostatic expansion value.
Courtesy of Alco Controls Div., Emerson Electric Co.

evaporator in exact proportion to the rate of evaporation of the liquid refrigerant, thereby preventing the return of liquid refrigerant to the compressor. By being responsive to the temperature of the refrigerant vapor leaving the evaporator and the pressure in the evaporator, the thermostatic expansion valve can control the refrigerant vapor leaving the evaporator at a predetermined superheat.

Remember, a vapor is said to be superheated whenever its temperature is higher than the saturation temperature corresponding to its pressure. The amount of superheat is the temperature increase above the saturation temperature at the existing pressure.

Consider a refrigeration evaporator operating with R-12 as the refrigerant at 37-psi suction pressure (see Figure 5-24). The R-12 saturation temperature at 37 psi is 40°F. As long as any liquid refrigerant exists at this pressure, the refrigerant temperature will remain at 40°F.

As the refrigerant moves along in the evaporator, the liquid boils off into a vapor and the amount of liquid de-

creases. At point A in Figure 5-24, all the liquid has evaporated owing to the absorption of a quantity of heat from the atmosphere, which is equal to the latent heat of vaporization of the refrigerant. The refrigerant vapor continues along in the evaporator and remains at the same pressure (37 psi); however, its temperature increases owing to the continued absorption of heat from the surrounding atmosphere. By the time the refrigerant vapor reaches the end of the evaporator at point B, its temperature is 50°F. This refrigerant vapor is now superheated, and the amount of superheat is 50° −40°, or 10°F. The degree to which the refrigerant vapor is superheated is a function of the amount of refrigerant being fed into the evaporator and the load to which the evaporator is exposed.

Operation. Three forces govern the operation of the thermostatic expansion valve (see Figure 5-25): (1) the pressure created by the remote bulb and power assembly (P_1), (2) the evaporator pressure (P_2), and (3) the equivalent pressure of the superheat spring (P_3).

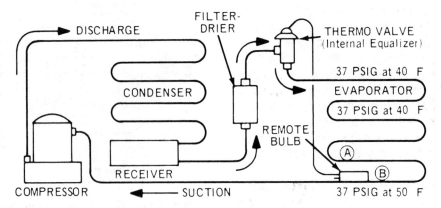

FIGURE 5-24. Basic refrigeration schematic. *Courtesy of Alco Controls Div., Emerson Electric Co.*

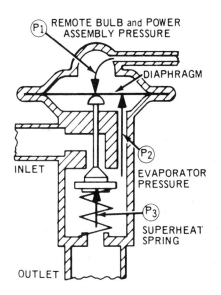

P₁ REMOTE BULB and POWER ASSEMBLY PRESSURE

DIAPHRAGM

INLET

P₂ EVAPORATOR PRESSURE

P₃ SUPERHEAT SPRING

OUTLET

FIGURE 5-25. Thermostatic expansion valve basic forces. *Courtesy of Alco Controls Div., Emerson Electric Co.*

The remote bulb and power assembly is a closed system; in the following discussion it is assumed that the remote bulb and power assembly charge is the same refrigerant as used in the system. The pressure within the remote bulb and power assembly, P_1 in Figure 5-25, corresponds to the saturation pressure of the refrigerant temperature leaving the evaporator and moves the pin in the opening direction. Opposed to this force on the underside of the diaphragm, and acting in the closing direction, is the force exerted by the evaporator (P_2), along with the pressure exerted by the superheat spring (P_3). The valve will assume a stable control position when these three forces are in equilibrium (that is $P_1 = P_2 + P_3$). As the temperature of the refrigerant vapor at the evaporator outlet increases above the saturation temperature, it becomes superheated. The pressure thus

generated in the remote bulb and power assembly increases above the combined pressures of the evaporator pressure and the superheat spring, causing the valve pin to move in the opening direction. Conversely, as the temperature of the refrigerant vapor leaving the evaporator decreases, the pressure in the remote bulb and power assembly also decreases, and the combined evaporator and spring pressures cause the valve pin to move in the closing direction.

The factory superheat setting of thermostatic expansion valves is made with the valve pin just starting to move away from the seat. These valves are so designed that an increase in superheat of the refrigerant vapor, leaving the evaporator, usually 4°F beyond the factory setting, is necessary for the valve pin to open to its full open position. For example, if the factory setting is 10°F superheat, the operating superheat at the rated open position (full-load rating of the valve) will be 14°F superheat. If the system is operating at half-load, with 50% compressor capacity reduction, the valve will operate at about 12°F superheat. It is important that the internally adjustable type of thermostatic expansion valves be ordered with the correct factory superheat setting. It is also recommended that an externally adjustable valve be used in a pilot-model test to determine the correct factory superheat setting before this type of valve is ordered.

As the operating superheat setting is raised, the evaporator capacity decreases, since more of the evaporator surface is needed to produce the superheat necessary to open the valve (see Figure 5-26). It is obvious, then, that it is most important to adjust the operating superheat correctly. It is vital that a

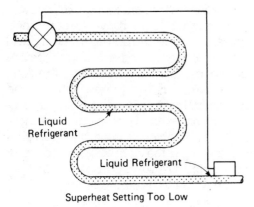

Liquid Refrigerant

Liquid Refrigerant

Superheat Setting Too Low

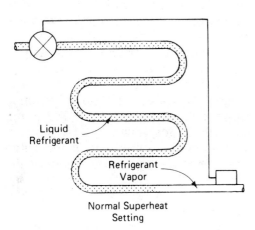

Liquid Refrigerant

Refrigerant Vapor

Normal Superheat Setting

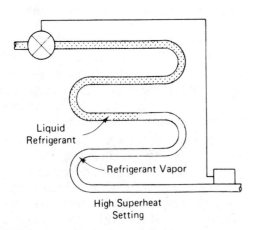

Liquid Refrigerant

Refrigerant Vapor

High Superheat Setting

FIGURE 5-26. Superheat setting and evaporator capacity.

minimum change in the superheat be required to move the valve pin to the full open position, because this provides savings in both the initial evaporator cost and cost of operation. Accurate and sensitive control of the liquid refrigerant flow into the evaporator is necessary to provide maximum evaporator capacity under all load conditions.

Adjustment. On most thermostatic expansion valves used on automotive air-conditioning systems, external adjustment is not possible. However, it is desirable that the service technician know how the valve works and what conditions affect its operation.

How to Determine Superheat. Thermostatic expansion valve performance cannot be analyzed properly by measurement of the suction pressure or by observation of the frost formation on the suction line. The initial step in correctly determining whether or not a thermostatic expansion valve is functioning properly is to measure the superheat setting:

1. Measure the temperature of the suction line at the point where the bulb is clamped.
2. Obtain the suction pressure that exists in the suction line at the bulb location by either of the following methods:
   (a) If the valve is externally equalized, a gauge in the external equalizer line will indicate the desired pressure directly and accurately.
   (b) Read the gauge pressure at the suction valve of the compressor. To the pressure reading, add the estimated pressure drop through the suction line be-

tween the valve location and the compressor suction valve. The sum of the gauge reading and the estimated line pressure drop will equal the approximate line pressure at the bulb.

3. Convert the pressure obtained in step 2(a) or 2(b) to the saturated evaporater temperature by using a temperature–pressure chart as shown in Table 5-1.

4. Subtract the two temperatures obtained in steps 1 and 3. The difference is the superheat.

Figure 5-27 illustrates a typical example of superheat measurement on an air-conditioning system using R-12 refrigerant. The temperature of the suction line at the bulb location is read at 51°F. The suction pressure at the compressor is 35 psi and the estimated pressure drop is 2 psi. The total suction pressure is 35 psi plus 2 psi, which equals 37 psi. This is equivalent to a 40°F saturation temperature; 40°F subtracted from 51°F equals 11°F superheat setting.

Notice that subtracting the difference between the temperature at the inlet of the evaporator and the temperature at

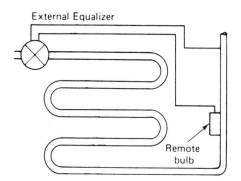

FIGURE 5-28. Remote bulb installation on vertical tubing.

the outlet is not an accurate measurement of superheat. This method is not recommended because any evaporator pressure drop will result in an erroneous superheat indication.

Bulb Location and Installation. The location of the remote bulb is extremely important and in some cases determines the success or failure of the air-conditioning unit. For satisfactory expansion valve control, good thermal contact between the bulb and the suction line is essential. The bulb should be securely fastened with two straps to a clean, straight section of the suction line.

Installation of the bulb on a horizontal run of suction line is preferred. If a vertical installation cannot be avoided, the bulb should be mounted so that the capillary tube comes out the top, as shown in Figure 5-28.

To install, clean the suction line thoroughly before clamping the remote bulb in place. When a steel suction line is used, it is advisable to paint the line with aluminum paint to minimize future corrosion and faulty remote bulb contact with the suction line. On lines under ⅞ in. OD, the remote bulb may be installed on

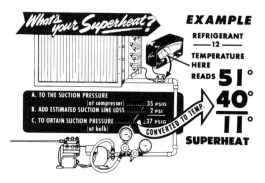

FIGURE 5-27. Determination of superheat.
Courtesy of Sporlan Valve Co.

TABLE 5-1. Temperature-Pressure Chart

BOLD FIGURES = INCHES MERCURY VACUUM   LIGHT FIGURES = PSIG

°F	R-12	R-13	R-22	R-500	R-502	R-717 Ammonia
-100	**27.0**	7.5	**25.0**	—	**23.3**	**27.4**
-95	**26.4**	10.9	**24.1**	—	**22.1**	**26.8**
-90	**25.7**	14.2	**23.0**	—	**20.7**	**26.1**
-85	**25.0**	18.2	**21.7**	—	**19.0**	**25.3**
-80	**24.1**	22.2	**20.2**	—	**17.1**	**24.3**
-75	**23.0**	27.1	**18.5**	—	**15.0**	**23.2**
-70	**21.8**	32.0	**16.6**	—	**12.6**	**21.9**
-65	**20.5**	37.7	**14.4**	—	**10.0**	**20.4**
-60	**19.0**	43.5	**12.0**	—	**7.0**	**18.6**
-55	**17.3**	50.0	**9.2**	—	**3.6**	**16.6**
-50	**15.4**	57.0	**6.2**	—	**0.0**	**14.3**
-45	**13.3**	64.6	**2.7**	—	2.1	**11.7**
-40	**11.0**	72.7	0.5	**7.9**	4.3	**8.7**
-35	**8.4**	81.5	2.6	**4.8**	6.7	**5.4**
-30	**5.5**	91.0	4.9	**1.4**	9.4	**1.6**
-28	**4.3**	94.9	5.9	0.0	10.6	**0.0**
-26	**3.0**	98.9	6.9	0.7	11.7	0.8
-24	**1.6**	103.0	7.9	1.5	13.0	1.7
-22	**0.3**	107.3	9.0	2.3	14.2	2.6
-20	0.6	111.7	10.1	3.1	15.5	3.6
-18	1.3	116.2	11.3	4.0	16.9	4.6
-16	2.1	120.8	12.5	4.9	18.3	5.6
-14	2.8	125.7	13.8	5.8	19.7	6.7
-12	3.7	130.5	15.1	6.8	21.3	7.9
-10	4.5	135.4	16.5	7.8	22.8	9.0
-8	5.4	140.5	17.9	8.8	24.4	10.3
-6	6.3	145.7	19.3	9.9	26.0	11.6
-4	7.2	151.1	20.8	11.0	27.7	12.9
-2	8.2	156.5	22.4	12.1	29.5	14.3
0	9.1	162.1	24.0	13.3	31.2	15.7
2	10.2	167.9	25.6	14.5	33.1	17.2
4	11.2	173.7	27.3	15.7	35.0	18.8
6	12.3	179.8	29.1	17.0	37.0	20.4
8	13.5	185.9	30.9	18.4	39.1	22.1
10	14.6	192.1	32.8	19.8	41.1	23.8
12	15.8	198.6	34.7	21.2	43.3	25.6
14	17.1	205.2	36.7	22.7	45.5	27.5
16	18.4	211.9	38.7	24.2	47.8	29.4
18	19.7	218.8	40.9	25.7	50.1	31.4
20	21.0	225.7	43.0	27.3	52.5	33.5
22	22.4	233.0	45.3	29.0	55.0	35.7
24	23.9	240.3	47.6	30.7	57.5	37.9
26	25.4	247.8	49.9	32.5	60.1	40.2
28	26.9	255.5	52.4	34.3	62.8	42.6
30	28.5	263.2	54.9	36.1	65.4	45.0
32	30.1	271.3	57.5	38.0	68.3	47.6
34	31.7	279.5	60.1	40.0	71.2	50.2
36	33.4	287.8	62.8	42.0	74.1	52.9
38	35.2	296.3	65.6	44.1	77.2	55.7
40	37.0	304.9	68.5	46.2	80.2	58.6
45	41.7	327.5	76.0	51.9	88.3	66.3
50	46.7	351.2	84.0	57.8	96.9	74.5
55	52.0	376.1	92.6	64.2	106.0	83.4
60	57.7	402.3	101.6	71.0	115.6	92.9
65	63.8	429.8	111.2	78.2	125.8	103.1
70	70.2	458.7	121.4	85.8	136.6	114.1
75	77.0	489.0	132.2	93.9	148.0	125.8
80	84.2	520.8	143.6	102.5	159.9	138.3
85	91.8	—	155.7	111.5	172.5	151.7
90	99.8	—	168.4	121.2	185.8	165.9
95	108.3	—	181.8	131.2	199.7	181.1
100	117.2	—	195.9	141.9	214.4	197.2
105	126.6	—	210.8	153.1	229.7	214.2
110	136.4	—	226.4	164.9	245.8	232.3
115	146.8	—	242.7	177.3	262.6	251.5
120	157.7	—	259.9	190.3	280.3	271.7
125	169.1	—	277.9	203.9	298.7	293.1
130	181.0	—	296.8	218.2	318.0	315.0
135	193.5	—	316.6	233.2	338.1	335.0
140	206.6	—	337.3	248.8	359.1	365.0
145	220.6	—	358.9	265.2	381.1	390.0
150	234.6	—	381.5	282.3	403.9	420.0
155	249.9	—	405.2	300.1	427.8	450.0
160	265.12	—	429.8	318.7	452.6	490.0

Courtesy of Alco Controls Division.

top of the line. On ⅞ in. OD and larger, the bulb should be installed at about the 4 o'clock position (see Figure 5-29).

It is necessary to protect the remote bulb from the effects of the outside airstream after it is clamped to the line; use a material such as sponge rubber that will not absorb water when evaporator temperatures are above 32°F.

Thermostatic Expansion Valve Equalizer. The operation of the thermostatic expansion valve is dependent on the relationship of three fundamental pressures. That is, the bulb pressure acting on top of the diaphragm must always equal the sum of the suction pressure (or evaporator pressure) and the spring pressure applied to the evaporator side of the diaphragm.

On externally equalized valves, the pressure at the valve outlet (or evaporator outlet) is transmitted to the evaporator side of the diaphragm via a passageway within the valve through a clearance around the push rods (see Figure 5-30).

On an externally equalized expansion valve, the evaporator side of the diaphragm is isolated from the valve outlet pressure by packing around the

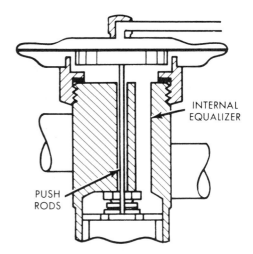

FIGURE 5-30. **Internally equalized expansion valve.** *Courtesy of Sporlan Valve Co.*

push rods. The suction pressure is transmitted to the evaporator side of the diaphragm by a line usually connected between the suction line near the evaporator outlet (preferably downstream of the bulb) and an external fitting on the valve (see Figure 5-31).

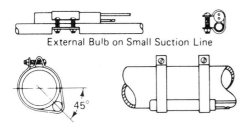

External Bulb on Small Suction Line

45°

External Bulb on Large Suction Line

FIGURE 5-29. **Remote bulb installation on horizontal tubing.** *Courtesy of Alco Controls Div., Emerson Electric Co.*

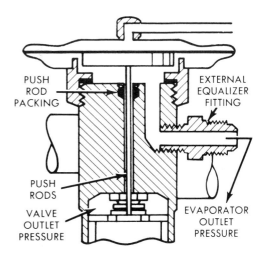

FIGURE 5-31. **Externally equalized expansion valve.** *Courtesy of Sporlan Valve Co.*

EVAPORATOR

The evaporator is the device that cools and dehumidifies the air before it enters the passenger compartment of the car (see Figure 5-32). The high-pressure liquid refrigerant from the condenser flows through the flow-control device orifice into the low-pressure area of the evaporator. This regulated flow of refrigerant starts boiling immediately as it is absorbing heat from the evaporator. The air passing over the evaporator loses its heat to the cooler coil, and the air is cooled and dehumidified. The moisture that is condensed by the evaporator coil is drained off through a condensate drain line to the outside of the car.

ACCUMULATOR

On almost all later-model automobiles, an accumulator is used to prevent liquid refrigerant returning to the compressor and causing damage to it. Refrigeration

FIGURE 5-32. Evaporator. *Courtesy of AC Delco/General Motors Corp.*

compressors are designed to pump a vapor, not a liquid. Accumulators are used on GM clutch cycling systems with the orifice tube flow-control device, and on some Ford systems that use the suction throttling valve-type control. Its purpose is to collect or "accumulate" any liquid refrigerant that might pass through the evaporator on these types of systems and prevent its entering the compressor. Only the vapor is allowed to pass into the compressor suction valves.

Thus, with an ideal accumulator without a bleed hole, and a correctly designed system, little or no liquid can get to the compressor, which allows the compressor to operate as it was designed. However, in an actual accumulator, there is always some entrained liquid refrigerant in the vapor stream to the compressor. What determines a good accumulator is how well it separates vapor from the liquid and how little liquid is released to the compressor. Also, an actual accumulator is equipped with an oil bleed hole to prevent trapping oil in the bottom of the accumulator. Some liquid refrigerant bleeds through this hole with the oil. Thus, the refrigerant flow out of the accumulator to the compressor is made up of mostly vapor with some entrained liquid and some oil passing out of the bleed hole.

On GM automobiles a bag of desiccant is placed in the accumulator. This desiccant is used to absorb any moisture in the refrigeration system.

BLOWER AND MOTOR

A blower and motor are located in the evaporator housing and are used to force the air through the coil, the air ducting, and into the passenger compartment. The blower draws the warm air from inside the passenger compartment, or from the outside, and forces the air through the evaporator, where it is cooled and dehumidified, and then through the ducts to the passenger compartment. The speed of the motor is controlled by a switch on the instrument panel inside the car. Various speeds from low to high can be selected by the switch.

When the blower is operated in the high speed position, the blower will provide the greatest amount of air to the compartment. When the blower switch is positioned in one of the other positions, the airflow will be reduced. A slower blower speed will allow the air to remain in contact with the evaporator for a longer period of time, reduce the temperature still lower, and remove more of the moisture. However, the lower speeds may not provide adequate air circulation to satisfy the ventilation requirements of the passengers.

WATER CONTROL VALVE

The water control valve is located in the heater core inlet hose (see Figure 5-33). It is made up of a brass tube, piston

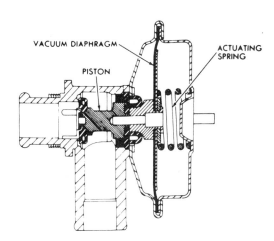

FIGURE 5-33. Water control valve. *Courtesy of AC Delco/General Motors Corp.*

assembly, and a vacuum diaphragm assembly.

The water control valve is generally used in air-conditioning systems that are controlled by an evaporator pressure regulator. Its function is to regulate the flow of radiator coolant into the heater core. Depending upon the make and model of the car, it is either opened or closed when a vacuum is applied to the diaphragm. On most applications, the water valve is closed when the air-conditioning controls are set to the maximum cooling position.

REVIEW QUESTIONS

1. What is the function of the evaporator?

2. How many states does the refrigerant enter in a refrigeration system?

3. What happens to the refrigerant when it absorbs heat?

4. What are the two purposes of a refrigeration compressor?

5. What is the purpose of the condenser?

6. What are the main working parts of an automotive air-conditioning system?

7. What is the purpose of the flow-control device?

8. What types of compressors are used in automotive air-conditioning systems?

9. What component permits the compressor to engage or disengage?

10. Where is the muffler located in an automotive air-conditioning system?

11. Why is the condenser located in front of the radiator?

12. Define the term superheat.

13. What three forces govern the operation of a thermostatic expansion valve?

14. Is it recommended that the superheat setting of a thermostatic expansion valve be checked by subtracting the evaporator inlet temperature from the evaporator outlet temperature?

15. How should the thermostatic expansion valve bulb be mounted?

16. What is the purpose of an accumulator?

17. What is the purpose of the bleed hole in an accumulator?

18. What is the purpose of the desiccant in a refrigeration system?

19. What may be a problem when running the blower on a lower speed?

20. What is the function of the water control valve?

Basically, there are two types of automotive air-conditioning systems. These units are classified according to the method used in providing temperature control. These systems are the cycling clutch system and evaporator pressure control system. It is important that the technician be able to tell the difference between the two types of systems so that the proper procedures may be employed when working on the unit.

CYCLING CLUTCH SYSTEM

This type of system may be used with different types of refrigerant flow-control devices, including the thermostatic expansion valve and a receiver–drier. Or it may employ an expansion orifice tube and an accumulator.

In all systems using this type of temperature control, the compresssor is operated on an intermittent basis. This is accomplished by engaging and disengaging the clutch with a thermostat inside the passenger compartment. The thermostatic switch operates in response to the temperature in the passenger compartment through a capillary tube, which is an integral part of the switch assembly. When the temperature inside the car rises to a predetermined degree, the switch will close a set of electrical contacts, which in turn completes a supply of electricity to the compressor clutch, causing the compressor to operate. As the temperature inside the compartment is reduced to a predetermined degree, the thermostat switch contacts open the electrical circuit to the clutch and the compressor stops operating. The system is now awaiting another signal from the thermostat that more cooling is needed. This operation provides the name "cycling clutch system." In these types of systems the thermostat is adjusted

6

Control Systems Components

to provide the lowest possible air temperature coming out of the evaporator without freezing of the condensate on the evaporator coil.

Cycling Clutch System with a Thermostatic Expansion Valve. Often, when these systems are installed at the factory, a thermostatic expansion valve (TXV) and a receiver–drier type of system will be used (see Figure 6-1). The evaporator is usually mounted in the housing for the heater core, and both systems use a common blower and ductwork for both applications. The refrigerant flow-control device, in this case the thermostatic expansion valve, may be either mounted in the cowling with the evaporator, or it may be installed in the engine compartment.

In most of these applications, the thermostatic switch is not adjustable from inside the passenger compartment and is mounted on the evaporator case. The temperature is varied to provide passenger comfort by using fresh or recirculating air and by reheating the cooled air before it leaves the evaporator housing.

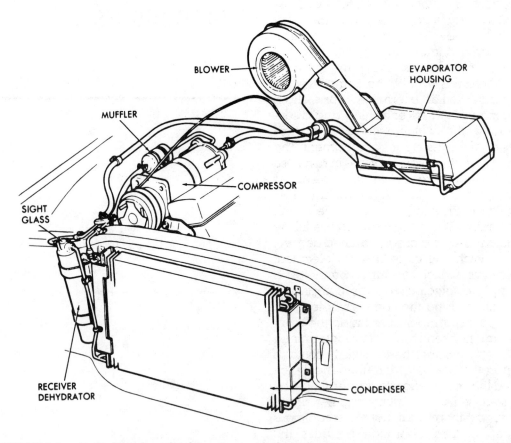

BLOWER

EVAPORATOR HOUSING

MUFFLER

COMPRESSOR

SIGHT GLASS

RECEIVER DEHYDRATOR

CONDENSER

FIGURE 6-1.   Typical "cycling clutch" system with thermostatic expansion valve. *Courtesy of AC Delco/General Motors Corp.*

In this case, the compressor is cycled only to prevent icing of the evaporator.

The field-installed unit is another system that uses the cycling clutch system. In these types of systems, the evaporator, thermostatic expansion valve, and blower are installed under the dash as an integral unit. These types of systems do not have the fresh-air option that is available with factory-installed systems. They operate solely on recirculated air. The compartment temperature is controlled by the intermittent operation of the compressor. The thermostatic switch has a control knob that the passengers can adjust to satisfy their particular requirements.

The components that make up the cycling clutch system with a thermostatic expansion valve are shown in Figure 6-2. Note that the receiver–dehydrator is used with this particular system. The receiver–dehydrator has two functions: to store refrigerant until it is needed, and to remove any moisture that may have gotten into the system during installation or service operations.

Cycling Clutch System with an Expansion Orifice Tube (CCOT). The typical CCOT system is usually factory installed and can use one of two types of temperature controls: the thermostat inside the passenger compartment, or a pressure cycling switch that is mounted on the accumulator shell (see Figure 6-3). On this type of system an expansion orifice tube is used as the refrigerant flow-control device (see Figure 6-4).

Notice that this system has an accumulator at the evaporator outlet. The purpose of the accumulator is to prevent

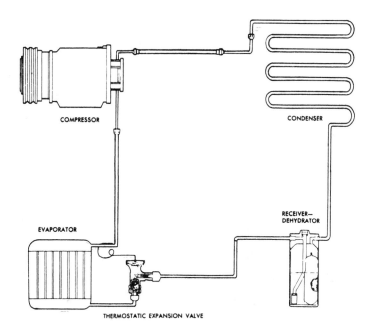

FIGURE 6-2. Basic components of cycling clutch system thermostatic expansion valve. *Courtesy of AC Delco / General Motors Corp.*

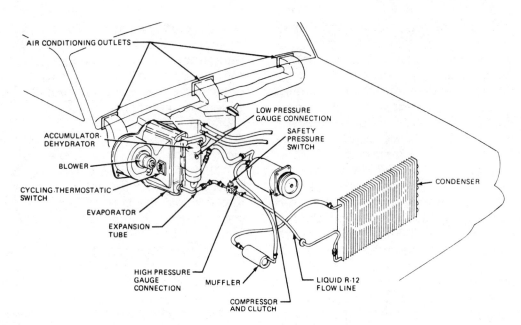

FIGURE 6-3. **Typical cycling clutch system with expansion (orifice) tube (CCOT).** *Courtesy of AC Delco / General Motors Corp.*

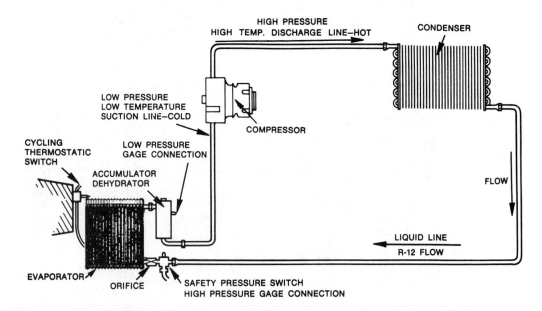

FIGURE 6-4. **Basic components of cycling clutch system with expansion (orifice) tube (CCOT).** *Courtesy of AC Delco / General Motors Corp.*

liquid refrigerant from entering the compressor. On some systems a bag of desiccant is installed in the accumulator to absorb any moisture that may have entered the system. There is no receiver–dryer or sight glass used in these systems.

EVAPORATOR PRESSURE CONTROL SYSTEMS

When this type of system is used, the compressor operates continuously when the dash controls are placed in the cooling position. The temperature of the air from the evaporator is controlled by an evaporator pressure control valve such as the STV, POA, or the EPR valve. These valves are used to control the flow of refrigerant through the system as

required by the evaporator to maintain the minimum evaporator pressure possible without freezing of the condensate on the evaporator coil during operation. These valves also control the maximum evaporator pressure to allow proper cooling of the passenger compartment.

Pilot-Operated Absolute (POA) Valve System. In the POA system, both the evaporator and the heater cores are placed in the air-distribution duct system, which is an integral part of the cowling and dash assembly (see Figure 6-5). The operator controls actuate a series of doors inside the ductwork, which makes it possible to select the maximum air conditioning or the maximum heater air flow, as well as any combination of the

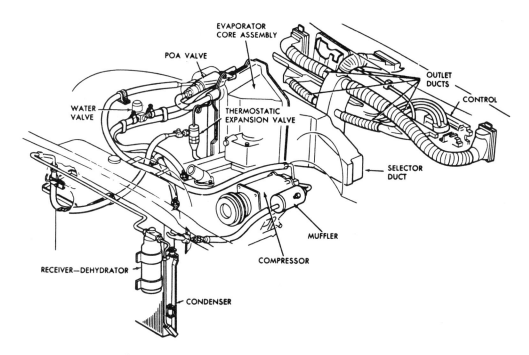

FIGURE 6-5. Typical evaporator pressure control system with POA valve. *Courtesy of AC Delco / General Motors Corp.*

two that will provide the desired passenger comfort.

When the technician is troubleshooting one of these types of systems, it is necessary to differentiate between any malfunctions that are caused by the air-distribution system and those that are caused by the refrigeration system. The refrigeration components for this type of system are shown in Figure 6-6.

Remember that the compressor operates continuously and that evaporator de-ice control is accomplished by the POA valve. This valve is located in the refrigerant tubing at the outlet of the evaporator and before the compressor. There is an equalizer line connected between the POA valve and the thermostatic expansion valve to sense the re-

frigerant pressure as it leaves the evaporator. Also, there is an oil bypass or a liquid bleed line reaching from the bottom of the evaporator to the POA valve. The purpose of this line is to ensure that a sufficient amount of oil is circulating through the system to lubricate the compressor at all times. There is also a connection on the POA valve for taking pressure readings for analyzing system operation.

Note that this system uses a receiver-dehydrator, sight glass, and a thermostatic expansion valve in the high side of the system.

Valves-In-Receiver (VIR) System. This type of system incorporates the POA, TXV, and the receiver–dehydrator in one

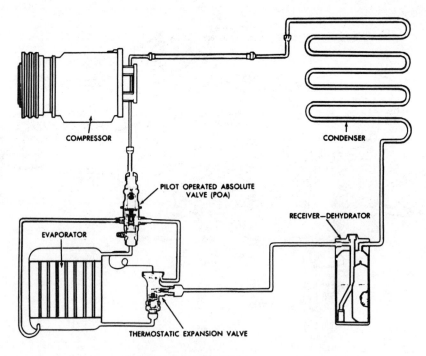

FIGURE 6-6. Basic components of evaporator pressure control system with POA valve. *Courtesy of AC Delco/General Motors Corp.*

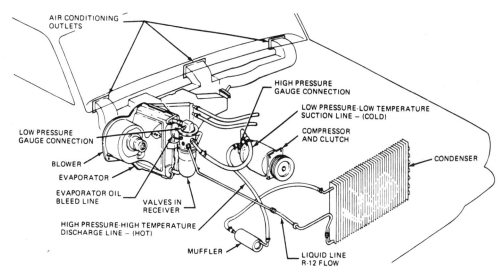

FIGURE 6-7. Typical evaporator pressure control system with VIR assembly. *Courtesy of AC Delco / General Motors Corp.*

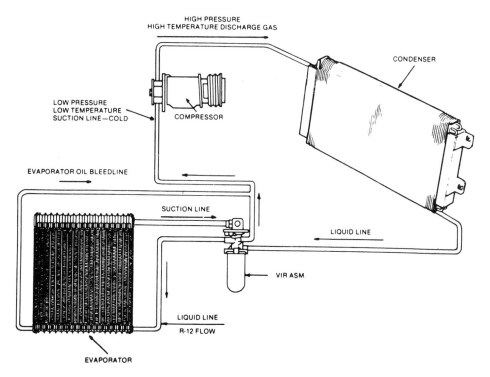

FIGURE 6-8. Basic components of evaporator pressure control system with VIR assembly. *Courtesy of AC Delco / General Motors Corp.*

assembly (see Figure 6-7). The VIR assembly is mounted close to the evaporator and has connections to both the evaporator inlet and outlet tubing. Figure 6-8 shows the basic refrigeration system components.

The external equalizer line for the thermostatic expansion valve is located inside the VIR assembly. Its function is accomplished by a bypass hole drilled into the assembly housing. The oil bypass line and the liquid bleed line are connected from the VIR outlet to the evaporator bottom.

REVIEW QUESTIONS

1. Name the two types of control systems discussed in this chapter.

2. What is the purpose of the thermostat in the passenger compartment?

3. At what temperature is the thermostat adjusted?

4. What does the thermostat energize to cause the unit to operate?

5. What is the purpose of the expansion orifice tube?

6. Do field-installed units have the fresh-air option?

7. Name two types of temperature controls that are used on CCOT systems.

8. Name the types of controls used on the evaporator pressure control systems.

9. What is the purpose of the controls listed in question 8?

10. Where is the thermostatic expansion valve located in the VIR system?

In addition to the components discussed in Chapter 6, there are those that control the operation of the basic components. They are devices such as evaporator pressure controls and the various switches that are used depending on the type of system used. The following is a description of these basic components or assemblies that contain more than one component.

EVAPORATOR PRESSURE (TEMPERATURE) CONTROLS

The various automobile air-conditioning systems that are referred to as evaporator pressure control systems use different types of valves at the evaporator outlet to maintain the pressure high enough to prevent icing of the evaporator coil. They are the suction throttling valve (STV), pilot-operated absolute valve (POA), evaporator pressure regulator (EPR), or evaporator temperature regulator (ETR).

Regardless of which valve is used, its purpose is to maintain a "suction pressure" in the evaporator high enough to provide satisfactory operation. This is possible because of the pressure–temperature relationship, discussed previously. The temperature is controlled at a sufficiently high point to provide effective air conditioning while preventing the formation of ice on the evaporator.

Suction Throttling Valve (STV). The suction throttling valve controls the evaporator temperature by limiting the minimum evaporator pressure to prevent freezing the condensate. The prevention of evaporator freeze-up is important because any obstruction to the flow of air through the evaporator reduces the cooling effect of the system. Plus there is a loss of efficiency from the refrigeration standpoint. When the system is operating, the

——— 7 ———

System Control Component Descriptions

evaporator pressure will be maintained at a minimum pressure of 28 psi, which will provide maximum cooling at all times. This pressure is maintained as long as the system controls are set at the cooling position.

The STV valve is located in the suction line where it leaves the evaporator (see Figure 7-1). It operates on the spring pressure against the evaporator pressure principle. In operation, the flow of refrigerant from the evaporator to the compressor is controlled by the position of the piston in the valve body, which is, in turn, determined by the balance of the forces that are applied to the diaphragm. The low-pressure refrigerant vapor flows into the valve inlet through three openings in the lower skirt of the piston, then through the valve outlet, and through the suction line to the compressor suction. A very small part of the refrigerant is diverted to the inside of the piston through holes drilled in the piston wall. The pressure caused by this refrigerant is transmitted to the inner side of the diaphragm, allowing it to sense the actual pressure in the evaporator. The evaporator pressure thus applied on the inner side of the diaphragm and piston assembly is balanced and opposed by the spring load plus the atmospheric pressure applied to the outer surface of the diaphragm. An increase of pressure (temperature) in the evaporator will cause the piston to move against the

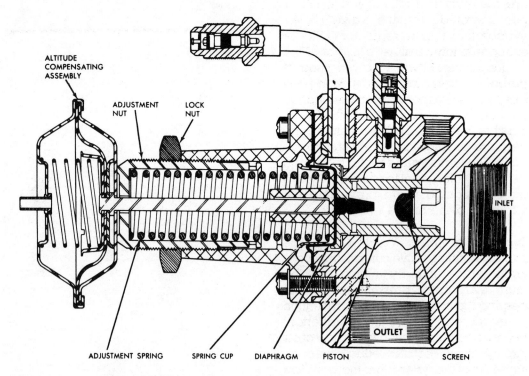

FIGURE 7-1. Suction throttling valve—sectional view. *Courtesy of AC Delco/General Motors Corp.*

opposing spring pressure and thus open the valve, allowing more vapor to flow through to the compressor suction. This allows the compressor to lower the evaporator pressure, which allows the piston to close as required to maintain the proper pressure. The evaporator pressure is thus controlled by "throttling," or choking off, the suction line when the evaporator pressure drops below the established setting. When the refrigerant flow is thus restricted, the evaporator pressure will rise because of the boiling off of the refrigerant. As the pressure increases above the valve setting, the valve will be caused to open as required to lower the pressure to the proper level.

The temperature lever on the dash may be moved at this point to mix heated air with the cooled air and thus temper the outlet air to the desired temperature. Thus, indicating that maximum cooling is no longer needed, the control cable and linkage move to close a vacuum valve through which 4½ in. of vacuum has been applied to the vacuum head on the STV. The loss of this vacuum allows an increase in internal spring pressure, which is applied to the STV piston and effectively increases the minimum evaporator pressure approximately 3 lb, to 31 psi, thus reducing the evaporator cooling capacity.

NOTE: The primary purpose of the vacuum connection is to guard against evaporator freeze-up at higher elevations. When the system is operated at elevations above 4000 ft, the temperature lever should be moved about ½ in.

STV valves are equipped with two Schrader valve ports on the outside of the assembly. One is capped and used for checking the low-side pressure with the gauge manifold set. The other is used to connect the oil bypass line from the bottom of the evaporator. The small threaded opening near the oil bypass fitting is used to connect the external equalizer line from the thermostatic expansion valve.

Pilot-Operated Absolute (POA) Valve.

The function of this valve is to control the evaporator pressure during operation. This is accomplished by restricting the evaporator outlet so that the desired pressure is maintained in the evaporator, just as with the STV valve. Even though the result is the same with this valve as with the STV valve, their operation is nothing alike.

The POA valve, as its name applies, contains a pilot valve. This valve is equipped with a bronze bellows that has been evacuated. The valve is controlled by this nearly perfect vacuum rather than by the atmospheric pressure around the valve, as is the case with the STV valve. Because of this, an external altitude correction device is not needed with the POA valve (see Figure 7-2).

When the system is in normal operation, the evaporator pressure at point A in Figure 7-2 is applied to the inlet fitting of the valve. As the refrigerant passes through the piston screen and the drilled holes in the piston, pressure is applied to the area beneath the piston ring. As the evaporator pressure increases, the force of the piston ring will be overcome and the piston will begin to move, gradually opening the valve's main port and allowing more refrigerant to flow at point B. This action is possible because the pressure in area C behind the piston is lower than the evaporator pressure.

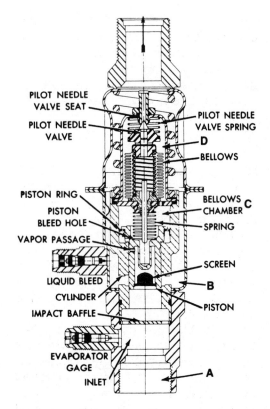

PILOT NEEDLE
VALVE SEAT

PILOT NEEDLE
VALVE

PILOT NEEDLE
VALVE SPRING

D

BELLOWS

PISTON RING

PISTON

BLEED HOLE

VAPOR PASSAGE

BELLOWS
CHAMBER C

SPRING

SCREEN

LIQUID BLEED

CYLINDER

IMPACT BAFFLE

B

PISTON

EVAPORATOR
GAGE

INLET

A

FIGURE 7-2. Pilot-operated absolute valve (POA)—*sectional view. Courtesy of AC Delco/ General Motors Corp.*

However, as the valve is opening, the refrigerant from the evaporator is flowing through the piston bleed port into the area C above the piston. As the pressure in area C increases and approaches the evaporator pressure, point A, the piston spring will cause the piston to move toward the closed position, reducing the flow of refrigerant. When the pressure becomes equal on both sides of the piston, the main port will normally be closed and the valve would be inoperative. This is where the bellows and the pilot valve are coming into use. The area surrounding the pilot bellows and the

needle valve, point D, is connected to the area above the piston C by a hole to that area. Therefore, the pressures in area C and area D will be equal. As refrigerant pressure builds up in area C, the piston spring allows the piston to move toward the closed position. At the same time, pressure builds up in area D, which surrounds the evacuated bellows. The higher pressure in this area causes the bellows to collapse, pulling the needle from the needle seat. The pressure in area D will be reduced by refrigerant flowing through the needle valve, and at a predetermined point the bellows will expand and close the pilot needle valve. When the pressure is again reduced in area D, the pressure will also be reduced in area C. The reduced pressure will allow the evaporator pressure to overcome the force of the piston spring and cause the piston to move and open the main port of the valve. In actual operation, the valve parts balance out and hold the piston in the proper modulated position to maintain the predetermined pressure and temperature in the evaporator at all times.

The POA valve is set at the factory and is not field repairable. When found to be faulty, the valve should be replaced as a complete unit.

There are three external connections in addition to the inlet and outlet ports. There are two valves equipped with Schrader valves; one is used to connect the oil bypass line from the evaporator and the other is used to make gauge manifold connections for servicing the unit. The valve core in the pressure gauge connection and the one in the bleed line valve are not interchangeable because they have different spring ratings. The small threaded connection is for the external equalizer line from the thermostatic expansion valve.

Valves-in-Receiver (VIR) Assembly. The valves-in-receiver assembly contains the POA valve, the thermostatic expansion valve, the desiccant (drying agent), and the sight glass in a single housing (see Figures 7-3 and 7-4). The VIR assembly

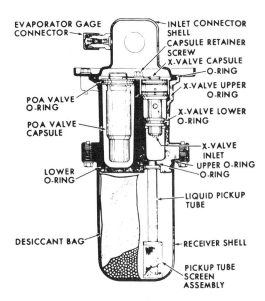

FIGURE 7-4.   Sectional view of EEVIR. *Courtesy of AC Delco/General Motors Corp.*

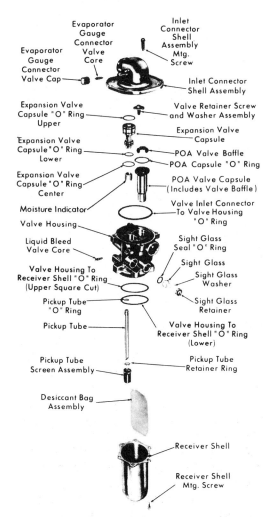

FIGURE 7-3.   Components of VIR assembly. *Courtesy of AC Delco/General Motors Corp.*

has, as mentioned earlier, port connections to and from the evaporator, the compressor, and from the condenser (see Figure 7-5).

The desiccant is in a bag placed in the receiver tank (see Figure 7-4). The desiccant is replaceable. The expansion valve and the POA valves are also replaceable, as will be discussed later.

VIR and EEVIR Assemblies. There are two basic designs of the VIR and a third variation. The original design, indicated by a black label, has an external equalizer port between the POA capsule cavity and the thermostatic expansion valve capsule diaphragm of the valve body. The latest design, which is designated the EEVIR and has a red label, does not have the equalizer port between the valve cavities but the top O-ring is left off the thermostatic expansion valve to permit

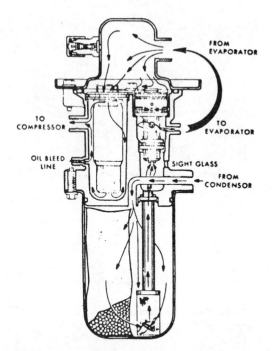

FIGURE 7-5.   Port connections. *Courtesy of AC Delco/General Motors Corp.*

the evaporator pressure to pass through the diaphragm area. The EEVIR will replace the VIR as an assembly only. The two specific components that cannot be used interchangeably when making a repair to the system are the valve housing and the thermostatic expansion valve capsule. If these parts are improperly changed, all the catalog information for service operations is nullified.

Moisture Indicator EEVIR Assembly. There is a moisture indicator ring installed on the bottom of the expansion valve capsule on some EEVIR assemblies. This ring, which is sensitive to moisture, can be seen through the sight glass to determine if the system has excessive moisture inside it. When the system is dry

the color is blue; when wet the color is pink.

VIR Identification and Parts Interchangeability. For identification purposes, the differences between the original VIR assembly and the current EEVIR assembly are given in tables (see Table 7-1). The illustrations and procedures given in this text are for the EEVIR.

NOTE: Two specific components of the EEVIR must not be interchanged with the early design: (1) the valve housing, and (2) the thermostatic expansion valve capsule. Also, in the original VIR the expansion valve has an O-ring in the upper grove of the assembly that must not be used in the EEVIR assembly. Be sure to consult the parts catalog when making repairs to these assemblies.

VIR Refrigerant Flow. During the operating cycle, the refrigerant from the condenser enters the valve as a liquid at the inlet port and flows into the receiver shell, where it comes into contact with the desiccant to remove any moisture it might contain (see Figure 7-6). The liquid refrigerant then flows through the filter screen at the bottom of the pickup tube to the lower portion of the expansion valve cavity. The expansion valve then meters the liquid refrigerant into the evaporator.

The refrigerant vapor then returns from the evaporator through the inlet connection in the shell assembly at the top of the VIR assembly. The POA then regulates the flow of refrigerant back to the compressor.

The evaporator gauge fitting incorporates a valve located in the inlet connection of the shell assembly at the top of the VIR assembly (see Figure 7-4).

TABLE 7-1.   VIR and EEVIR Differences

Item	VIR (Original)	EEVIR (Current)
Expansion valve O-rings	3 Total 1 in topmost valve body groove 1 in lower valve groove 1 in valve housing at "jam seal fit"	2 Total 1 in lower valve body groove 1 in valve housing at "jam seal fit"
Information label color	Black	Red (color dots are indicated on moisture-indicator version).
Expansion valve capsule color	Silver	Gold
Valve housing identification	Equalizer passage between capsule cavities. Colored silver.	Color gold or letter E stamped below sight glass.

Courtesy of AC Delco/General Motors Corp.

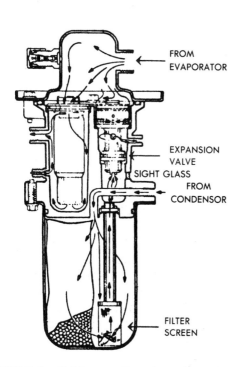

FIGURE 7-6.   Refrigerant flow through EEVIR.
Courtesy of AC Delco/General Motors Corp.

The oil bleed line fitting is located in the VIR valve housing and is connected directly to the POA valve cavity outlet (see Figure 7-6).

CAUTION: These two Schrader valve cores cannot be used interchangeably because they have different spring ratings.

VIR Expansion Valve. The thermostatic expansion valve is a pressure- and temperature-sensitive automatic device used to control the flow of refrigerant into the evaporator (see Figure 7-7). The valve controls the flow by sensing the temperature and pressure of the refrigerant vapor as it passes through the VIR assembly on its return to the compressor.

The thermostatic expansion valve is factory adjusted and cannot be changed during field-service operations. When the valve is found to be faulty, the entire expansion valve capsule should be replaced.

The equalizer port aids the valve under certain operating conditions. In

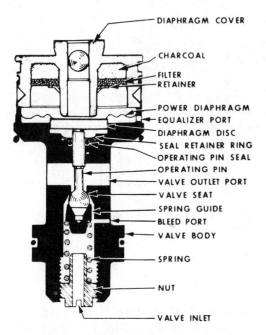

DIAPHRAGM COVER
CHARCOAL
FILTER
RETAINER
POWER DIAPHRAGM
EQUALIZER PORT
DIAPHRAGM DISC
SEAL RETAINER RING
OPERATING PIN SEAL
OPERATING PIN
VALVE OUTLET PORT
VALVE SEAT
SPRING GUIDE
BLEED PORT
VALVE BODY
SPRING
NUT
VALVE INLET

FIGURE 7-7.   Expansion valve capsule. *Courtesy of AC Delco/General Motors Corp.*

the VIR, the main equalizer function is accomplished through an equalization port, which is drilled between the two cavities in the assembly. This port exposes the diaphragm to the suction pressure of the compressor. On the EEVIR assembly, this equalization is accomplished by leaving the top O-ring off the expansion valve body, permitting the evaporator pressure to be exerted on the valve diaphragm.

VIR POA Valve. The POA capsule is located in the VIR assembly adjacent to the expansion valve capsule. Its function is to control the flow of refrigerant from the evaporator and to maintain the evaporator pressure above 30 psi or 32°F temperature. The evaporator pressure may be well above 30 psi depending on

the heat load, the compressor speed, and so on.

The POA valve capsule is set at the factory and cannot be changed during field-service procedures. When it is determined that the POA valve is defective, the capsule must be replaced as an assembly.

Combination Expansion Valve and Suction Throttling Valve. Some Ford systems use a combination valve, combining the thermostatic expansion valve and a suction throttling valve in a single assembly (see Figure 7-8). This combination valve is mounted at the evaporator. This system does, however, have a separate receiver–dehydrator mounted at the outlet of the condenser. No sight glass is used on these units. Other than this difference, the assembly functions just like the VIR assembly. The original designs of the combination valve had an equalizer port between the thermostatic expansion valve and the suction throttling valve. The later designs have a notch in the valve seat to eliminate the equalizer port.

A liquid bleed valve using a calibrated Schrader valve is part of the combination valve assembly. A pressure gauge port is also used, but it does not have a calibrated Schrader valve.

EPR and ETR VALVES. Chrysler Corporation uses an evaporator pressure regulator valve (EPR) or an evaporator temperature regulator valve (ETR) installed in the suction of the compressor (see Figure 7-9). It is accessible after the compressor suction fitting is removed.

For a short while during the early 1970s the ETR valve was used with the automatic temperature control systems.

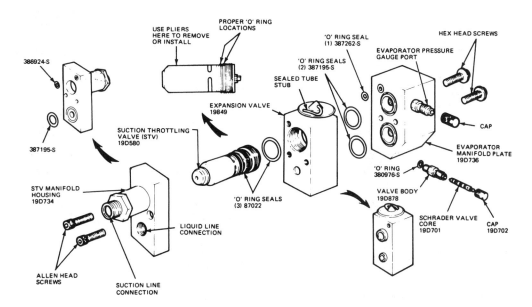

FIGURE 7-8. **Combination valve (TXV & STV), Ford.** *Courtesy of AC Delco/General Motors Corp.*

FIGURE 7-9. **Early model evaporator pressure regulator valve (EPR).** *Courtesy of AC Delco/General Motors Corp.*

In present use, all Chrysler systems using evaporator pressure control devices use a slightly modified EPR valve (see Figure 7-10). The modified valve is fully interchangeable with the early design EPR and ETR valves.

EPR Valve Operation. The EPR valve is operated by a gas-filled bellows. When the evaporator pressure is above 26 psi, the pressure acting on the diaphragm will compress the spring and hold the valve in the open position and permit free passage of the refrigerant through the valve assembly. When the refrigerant pressure drops below 26 psi, the valve tends to close and restrict the flow of refrigerant through the valve. The evaporator pressure and, therefore, the temperature is increased, preventing freezing of the condensate on the evaporator coil. This valve will maintain a minimum evaporator pressure between 22 and 26

FIGURE 7-10. Late model evaporator pressure regulator valve (EPR). *Courtesy of AC Delco/General Motors Corp.*

psi. This pressure can be determined by the use of a gauge manifold connected to the service port on the compressor suction fitting.

The main function of the EPR valve is the same as the POA valve or the STV valve, that is, to maintain the evaporator pressure high enough to prevent moisture on the evaporator from freezing, while providing maximum efficiency of the system.

ETR Valve Operation. The ETR does not regulate pressure. It is simply an on–off valve. It is located in the same place as the EPR valve, but it is operated by a solenoid coil. A thermostatic switch located in the evaporator, similar to the clutch cycling thermostat, controls operation of the solenoid. When the evaporator gets cold enough to cause moisture to condense on the coil surface, the thermostat causes the solenoid to close the ETR

valve. This closing restricts the refrigerant flow to the compressor until the valve is opened. The compressor continues to run, but because there is little refrigerant to compress, it has a low load. This action has almost the same effect as the cycling clutch system.

The ETR valve can be identified by the electrical lead to the solenoid coil. There are no electrical connections to the EPR valve.

The EPR valves and ETR valves are replaced by the new-design EPR valve shown in Figure 7-10. When installing the new EPR valve in place of the ETR valve, replace the old gasket, and tape the ETR control wire to the engine harness. Do not reuse the old suction screen.

Expansion (Orifice) Tube. The expansion (orifice) tube, usually referred to as the orifice tube, is used in place of the thermostatic expansion valve on the clutch cycling (CCOT) type of systems (see Figure 7-11). Like any other type of refrigerant flow-control device, the orifice tube is the dividing point between the high and the low side of the system. Its metering or flow rate control, however, does not depend upon the comparing of

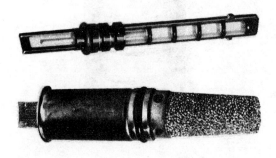

FIGURE 7-11. Expansion tube orifice. *Courtesy of AC Delco/General Motors Corp.*

the evaporator pressure or temperature. It is a fixed orifice, and the flow is determined by the difference in pressure across the orifice and by subcooling of the refrigerant. (*Subcooling* is the additional cooling of the liquid refrigerant in the bottom of the condenser after the vapor has changed to a liquid.) The flow rate through the orifice is affected more by the amount of subcooling than by the pressure differential across the orifice.

COMPRESSOR CONTROLS

Compressor controls are the controls that signal the compressor when or when not to operate. They generally complete or break an electrical circuit to the compressor clutch in response to some external force, such as temperature or system refrigerant pressure.

Compressor Clutch and Pulley Assembly. Every automotive air-conditioning compressor is equipped with a magnetic clutch assembly that is part of the compressor pulley (see Figure 7-12). The clutch is designed to connect the pulley to the compressor shaft when the coil is energized by the passenger compartment controls. The clutch is used to transmit the power from the engine crankshaft to the compressor by being engaged or disengaged.

The compressor is caused to turn by one or more belts extending from the clutch pulley to the engine crankshaft. Whenever the engine is running and the clutch is engaged, power is transmitted to the compressor through the clutch assembly. When the clutch is not engaged, the compressor shaft does not rotate and the pulley freewheels without transferring any power.

FIGURE 7-12. Typical clutch used on reciprocating compressors. *Courtesy of AC Delco/ General Motors Corp.*

A magnetic field is created when the passenger compartment controls are switched to the cooling position and the clutch is engaged. When the clutch is disengaged, springs force the clutch components apart, allowing the compressor to stop turning. In operation, when the controls call for cooling, the electrical circuit is closed and the clutch is engaged, causing the compressor to turn, producing refrigeration. When the controls are satisfied, the electrical circuits open, disengaging the clutch and stopping the compressor.

Almost all different compressor types use a different type of clutch. The General Motors clutch and pulley assemblies are made up of several different components that can be replaced individually (see Figures 7-13 and 7-14). The typical clutch and pulley assembly used on reciprocating compressors is serviced by replacing

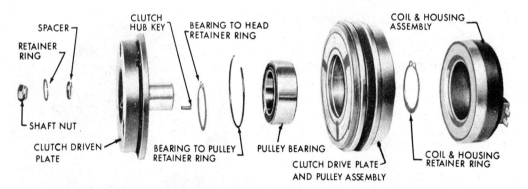

FIGURE 7-13.   GM 6-cylinder compressor clutch and pulley assembly.
Courtesy of AC Delco/General Motors Corp.

either the bearing or the pulley and clutch assembly (see Figure 7-12).

When the cycling clutch type of system is used, the clutch is intermittently energized and deenergized by the thermostatic switch or the pressure switch in the electrical control circuit. When the evaporator pressure control valve type of system is used, the clutch is electrically energized when the controls are set for cooling, and the compressor turns until the controls are moved away from the cooling position. Also, in addition to the manually operated controls, the com-

pressor may be protected by other controls such as the ambient switch, thermal limiter, superheat switch, and a low-pressure cutoff switch.

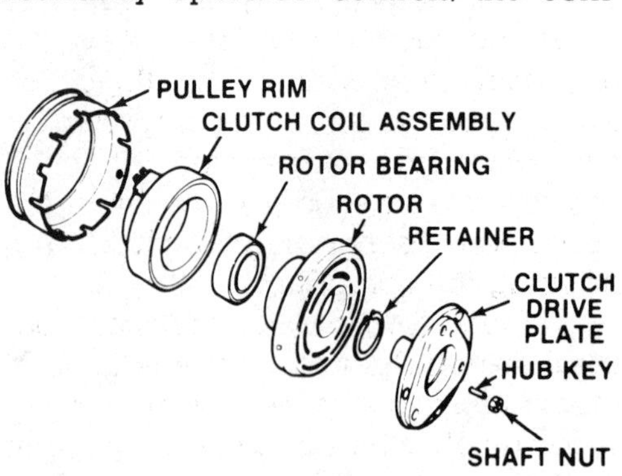

Thermostatic Switch. When cycling clutch systems are used, the thermostatic switch is placed in an electrical series with the compressor clutch circuit so that it can start or stop the compressor on demand from the compartment temperature (see Figure 7-15). The thermostatic switch has two purposes: (1) to de-energize the clutch and stop the compressor if the evaporator is at the freezing point, thus acting as a de-ice control; (2) on field-installed units or systems without reheat temperature control, it also controls the air temperature by intermittently starting and stopping the compressor. There is a control knob for changing this setting.

The thermostatic switch uses a metallic sensing tube that is filled with a very expansive gas. This sensing tube is inserted into the evaporator coil between the fins to have good contact. It may also be located in the discharge airstream from

FIGURE 7-14.   GM 4-cylinder compressor clutch and pulley assembly. *Courtesy of AC Delco/General Motors Corp.*

FIGURE 7-15. **Thermostatic switch.** *Courtesy of AC Delco/General Motors Corp.*

the evaporator. The other end of the tube is connected to a bellows, which is part of the switch mechanism. As the temperature of the air rises, the gas inside the tube expands, increasing the pressure inside the bellows, which in turn closes the switch contacts, energizing the compressor clutch. As the discharge air temperature is lowered to the point of freezing or to the low-temperature setting of the switch, the thermostatic switch opens the electrical circuit, disengaging the compressor clutch. The compressor is not turning to produce refrigeration and remains idle until the evaporator temperature rises to the preset temperature of the switch to restart the compressor.

Some thermostatic temperature controls, which do not have the adjustment knob, are equipped with an internal adjustment screw. This screw can be adjusted by service personnel to change the temperature at which the clutch cycles.

Pressure Cycling Switch. The pressure cycling switch is connected in series electrically with the compressor clutch. It controls the cycling of the compressor just like the thermostatic switch (see Figure 7-16). This switch is mounted on the accumulator tank and has three functions:

1. The switch will interrupt the electrical circuit to the clutch when the low-side pressure drops to 27 psi, thus preventing evaporator freeze-up. The switch will energize the electrical circuit when the refrigerant pressure reaches approximately 35 psi.

2. The pressure switch will stop operation of the compressor when the accumulator pressure drops below 27 psi on a system that is low on refrigerant. This prevents compressor operation without proper lubrication and cooling.

3. The switch will prevent operation of the compressor when the evaporator pressure is too low for safe compressor operation.

This control incorporates a spring-loaded diaphragm that is referenced to the atmospheric pressure.

Manually Operated Controls. A typical General Motors control panel for an

FIGURE 7-16. **Pressure cycling switch.** *Courtesy of AC Delco/General Motors Corp.*

evaporator pressure control system is shown in Figure 7-17. When the top horizontal selection lever is in any of the air-conditioning positions, the compressor operates continually and the evaporator temperature is controlled by the POA valve or the VIR.

The lower horizontal selection lever actuates the "air door" in the air-distribution ductwork. This door deflects cooled air from the evaporator through the heater core in whatever proportions that might be desirable for passenger comfort. The vertical lever on the left side of the control is for blower speed selection.

Ambient Switch. The ambient switch senses the temperature of the outside air and prevents operation of the compressor when air conditioning is not required or when operation of the compressor might do internal damage to the seal or other parts.

The switch is in electrical series with the compressor clutch. It closes at about 37°F. At all temperatures below this, the switch is open, preventing clutch engagement.

On General Motors cars, the ambient switch is located in the air inlet duct of the air-conditioning systems that are regulated by the evaporator pressure controls. Other makes of cars have this switch installed near the car radiator. It is not

SUPERHEAT SWITCH   THERMAL FUSE

FIGURE 7-18. Superheat switch and thermal limiter. *Courtesy of AC Delco/General Motors Corp.*

used on systems using the thermostatic switch.

Thermal Limiter and Superheat Switch. Some General Motors cars use a thermal limiter, or fuse, and superheat switch to protect the compressor against damage when a part, or all, of the refrigerant charge is lost (see Figure 7-18). The thermal limiter is placed in various locations under the hood, and the superheat switch is located in the rear head of the compressor. The fuse and thermal limiter switch are connected in electrical series to the compressor clutch.

The thermal limiter should not be moved from its original location because varying underhood ambient conditions could result in improper operation of the switch.

A wiring diagram of the electrical circuit for the switch and fuse is shown in Figure 7-19. During normal operation of the air-conditioning system, electrical current flows through the head switch, ambient switch, and the thermal limiter to the clutch coil to engage the clutch. Should a partial loss of refrigerant occur, the contacts of the superheat switch close

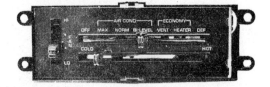

FIGURE 7-17. Manual control. *Courtesy of AC Delco/General Motors Corp.*

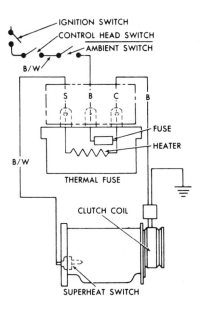

FIGURE 7-19. Fuse and switch electric circuit.
Courtesy of AC Delco/General Motors Corp.

as the switch senses a loss of refrigerant, resulting in a high suction vapor temperature. When the contacts close, electrical current flows through a resistor-type heater in the thermal fuse. The heat from the resistor melts the fuse link, opening the electrical circuit to the clutch coil. Operation of the compressor is stopped to prevent damage to the compressor due to overheating or the lack of lubrication.

Before the thermal fuse is replaced, the refrigerant leak must be found and corrected and the system recharged with refrigerant. It is serviceable only as a unit.

The superheat switch is located in the rear compressor head and is sealed by means of an O-ring between the switch housing and the compressor head. A specially formed retainer ring holds the switch in place and electrically grounds

the switch housing to the compressor. Replacement switches are available in a kit consisting of a switch, O-ring, and a retainer ring.

Discharge-Pressure (Low-Pressure) Switch. Late-model General Motors and Chrysler units use a pressure switch in the compressor discharge to provide compressor protection. This switch is referred to as a discharge pressure switch or a low-pressure cutoff switch. On General Motors cars, it is installed in the compressor discharge line, and on Chrysler units it is installed in the receiver–dehydrator (see Figure 7-20).

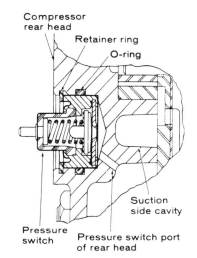

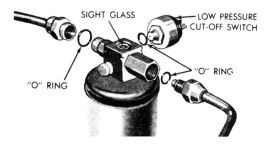

FIGURE 7-20. Low pressure cut-off switch.
Courtesy of AC Delco/General Motors Corp.

NOTE: The low-pressure cut-out switch located in the rear head of General Motors compressors should not be confused with the superheat switch. The superheat switch is installed in the same location in earlier-model compressors. The two switches have a similar appearance.

The pressure switch is wired in electrical series with the compressor clutch coil. It provides the same protection as the ambient switch. When the switch senses a low discharge pressure, its contacts open and the electrical circuit to the clutch is interrupted. This action can occur under two conditions: (1) Cold outside ambient air, because of the refrigerant pressure–temperature relationship, causes the pressure to be low. Because of this, the compressor will not start up in cold weather. (2) The loss of refrigerant causes a low pressure. The compressor is stopped under these conditions to prevent damage to the compressor from the loss of lubricating oil should a major leak occur.

Complete replacement of the switch is the only service possible.

High-Pressure Relief Valve. The high-pressure relief valve is a reseating type of valve that is designed to open the refrigerant circuit when an abnormally high pressure exists. They usually open at about 475 to 500 psi to prevent damage to the system components. The valve will reseat when the pressure is reduced to a predetermined safe level. The venting port of this valve is covered with a Mylar disc that is used to protect the valve from corrosion and dirt. If this disc is missing or is damaged, it should be replaced. Use a disc that has been cut from an adhesive-type Mylar tape.

CAUTION: Do not use electrical tape or masking tape for this purpose.

REVIEW QUESTIONS

1. What is the purpose of the evaporator pressure controls used on automotive air-conditioning systems?

2. Name the four evaporator pressure controls used on automotive air-conditioning systems.

3. Why is the prevention of evaporator freezing important?

4. What is the minimum evaporator pressure permitted with the STV?

5. What does the loss of vacuum on the ETV cause?

6. What type of altitude correction should be made on the POA valve?

7. Are the Schrader valve cores on a POA valve interchangeable?

8. On the POA valve, where does the external equalizer line from the TXV connect?

9. How is the original VIR valve marked?

10. What two components cannot be interchanged between the VIR and the EEVIR?

11. Where are the EPR and the ETR valves installed on Chrysler units?

12. What is the opening pressure of the EPR valve?

13. Does the ETR valve regulate pressure?

14. How can the ETR valve be distinguished from the EPR valve?

15. What is the purpose of the orifice tube?

16. What is the purpose of the compressor controls?

17. On what type of automotive air-conditioning unit does the clutch cycle?

18. Where is the thermostat sensing bulb located?

19. Where is the pressure cycling switch located?

20. What is the purpose of the ambient switch?

For any piece of machinery to operate at its peak efficiency, it must be properly maintained and serviced. Air-conditioning equipment is no exception to this theory. Therefore, those who work on these units must have a good sound understanding of the proper procedures involved.

SAFETY PROCEDURES

The old saying "Safety doesn't cost, it pays" is certainly true. It is most important that proper safety procedures be followed, especially by workers in industry. Since these people usually work alone, help may be difficult to obtain should a serious injury occur.

Safety may be divided into three general categories: safety of the worker, safety of the equipment, and safety of the contents.

Safety of the worker is, of course, of prime importance. Machinery can always be replaced, but human life cannot. If the equipment is properly used, there is little danger to the worker.

1. Always use your leg muscles when lifting heavy objects; never use the back muscles.

2. Ask for help in lifting objects weighing more than 30 to 35 lb.

3. Keep the floor clear of water and oil. A slip while carrying heavy objects usually means serious injury.

4. Air-conditioning and refrigeration equipment use electricity as their source of power. Be sure that all electrical circuits are disconnected from the power source before working on them. The disconnect switch or circuit breaker will usually break the circuit. Never work on a "hot" circuit.

—— **8** ——

System Maintenance and Standard Service Procedures

5. Always wear safety goggles when working with refrigerants. Refrigerants in the eye cause freezing. If a refrigerant gets in your eye, gently wash it with tap water, and see a physician as soon as possible.

6. Protect your skin from frostbite when working with refrigerants.

Safety of the equipment is also of great importance. Many components on air-conditioning and refrigeration equipment are easily broken. Some of these components are very expensive to replace.

1. Use the proper torque and sequence when tightening bolts and nuts.

2. Before operating equipment, be sure that all fan blades and belts are clear of all objects.

Safety of the contents is a basic requirement and will depend to a great extent on the care given to the equipment during installation and servicing. Keep the contents of a given installation at the desired temperature; this is the responsibility of the service technician. He or she must know what the required conditions are and maintain the equipment to produce these conditions. Most manufacturers provide tables and charts showing the desired operating conditions and the required control settings.

HANDLING REFRIGERANT 12

Refrigerant 12, or R-12 as it is sometimes known, is a colorless, transparent fluid in both the liquid and vapor state. It has a boiling point of $-21.6°F$. Therefore, it will be a vapor at all normal temperatures and pressures at which we will be using the refrigerant. The vapor is heavier than

air, and it is noninflammable, nonexplosive, and nonpoisonous, except when subjected to an open flame; it is then transformed into phosgene gas, which is very toxic and will cause many health problems if breathed. R-12 is available in many different types of containers (see Figure 8-1).

The following precautions should be observed at all times when handling any type of refrigerant:

1. Do not transport R-12 in the passenger compartment of the car.

2. Do not subject the R-12 containers to high temperatures.

3. Do not weld or steam clean on or near an air-conditioning system with R-12 inside.

4. Do not discharge R-12 vapor into an area that has an open flame in it.

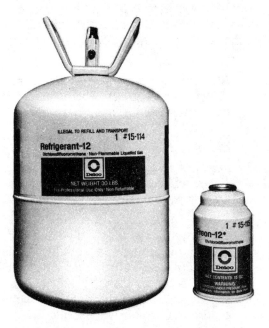

FIGURE 8-1.   Refrigerant-12. *Courtesy of AC Delco/General Motors Corp.*

5. Avoid all eye contact with the R-12 liquid because severe eye burn is almost certain.

Should it become necessary to transport R-12 in the car, put it in the trunk. If the container should become exposed to extremely high temperatures, such as the sun's rays, the pressure inside the container may become so high that the container could possibly burst.

The R-12 container should never be exposed to high temperatures when charging a system with refrigerant. The container should never be heated above 125°F. This heating should be done with a container of warm water, never a welding torch or an open flame.

Any welding or steam cleaning on or near the refrigerant lines with refrigerant pressure inside could result in excessive pressure buildup and rupture of one of the system components.

Never fill a refrigerant container completely full of refrigerant. The system should never be discharged into a cylinder to save the refrigerant because excessive pressures could result from the hot vapor and the pressure caused by the compressor. In any case, there should always be space above the liquid for expansion. When the cylinder is completely full, there will be tremendous pressure buildup with any increase in temperature.

R-12 vapor can usually be safely discharged into the room without any ill effects. However, certain precautions must be taken to prevent the vapor from being burned by an open flame or by a running engine. Also, a heavy concentration of R-12 vapor in an enclosed room should be avoided because the vapor will displace the air in the room. The gas caused by a burning refrigerant will attack bright surfaces such as bumpers and wheel covers.

CAUTION: Always wear goggles to protect your eyes when working with refrigerant containers, when discharging a system, or when opening the system service valves.

If liquid refrigerant should get into your eye, use the following precaution and steps:

1. Call the doctor immediately and follow his instructions along with the following immediate steps.

2. Do not rub the eyes. Splash tap water onto the face and into the eyes to help get them above the freezing point.

3. The use of an antiseptic oil in the eyes may prove a benefit in protecting against infection.

If liquid refrigerant should come into contact with the skin, flush the affected area immediately with tap water and treat the area for frostbite.

Refrigerant in Cans. Refrigerant cans are delivered from the factory sealed; a can should be opened only after it has been properly attached to the can valve. The can valve is then used to puncture the can. These cans are available in flat-top or screw-type seal cans, and the proper valve must be used for each type of can connection. The sealing gasket and the valve must be maintained in good condition at all times to prevent possible injury or loss of refrigerant.

These can valves are available in either single or multiple dispensing valve assemblies (see Figure 8-2). The multiple can dispenser assemblies make it possi-

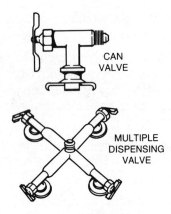

FIGURE 8-2. Can valve assemblies. *Courtesy of Superior Valve Co.*

ble to completely charge a system without the constant changing of the refrigerant can. There is a can valve located on each leg of the manifold so that the assembly may be used as a single-type unit if desirable. The cans are installed on each leg the same as if only one can were being installed (see Figure 8-3).

The following procedures should be used when installing the valve assemblies on the cans:

Screw-Type Seal Cans. Be sure that the valve is fully closed before placing it on the can. Screw the valve onto the can until the assembly is tight. This step will pierce the can. Connect the center hose on the gauge manifold to the can valve. Do not open the can valve until you are ready to use the refrigerant.

Flat-Top Seal Cans. There are several types of valve assemblies in common use for this type of can. Be sure that the one being used is in good working order. When the cam lock type is being used, open the can valve all the way. Securely place the locking lugs over the can flange and lock the can valve by turning

the cam lock or by tightening the locking nut. Turn the valve handle in completely. This step will close off the valve and pierce the can at the same time. When you are using the two-piece can valves, make certain that the valve handle is turned in fully to close the valve. Make certain that the locking base is turned to the outer limit. Securely place the locking lugs over the can flange. Turn the entire valve assembly, being careful not to disturb the valve handle, down onto the locking base and pierce the can. Do not open the valve handle until you are ready to use the refrigerant.

PERIODIC SYSTEM CHECKS

As with all machinery, certain periodic checks and inspections should be done to keep the system operating efficiently:

1. Inspect the condenser on a regular basis to make certain that there is no debris in the fins that would restrict the airflow, which would keep the condenser from functioning properly.

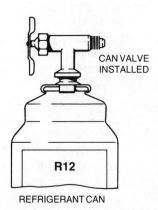

FIGURE 8-3. Valve installed on a refrigerant can. *Courtesy of Superior Valve Co.*

2. Check the refrigerant charge on no less than a yearly basis. Add if necessary. Check the refrigerant hoses for brittleness, wear, or leaks. Replace as necessary.

3. Check the evaporator drain tubes regularly and remove any restrictions.

4. Check the compressor belt tension regularly. Replace as necessary.

5. Check the blower motor operation in all speeds.

6. Check the operation of the air door in all selector positions.

7. Check the discharge air temperature with the system operating in maximum A/C.

8. If the air temperature is not within the desired specifications, make a system performance test. (See Performance Testing.)

SYSTEM SERVICE VALVES

System service valves provide for connecting the manifold gauge set to the system for service operations. There is a port for the low side and one for the high side of the system. They may be either stem-type valves or they may be Schrader valves.

Stem-Type Service Valves. These are three-way valves and are double-seating-type valves (see Figure 8-4). This valve has a stem located under a cap opposite the hose connection. These valves have three positions, as follows:

The *back-seated position* is the normal operating position with the valve stem backed all the way out of the valve body. The stem is rotated in a counter-

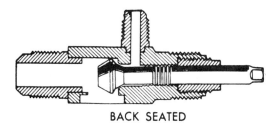

BACK SEATED

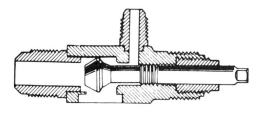

MID POSITION

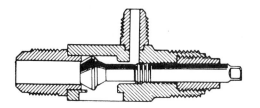

FRONT SEATED

FIGURE 8-4. Service valve positions. *Courtesy of AC Delco/General Motors Corp.*

clockwise direction to the rear valve seat and to seal off the gauge port.

NOTE: A special service valve wrench should be used on the valve stem when turning it. Crescent wrenches and other such wrenches will likely ruin the valve stem.

The *mid-position* is the test position when the valve stem is turned in a clockwise direction about one and a half to two turns. Before moving the valve to this position, be sure that the gauge connection cap is in place or that the gauge manifold is properly connected to the system. When the valve is in the mid-position, service operations can be performed on the system. Do not remove the service gauge hose until the valve stem is completely back-seated; then bleed the pressure from the hose carefully.

The *front-seated position* moves the valve seat all the way to the front seat, stopping the flow of refrigerant into the compressor. This position is used to isolate the compressor from the remainder of the system for service operations. The service valve port is now fully open. Do not attempt to remove the service hose from the system when the service valve is in the front-seated position.

Schrader-Type Service Valves. Systems that are not equipped with stem-type service valves make use of Schrader-type service valves (see Figure 8-5). These valves are located in both the high and the low sides of the system for testing and servicing purposes.

On General Motors cars, the Schrader valve locations may be as follows:

1. High-pressure valve: located at the compressor discharge fitting or in the

liquid line just ahead of the TXV or the CCOT orifice.

2. Low-pressure valve: Located in the compressor inlet fitting, on the POA valve, on the VIR inlet connector shell, or on the accumulator.

On most other types of automobiles, the gauge connections are on the compressor itself.

Most of the gauge hoses in use today have a depressor in the hose fitting that will depress the valve core and unseat the valve as the hose is being connected. If not, a separate fitting must be installed before connecting the hose.

NOTE: On late-model General Motors cars, the high- and low-pressure Schrader valve fittings are of a different size. This minimizes the possibility of making wrong hose connections.

MANIFOLD GAUGE SET

The manifold gauge set is one of the most important tools in the service technician's tool chest (see Figure 8-6). It is used when performing service operations on the refrigeration system. One of the gauges is

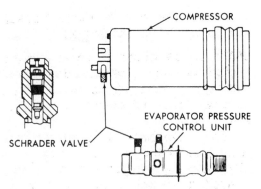

FIGURE 8-5. Schrader-type service valve. *Courtesy of AC Delco/General Motors Corp.*

FIGURE 8-6. Manifold gauge set. *Courtesy of Superior Valve Co.*

known as the low-pressure, or compound, gauge, and the other one is the high-pressure gauge. The low-pressure gauge dial is graduated from 30 in. of vacuum to 250 psi. The graduations are available in many different ratings, and the one that best suits the needs of the user should be purchased. Use this gauge when taking pressure readings on the low side of the system (see Figure 8-7).

The pressure gauge is graduated from 0 to 500 psi in 10-lb graduations. This gauge is used for taking pressure readings on the high side of the system. This gauge will not indicate pressures below atmospheric pressure (see Figure 8-8).

The center manifold connection is a common connection between both the gauges. It is used for evacuating, adding refrigerant to the system, adding oil to the system, or other service operations. This fitting should be capped when it is not in use, as is the case with all the gauge fittings.

The hose that is connected directly below the low-side gauge is used to connect the gauge to the low side of the system. The one directly below the high-side gauge is used to connect the gauge to the high side of the system.

The gauge manifold is designed to control the refrigerant flow. When the

P877-21

FIGURE 8-8. **Pressure gauge.** *Courtesy of Superior Valve Co.*

manifold set is connected to the system, pressure is always registered on both gauges. When making tests, both hand valves are in the closed position (see Figure 8-9). The refrigerant will flow around the valve stem and indicate the system pressure on the proper gauge. The hand valves isolate the low and high side from the central portion of the manifold.

When connecting the gauges to the system, the hoses should always be

P877-22

FIGURE 8-7. **Compound gauge.** *Courtesy of Superior Valve Co.*

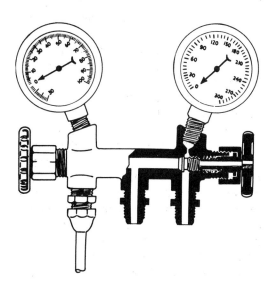

FIGURE 8-9. **Manifold gauge set cut-away.** *Courtesy of AC Delco/General Motors Corp.*

purged (blow a small amount of refrigerant through the hoses) before tightening the connections to the valve fitting. Purging is done by "cracking" each valve on the gauge set to allow the refrigerant pressure in the system to force the air out of the manifold through the center hose. If the hoses are not purged, air and other contaminants will enter the system.

CAUTION: Do not open the high-side pressure gauge hand valve while the system is operating. If this valve should be opened while the system is operating and a refrigerant can is connected to the center hose, the refrigerant will flow out of the system and into the can under high pressure. This pressure is between 150 and 300 psi and may cause the can to burst.

Opening the low-side hand valve while the system is operating and with a refrigerant can connected to the center hose will allow the refrigerant to flow from the can and into the system, resulting in a possible system overcharge of refrigerant.

The only occasion when both hand valves would be opened would be when evacuating the system.

Some gauge sets may have a separate compound gauge mounted on the right side of the pressure gauge. This gauge is not connected to the other manifold gauge set. It operates independently and is used only in checking the EPR valve on Chrysler systems (see Figure 8-10). The third gauge may also be used for checking the STV valve used on Ford systems. These systems have low-pressure gauge ports both on the valve and in the suction line to the compressor.

Connecting the Manifold Gauge Set. Be sure to wear safety goggles when per-

FIGURE 8-10. Compound manifold gauge set. *Courtesy of AC Delco / General Motors Corp.*

forming service operations. Use the following steps when connecting the gauge set to the system:

1. With the engine not running, remove the caps from the service valve fittings.

2. Close all the hand valves in the gauge manifold set.

3. Leave the center hose connection on the manifold capped or connected to a hose, which is in turn connected to a refrigerant cylinder.

4. Connect the high-pressure gauge hose to the service valve on the high side of the system.

5. Purge the test hoses by opening each hand valve, one at a time, one turn, and allow a small amount of refrigerant to escape out of the center hose; then close the hand valves. Tighten all the hose connections.

6. Before accurate tests can be made the system must be stabilized.

SYSTEM STABILIZING PROCEDURE

To stabilize the system, use the following procedure:

1. Start the engine and set it to idle at about 1500 to 2000 rpm.

2. Turn on the air-conditioner and set the controls for maximum cooling with the blower on high speed.

3. Close the car doors and windows.

4. Operate the air-conditioner for about 5 min to stabilize the refrigerant charge.

5. Check the refrigerant charge by noting the sight glass condition. (See *Sight Glass Quick Check Procedure* in Chapter 9).

6. Check the high- and low-side system pressures for normal operation. (Refer to the performance chart in *Performance Testing* in this chapter.) An insufficient refrigerant charge will be indicated by a high-side gauge reading lower than normal.

If there is a shortage of refrigerant as indicated by the gauge reading or the sight glass quick test method, the system should be checked for a leak, the leak repaired, and the system recharged before an accurate test can be performed to determine whether or not the system is operating normally.

There will be some refrigerant loss from one season to the next. This loss is accepted as being normal because of vibration, hose porosity, and the general construction of the components that are installed on a moving vehicle make a leakproof system almost impossible. The replacement of this refrigerant lost during the off-season will be a large part of the quick-service jobs in the springtime of the year.

Maintaining System Stability. The efficient operation of any air-conditioning or refrigeration system depends upon the pressure–temperature relationship of pure refrigerant in the system. As long as the system contains pure refrigerant, it is considered to be chemically stable.

When foreign materials, such as air, dirt, or moisture, are allowed to enter the system, the pressure–temperature relationship of the refrigerant is changed. The system will no longer operate at the proper pressures and temperatures, resulting in decreased efficiency. The following general practices should be followed to ensure a chemically stable system:

1. When servicing the system, wipe away any dirt and/or oil before making the connection. Be sure to cap both connections when the service procedures are finished.

2. Keep all tools clean and dry. Include all replacement parts.

3. When adding oil, be certain that no moisture, air, or foreign materials enter the system.

4. When it is necessary to open a system, have all tools and materials required to complete the job close at hand.

5. Be sure to evacuate any system that has been opened to the atmosphere.

LEAK TESTING THE SYSTEM

When it is suspected that a refrigerant leak is in the system, a leak test should be performed to determine its location. When making the leak test, be sure that there is sufficient pressure in the system to find the leak. The procedure used in repairing the leak will be determined by its location.

NOTE: Most manufacturers do not recommend the use of refrigerant containing a leak-detecting dye. The following is a list of their reasons:

1. It is possible to have a refrigerant leak without any loss of oil; therefore, the dye will not indicate a leak. A leak detector will indicate a leak when there is no loss of oil.

2. The addition of any type of additive may alter the chemical stability of the refrigerant and cause system malfunctions.

3. Because dye leak detectors are insoluble, they can form a curdle that can block the screens in the valves and other system components and restrict the flow of refrigerant through the system.

Two different types of leak detectors are in common use, the halide torch and the electronic leak detector. The electronic unit is much more sensitive and will usually produce better results.

Electronic Leak Detector. Several different types of electronic leak detectors are available, and the one chosen will depend on the requirements of the user (see Figure 8-11). A typical automotive air-conditioning system will leak approximately ½ ounce of refrigerant in the period of one year. Some electronic leak detectors are so sensitive that they will detect this normal leakage. Thus, the leak detector should be adjusted to detect leaks greater than this amount.

Be sure to use the detector manufacturer's recommendations for setting the sensitivity adjustment. Otherwise, the detector may not detect leaks properly.

The basic operation of these units is as follows:

FIGURE 8-11.   Electronic leak detector. *Courtesy of TIF Instruments.*

1. Turn on the control knob. Allow the unit to warm up to operating temperature.

2. Place the leak detector probe over a calibrated sample. This sample will indicate a leak of approximately ½ ounce per year. The detector will indicate a leak at this location.

3. Turn the sensitivity knob to a point when turning the knob only a small amount will cancel the indication and turning it back will indicate a leak. At this point the leak detector is ready to use. Be sure to use the recommended procedures when setting the unit up so that time will not be wasted in working on good components.

Halide Leak Detector. The halide leak detector is a gas-burning torch that is designed to locate a leak in any part of the refrigeration system. A sample of refrigerant vapor is drawn into the sampling tube, which is attached to the torch base (see Figure 8-12). As the refrigerant is drawn into the torch, the flame will change to a brilliant blue color. The larger the leak the bluer the flame. A very large leak will cause the flame to go out.

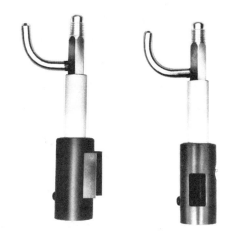

FIGURE 8-12. **Halide leak detector.** *Courtesy of Union Carbide Corp.*

Use the following steps to operate the halide leak detector:

1. Be sure that there is enough refrigerant in the system for proper leak detection.

2. Open the control valve until a slight hiss is heard; then light the propane gas at the chimney opening.

3. Adjust the flame until the flame just passes through the reactor plate in the chimney. This is the best flame for leak detection. The reactor plate should be heated to a cherry red color.

Checking For Refrigerant Leaks. After the leak detector flame has been adjusted and the reactor plate has been heated to operating temperature, check for leaks in an area that has a minimum amount of air flowing.

NOTE: Do not breathe the fumes produced by the burnt refrigerant leaving the leak detector. They are poisonous.

Anytime there is an open flame used near a car, there is the possible danger of fire because of gasoline. It is recommended that a fire extinguisher be close at hand.

Check for leaks by moving the sampling tube around all connections and points of possible leaks. Because R-12 is heavier than air, a leak will be more noticeable at the bottom of the suspected area.

To check for leaks in the evaporator core, remove the resistor from the case and insert the end of the sampling tube into the inside of the case. If a leak is present, this should indicate it. On models where this procedure cannot be used, remove the blower motor cooler tube and probe with the leak detector tube inside the evaporator case.

To check the condenser and the receiver–dehydrator, insert the sampling tube through the grille or through an access hole in the car body.

A slight leak around the compressor shaft seal is normal. Thus, a small amount of refrigerant around the shaft seal and pulley is normal and should cause no alarm. If a leak is indicated in this area, blow compressed air around the pulley and then recheck for a leak. If one is indicated immediately afterward, there is probably a serious leak at this point.

NOTE: A refrigerant leak in the high side of the system may be easier to locate if the unit is operated for a short period of time and then the engine is shut off. An immediate test will prove if a leak is present and that repairs are needed. This test should be made before the system pressures equalize.

DISCHARGING THE SYSTEM

When replacing any system component, except compressors with stem-type service valves, all the refrigerant must be discharged from the system. This procedure is accomplished by connecting the manifold gauge set to the system. It provides a means of controlling the refrigerant discharge and minimizing the amount of oil lost from the system.

Use the following procedures and steps when discharging a system. Refer to Figure 8-13.

1. Remove the protective cap from the low-side service valve.

2. Close the manifold gauge hand valves. Connect the low-side gauge to the system low-side fitting. A special adapter may be required on some units.

3. Place the open end of the center manifold hose in a container to receive any oil that may be discharged with the refrigerant.

4. Open the low-side gauge hand valve until refrigerant flows out of the end of the hose without any oil being discharged with the refrigerant.

5. Discharge until all the refrigerant has been removed from the system. Close the low-side valves to prevent contaminants entering the system.

6. Measure any oil that may have been discharged from the system so that it can be replaced with an equal amount of new oil when recharging the system.

COMPRESSOR OIL LEVEL CHECKS

It is not necessary, nor is it recommended, that the oil be checked during each service operation. In most cases, it is recommended that the oil level be

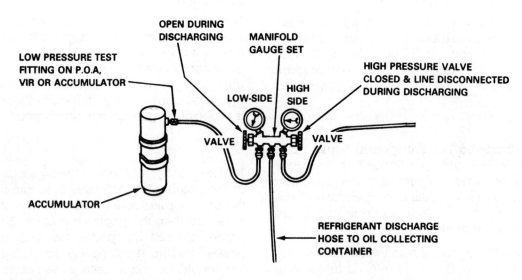

FIGURE 8-13. Discharging the system. *Courtesy of AC Delco/General Motors Corp.*

checked only when there is evidence that there has been a major loss of oil, such as might be caused by the following instances:

1. A severe refrigerant leak in the system.
2. Collision damage to the system components.
3. The changing out of major components of the system.

When checking the oil, all system manufacturers do not make the same recommendations. The recommendations made by the compressor manufacturer should be followed. The following is a list of these recommendations:

General Motors Compressor. The General Motors 6-cylinder compressor requires 11 fluid ounces of 525 viscosity refrigeration oil in the system. Their 4-cylinder compressor requires 6 fluid ounces. It is extremely important that only the specified type and amount be used in the compressor in question. When there is too much oil in the system, too much will circulate with the refrigerant, causing a reduction in the system capacity. Too little oil will result in poor lubrication of the compressor.

When there has been an excessively large leak in the system or when it is necessary to replace one of the refrigeration system components, certain procedures must be followed to make sure that the proper amount of oil is in the system after making these repairs.

When the compressor is placed in service, some of the oil will leave the compressor and circulate through the system with the refrigerant. After a period of time, the system will become balanced with a certain amount of oil in each part

of the refrigerant circuit. Thus, when a component is replaced after the system has been operated, some of the oil will leave the system with the part. This oil must be replaced before the system will be adequately lubricated. The procedure for adding oil to systems that use a receiver–dehydrator or a VIR is as follows:

1. Operate the system for about 5 min at about 2000 rpm with the air-conditioning controls set for maximum cooling and the blower on high speed. During this procedure, the oil is circulated and distributed throughout the system.
2. Turn off the air-conditioner and stop the engine. Discharge the refrigerant from the system.
3. Follow the outline in Table 8-1 to determine the correct amount of oil that should be added to the components or to the compressor depending upon the condition of the compressor. Note the different amount of oil to add depending on which type of compressor is used on the system.

The procedure for adding oil to the components or the compressor using the cycling clutch orifice tube (CCOT) system is as follows:

1. When there is no sign of excessive oil leak:
   (a) Compressor: remove the compressor, drain the oil, measure the amount drained, replace the same amount plus one fluid ounce (see note 1 below).
   (b) Evaporator: add 3 fluid ounces.
   (c) Condenser: add 1 fluid ounce.
   (d) Accumulator: remove accumulator, drain oil, measure the

TABLE 8-1.   Compressor Oil Change Procedure

Unit	Add Oil
Condenser	1 fluid ounce
Evaporator	3 fluid ounces
EE-VIR	1 fluid ounce

Compressor Condition	Amount of Oil Drained from Compressor	Amount of Oil to Install
Replacing compressor with a new compressor	More than: 4 fl oz in A-6 ½ fl oz in R-4	*Drain new compressor, refill with new oil (same amount as drained from old compressor except see Note)
	Less than: 4 fl oz in A-6 ½ fl oz in R-4	**Drain new compressor. Install new oil in new compressor: 6 fl oz in A-6 3 fl oz in R-4
Replacing compressor with a service rebuilt compressor	More than: 4 fl oz in A-6 ½ fl oz in R-4	*Same as above plus an additional fluid ounce (more oil is retained in a drained compressor than one that has been rebuilt)
	Less than: 4 fl oz in A-6 ½ fl oz in R-4	**Same as above plus an additional fluid ounce
Unable to run compressor being replaced, prior to removal from car	More than: 1½ fl. oz. in A-6 ½ fl. oz. in R-4 and system appears to have lost little or no oil	*Same as above
	Less than: 1½ fl oz in A-6 ½ fl oz in R-4 or system appears to have lost major amount of oil	**Same as above
Contaminated oil drained from system	Any amount	Drain as much oil as possible from system. Flush system with refrigerant-11. Replace drier desiccant and install new 525 viscosity oil in new compressor: A-6 comp: 10½ fl oz R-4 comp: 6 fl oz

Courtesy of AC Delco/General Motors Corp.

Note: For A-6 only, if the amount of oil drained is 8 fl. oz. or more, an overcharge of oil should be suspected. Flush the system with refrigerant-11, replace drier desiccant, and install new compressor with total compressor oil charge, 10½ fl. oz.

amount drained, replace the same amount plus 1 fluid ounce (see note 2 below).

2. When there are signs of an excessive oil leak:

(a) On A-6 compressor systems: remove the compressor and the accumulator (see note 2 below). Drain and measure the total amount of oil drained from both components. If less than 6 fluid ounces, add 6 fluid ounces to the system. If more than 6 fluid ounces, add the same amount as that drained.

(b) R-4 compressor systems: Remove only the accumulator (see note 2 below), drain the oil, and measure the amount drained. It is not necessary to remove and drain the compressor because the R-4 compressor contains only a very small amount of oil. If the amount drained is less than 3 fluid ounces, add 3 fluid ounces of oil. If the amount drained is more than 3 fluid ounces, add the same amount as that drained.

NOTE 1: If the amount of oil drained from the compressor alone is 8 oz. or more, an overcharge of oil should be suspected. Flush the system with R-11 refrigerant and replace the accumulator-dehydrator and install the new compressor with the total oil charge. 10½ fluid ounces.

NOTE 2: When installing a new accumulator, add 1 fluid ounce of additional oil to compensate for that retained by the original accumulator desiccant.

Chrysler Compressor. When a new compressor is factory installed, it contains 10 to 11 fluid ounces of a special wax-free refrigeration oil. When the air-conditioning system is operating, the oil is carried throughout the entire system by the refrigerant. Some of this oil will be trapped and retained in the various system components. Therefore, once the system has been in operation, the amount of oil that is left in the compressor will be less than the original charge of 10 to 11 fluid ounces.

Whenever the refrigerant charge has been purged from the system, the oil level should be checked as a matter of routine procedure. To check the oil level, use the following procedure:

1. Operate the system for about 15 min with the engine running at about 1000 rpm.

2. Start the air-conditioning system and turn the blower on high speed.

3. Open the car windows and keep the hood open.

4. After 15 min of operation, turn the air-conditioning unit off without changing any of the described settings.

Purge the refrigerant from the system, and wait 10 min for the refrigerant to completely bleed from the system. Then measure the oil in the system by inserting a dipstick through the crankcase oil filler hole. The proper oil level will be indicated between 1⅝ in. and 2⅜ in. on the dipstick when the compressor is in the vertical position: 1⅝ in. on the dipstick is equal to 6 fluid ounces in the compressor; 2⅜ in. is equivalent to 8 fluid ounces of oil in the compressor. It will be necessary to compensate for the dipstick measurements when the compressor is mounted on an angle (see Figure 8-14).

If the compressor oil sump contains less than 6 fluid ounces of oil, add fresh, clean oil to the compressor to bring the level back to the minimum level. Use the proper viscosity of oil. Remove any oil that is in excess of 8 fluid ounces.

Tecumseh or York Compressor. Under normal operating conditions, when the unit is cooling satisfactorily, there is no need to check the oil level. There is no place for the oil to go except through the system. When the air-conditioning unit is first started, the oil will travel into the rest of the system. However, after a few minutes of operation most of the oil will be returned to the compressor.

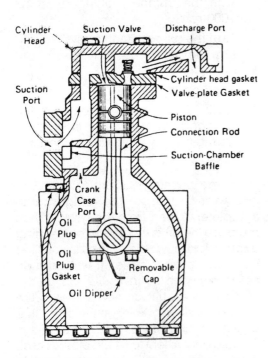

FIGURE 8-14. Compressor oil filler hole.

It is necessary to check the oil level only when a portion of the refrigerant is being replaced. Check the oil only after the system has been operating for 15 min with an engine speed of 1500 rpm in a 70°F, or above, ambient air temperature. Stop the car engine and isolate the compressor. Remove the oil filler plug from the compressor crankcase; insert a flattened ⅛-in. diameter rod into the oil filler hole until it bottoms out. The oil level should be indicated on the rod as shown in Table 8-2. It may be necessary to rotate the compressor crankshaft by hand until the stick clears the crankshaft. If additional oil is needed, add a 300 viscosity refrigeration oil to the compressor as needed.

Chrysler, Ford and Nippondenso 6-Cylinder Compressors. When the system is being inspected for an oil loss, be sure to check for signs of refrigerant leaks (leaks will usually be indicated by a wet, shiny looking place on the refrigerant line). Should an oil leak be found or if a component has been replaced, perform the oil level test procedures for the situation under question.

Replacing Component When No Oil Leak Is Noted. Purge the refrigerant from

TABLE 8-2. Compressor Oil Levels

	Inches	
	Min.	Max.
York		
Vertical mounted	⅞	1⅛
Horizontal mounted	13/16	1 3/16
Tecumseh		
Vertical mounted	⅞	1⅜
Horizontal mounted	⅞	1⅝

the system and replace the faulty component. Add the refrigeration oil to the replacement component as specified by the manufacturer.

Replacing Component When An Oil Leak Is Noted. If there has been an oil shortage noted because of a refrigerant leak, purge the system and repair or replace the faulty component. If the compressor is equipped with a drain plug, drain and discard the old oil. If there is no drain plug, remove the compressor from the car and pour the oil from the suction or discharge opening. If the compressor is used on a Ford car, add 13 oz of clean oil to the compressor crankcase. If the compressor is used on a Chrysler car, add 9 oz of clean oil to the compressor crankcase. Evacuate and recharge the system with refrigerant.

Compressor Failure and/or System Contaminated. If either of these conditions is present, purge the system and remove the compressor from the car. If the car is a Chrysler product, also remove the receiver–dehydrator and the H valve. If the car is a Ford product, also remove the accumulator and the expansion tube. Check each component for contamination. Clean or replace as the situation indicates. Install a new receiver-dehydrator or accumulator as required and a new compressor, if required. New or rebuilt compressors have the proper amount of oil charge in them from the factory. If reinstalling the old compressor, add the proper amount of oil for the application as noted above. Evacuate and recharge the system.

Sankyo 5-Cylinder Compressors. To check the oil level in this type of compressor, use the following steps:

1. Remove the oil filler plug. While looking through the oil filler hole, rotate the compressor, by hand, until the connecting rod is in the center of the oil filler hole.

2. Insert the dipstick into the oil filler hole (use dipstick part no. J-29642-12) to the right of the connecting rod until the dipstick hits the compressor housing.

3. Remove the dipstick from the compressor and count the number of increments that are covered by the oil. A properly filled compressor will cover from 4 to 6 of the increments on the dipstick.

SYSTEM EVACUATION

After the system has been evacuated, the low-pressure hose is to remain connected to the low-pressure side of the system. Both the high- and low-side hand valves on the gauge manifold remain closed.

The system must be completely discharged before connecting the gauge manifold to the vacuum pump. Pumping refrigerant through a vacuum pump can cause damage to the pump. Always wear safety goggles when working with refrigerant cylinders or when servicing air-conditioning units.

Before connecting the vacuum pump to the system, connect the low-side pressure gauge to the vacuum pump. Run the pump for a short time to get a reference vacuum reading, for which to watch in the following steps.

Use the following steps during the evacuation procedure:

1. Connect the high-pressure manifold gauge hose to the vacuum pump.

2. Connect the center manifold gauge hose to a refrigerant cylinder with the cylinder valve closed. The low-pressure hose is connected to the system (see Figure 8-15).

3. With the manifold gauge set and the vacuum pump connected as shown in Figure 8-15, begin the evacuation procedure by opening the high- and low-side manifold hand valves with the vacuum pump running.

4. Operate the vacuum pump for about 15 or 20 min after the low-side gauge shows a reading of 28 in. or below of vacuum (see Table 8-3).

TABLE 8-3. Boiling Point of Water under a Vacuum

Vacuum Inches of Mercury	Boiling Point, °F
27.32	110
29.18	70
29.76	30
29.90	−10

5. If the system has been left open to the atmosphere, it should have enough refrigerant put into it to raise the pressure a few pounds and be evacuated a second time.

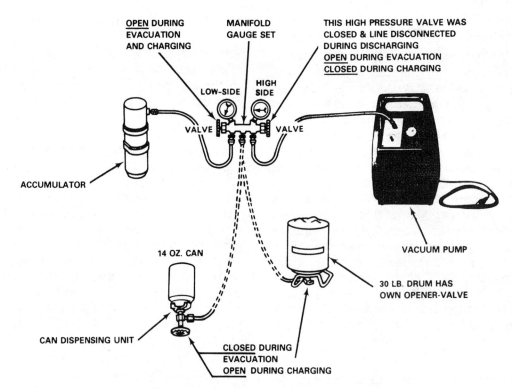

FIGURE 8-15. Evacuating and charging gauge connections. *Courtesy of AC Delco/General Motors Corp.*

6. Check the system for leaks by closing off the high- and low-side manifold hand valves and stopping the vacuum pump. There should be no more than a 2-in. vacuum loss in 5 min. A loss of more than this is a good indication that there is a leak in the system.

7. If a leak is indicated, put enough refrigerant in the system to raise the pressure above 50 psi. Check the system for leaks as outlined earlier in this chapter. Repair any leaks found.

8. Discharge the refrigerant from the system and reevacuate to the proper level.

   CAUTION: Do not discharge the refrigerant through the vacuum pump.

9. Allow the vacuum pump to operate for about 20 min after a vacuum of at least 28 in. has been reached. The system is now ready for charging.

CHARGING THE SYSTEM

The system should be charged only after the proper evacuation procedures have been completed as outlined under the previous heading. Two methods are used to charge an automotive air-conditioning unit with refrigerant. We will designate them (1) the General Motors method, and (2) the non-General Motors method.

Disposable Can Method for GM Units. After having discharged the system, made the necessary repairs, and evacuated the system, use the following charging procedure for disposable cans.

NOTE: To prevent blowing the thermal limiter fuse while charging the system on late-model GM units so equipped, remove the wire from the superheat switch at the rear head of the compressor, if accessible, or connect a jumper wire from terminal B to terminal C on the thermal limiter fuse. When the charging process has been completed, replace the wire at the switch or remove the jumper wire at the fuse. This switch should not be confused with a low-pressure cutoff switch, which on other applications might also be located in the rear compressor head. The latter should not be disconnected while charging the system. On cycling clutch systems, jump the thermostatic switch to keep the compressor from cycling.

Use the following steps in charging the unit. Always wear safety goggles:

1. Obtain the required quantity of the proper type of refrigerant.

2. Install the tapping valve on the container.

3. Connect the center hose of the manifold gauge set to the fitting on the tapping valve. Be sure to purge the air from the center manifold hose before putting refrigerant into the system through this line.

4. Start the engine; run it at fast idle speed and then reduce to normal idle with the air-conditioning control turned off.

5. With the refrigerant can inverted (turned upside down), open the can valve and the low-pressure hand valve on the manifold gauge set. Allow one can, 14 oz, of liquid refrigerant to flow into the system through the low-side service valve.

6. After one can of liquid R-12 has been admitted into the system, immedi-

ately engage the compressor clutch by setting the air-conditioning control lever to NORM and the blower speed on HI. Finish charging the system by using additional cans of refrigerant in the vapor form until the specified amount has been charged into the system.

7. Close off the source of R-12 at the cylinder. Run the engine for about 30 seconds to clear the lines and gauges of refrigerant. Then close off the low-side manifold gauge hand valve and disconnect the R-12 cylinder from the center hose. Place the hose in the stored place on the manifold gauge set. The air-conditioning system is now ready for performance testing.

NOTE: The charging process can be sped up by using a large-volume fan to blow air over the condenser.

Disposable Can Method for Non-GM Units. Many automotive air-conditioning units have a low-side service fitting at the compressor suction. When this is the case, the system should be charged with vapor only. One method of charging these systems is as follows:

1. Obtain the required quantity of refrigerant 12.

2. Install the can tapping valve on one can of refrigerant.

3. Connect the center hose of the manifold gauge to the tapping valve fitting. Purge the hose.

4. With the refrigerant can in the upright position, open the can valve and the manifold low-side hand valve. Let the refrigerant flow into the system until the can is empty

or until flow has stopped. Close the can valve. If the can is empty, replace it with a full one.

5. Start the engine and set the air-conditioning controls to the cooling position and the blower on high speed.

6. Slowly open the refrigerant can valve and allow vapor only to enter the compressor. Do not allow the charging pressure to exceed 40 psi on the low-side pressure gauge. Continue charging the system with the engine running at fast idle until the proper amount of refrigerant has been drawn into the system.

7. The charging by vapor process can be sped up by placing the refrigerant container in a pan of warm water (125°F maximum).

CAUTION: When using disposable cans to charge a system, do not connect any service hose to the high side of the system. To accidentally subject the can to the high discharge pressure of the compressor could cause the can to rupture, causing possible serious injury to those working on the unit or standing nearby. One-way safety valves can be installed in the charging line, and their use is recommended when low-side charging procedures are not followed.

Charging Station Method. The use of a charging stand has several advantages over the can method (see Figure 8-16). Some of these advantages are listed as follows:

1. The ability to measure an exact amount of refrigerant for any particular operation.

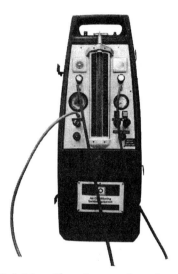

FIGURE 8-16. Charging station. *Courtesy of AC Delco/General Motors Corp.*

2. The ability to heat the refrigerant to 125°F with an internal heater to speed up the charging process.

3. A minimum number of connections must be made before the system can be discharged, evacuated, charged, and performance tested.

When a charging station is used to add refrigerant to a system, the manufacturer's instructions should be followed so that maximum efficiency can be reached during the service operation.

Adding Refrigerant. The following procedure is one method used when charging small amounts of refrigerant into a system. Before adding refrigerant to any system, be sure to check for any evidence of the loss of oil and add any oil that may be needed:

NOTE: This procedure is applicable only when the condenser air temperature is 70°F or above. If the condenser air temperature is below 70°F, there may be bubbles in the sight glass even though there is sufficient refrigerant in the system.

1. Close all service valves on the gauge manifold and the compressor. Connect the low-side pressure hose to the compressor service valve.

2. Purge the air from the hose.

3. Start the engine, turn on the air-conditioner, set the control lever to the coldest position, and set the blower for high speed. Operate the system for about 10 min at a speed of about 1500 to 2000 rpm to stabilize the system.

4. Check for any bubbles in the sight glass. If bubbles are present, there is a shortage of refrigerant. Add refrigerant as outlined.

5. Attach the center hose to a refrigerant cylinder. Purge the air from the hose.

6. Open fully the refrigerant cylinder valve and the low-pressure gauge manifold hand valve.

7. Add refrigerant until the bubbles disappear from the sight glass and then add an additional 14 oz of refrigerant.

8. When the charging process has been completed, continue to operate the system and make the necessary tests to determine if the system is functioning as it should, as described next under *Performance Testing.*

PERFORMANCE TESTING

The performance testing procedure provides us with information on the operating efficiency of the air-conditioning system. The manifold gauge set is connected to the system to determine both the high- and low-side operating pressures of the refrigeration system. While the unit is operating and the system pressures are being taken, a thermometer is placed in the discharge air from the distribution ducts in the passenger compartment to determine this temperature.

Before this test is completed, the operation of the air door is checked to make sure that it is operating as designed. The purpose of this door is to ensure that all the air flowing through the evaporator is directed to the air-distribution ducts and the air nozzles in the passenger compartment.

The following steps are used to perform this test:

1. Connect the high- and low-side gauges to the unit with the manifold gauge set. Be sure that all the valves are closed (see Figure 8-17, which shows the typical locations of the service valve fittings on GM units. When other brand units are being tested, the service valves will be found in various other locations).

2. Close all the car doors and windows. Keep the hood open so that free circulation of air through the engine compartment is possible.

3. Adjust the air-conditioning controls for maximum cooling. Set the blower on high speed.

4. Set the emergency brake and let the engine idle for about 10 min. Place a

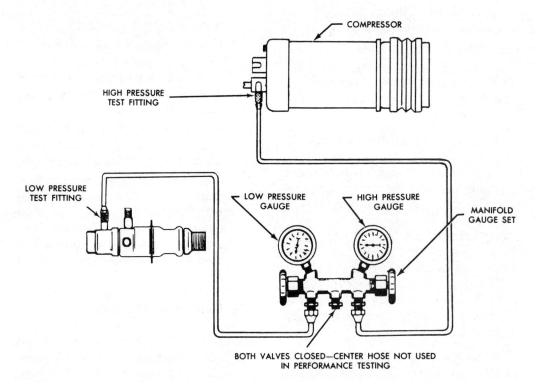

FIGURE 8-17.   Performance testing. *Courtesy of AC Delco / General Motors Corp.*

high-volume fan in front of the radiator to help cool the condenser.

5. Set the engine to run at about 1500 to 2000 rpm.

6. Measure the air temperature at the outlet of the air nozzle or the outlet grill in the passenger compartment. This temperature should be about 35° to 40°F.

7. Note the high and low refrigerant system pressures and compare them to those indicated in Table 8-4.

The refrigerant system operating pressures will vary with the humidity, as well as the outside air temperature. Therefore, on high-humidity days the operating pressures in the refrigerant system will be in the high operating range, as shown in the Table 8-4. When the humidity is lower, the operating pressures will also be lower.

When normal operating pressures are found, the system is normally considered to be operating as it should. As a further indication that the system is operating satisfactorily, check the discharge air temperature at the evaporator outlet. The temperature of the air at this location will also vary with the outside air temperature and humidity. Variations will also be found when the system uses a cycling clutch control or an evaporator pressure control valve. It is these variations that make it almost impossible to state an exact discharge air temperature on all units. As a general rule, however, when the outside air temperature is low (70°F) and the humidity is low (20%), the evaporator discharge air temperature should be around 35° to 40°F. When the outside

TABLE 8-4. Performance Chart: Approximate Test Pressure Ranges for Normal Functioning Systems

Ambient (Outside Air) Temperature °F	*At High Pressure Test Fitting (PSI)	STV, POA, or VIR Systems	**Cycling Clutch System with TXV and Rec.–Dehyd.	**Cycling Clutch System with Expansion (Orifice) Tubes and Accumulator (CCOT)	CCOT System with Pressure Cycling Switch	Chrysler Corp. with Evaporator Pressure Regulator Valve
60	120-170	28-31	7-15	—	—	—
70	150-250	28-31	7-15	24-31	24-31	22-30
80	180-275	28-31	7-15	24-31	24-31	22-37
90	200-310	28-31	7-15	24-32	24-31	25-37
100	230-330	28-35	10-30	24-32	24-36	—
110	270-360	28-38	10-35	24-32	—	—

Courtesy of AC Delco/General Motors Corp.

 *Pressures may be slightly higher on very humid days or lower on very dry days.

**Pressure just before clutch disengages (cycles off).

air temperature is high (80°F) and the humidity is also high (90%), the evaporator discharge air temperature should be around 55° to 60°F.

Because of these differences in system operating temperatures it is impossible to compile a chart to cover all units in all conditions. Therefore, it is necessary for the service technician to develop an experience factor for determining when the system is operating satisfactorily by comparing the refrigerant system pressures and the discharge air temperatures on the various units.

When the performance test indicates that the system is operating with pressure and temperature that are outside the normal operating range, there is some type of problem in the unit that must be corrected. A sound knowledge of the basics involved with the refrigeration system will help in this evaluation.

REFRIGERANT LINE REPAIRS

All the major components of an automotive air-conditioning unit have either flare fittings or fittings that will accommodate an O-ring type of connection. The refrigerant lines that connect these components are made up of the proper length of hose that has the appropriate type of fitting on each end (see Figure 8-18). In either case, the hose end of the fitting is made with sealing beads and will accommodate a hose clamp to aid in constructing a leakproof connection.

Repairing O-ring Connection Leaks. The following procedures are recommended when making repairs to O-ring connections:

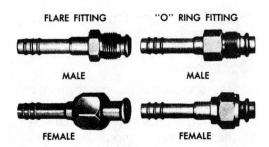

FIGURE 8-18. Flare and O-ring fittings.
Courtesy of AC Delco/General Motors Corp.

1. Check the torque on the fitting, and if found to be loose, tighten to the proper torque. Always use a backup wrench when tightening hose fittings. This will reduce the possibility of twisting the fitting. Do not overtighten these fittings because of the possibility of damage to the O-ring or the flare connection. After torquing the connection, leak test again to be certain that the leak has been repaired (see Table 8-5).

2. If the leak remains after the proper torque has been applied to the fitting, purge the entire refrigerant charge

TABLE 8-5. Recommended Fitting Torque Specifications

Metal Tube O.D.	Thread and Fitting Size	Steel Tubing Torque ft-lb	Alum. Tubing Torque, ft-lb
1/4	7/16	13	6
3/8	5/8	33	12
1/2	3/4	33	12
5/8	7/8	33	20
3/4	1 1/16	33	25

Courtesy of AC Delco/General Motors Corp.

from the system, as outlined under *Discharging the System.*

3. Inspect the fitting, and if damaged in any way, install a new one. Discard the old O-ring and replace it with a new one. Be sure to coat the new fittings with clean refrigeration oil.

4. Torque the fitting to the proper torque. Use a backup wrench.

5. Evacuate the system and charge in the proper amount of refrigerant.

Repairing Hose Clamp Connection Leaks. The following procedures are recommended when making repairs to hose clamp connections:

1. Check to be sure that the hose clamp is tight. If not, tighten as required. Retest for a leak.

2. If the leak still remains, purge the complete charge of refrigerant from the system as outlined under *Discharging The System.*

3. Loosen the hose clamp and remove the hose from the fitting by making an angular cut to the end of the hose (see Figure 8-19). This cut should loosen the hose so that it may be removed from the fitting more easily.

   CAUTION: Use extreme care when making this cut and avoid nicking or scoring the sealing beads on the fitting, which would possibly cause leaks.

4. If the old hose is to be reused, make a clean square cut at the rear of the angular cut made in removing the hose from the fitting.

5. Inspect the fitting, and if the sealing beads are scored or nicked, replace it with a new one.

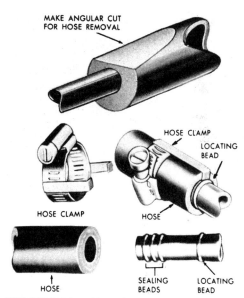

FIGURE 8-19. **Hose clamp connections.** *Courtesy of AC Delco/General Motors Corp.*

6. Dip the end of the hose in clean refrigeration oil and carefully slip it over the end of the fitting. Never push the hose past the locating bead.

7. Install the clamps on the hose. Hook the locating arms over the cut end of the hose.

8. Tighten the hose clamps to the proper torque of 35 to 42 in.-lb.

9. Evacuate the system and charge it with the proper amount of refrigerant.

Repairing Leaks in Crimped Hose Assemblies. Crimped hose assemblies are those in which the hose is permanently attached to the connection fitting. Many factory installations use this type of fitting. Two types of fittings can be used in repairing leaks that might appear in these fittings. They are the clamp-type splicer and the replacement connector fitting (see Figure 8-20 and 8-21). On

FIGURE 8-20. Typical splicer installation.
Courtesy of AC Delco/General Motors Corp.

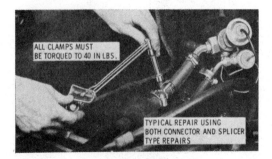

FIGURE 8-21. Combination splicer connector repair. *Courtesy of AC Delco/General Motors Corp.*

some repairs, it may be desirable to use a combination of both fittings when there is not enough of the hose left to make the desired connections.

A splicer-type connection should be used only when there is a leak in the middle of the hose. If the leak occurs at the crimped section and there is enough of the hose remaining to make the connections, a new hose clamp-type connector can be used. If the hose is too short, then the combination splicer–connector repair can be made.

THERMOSTATIC SWITCH ADJUSTMENT

The thermostatic switch is a device that opens or closes the electrical circuit to the compressor clutch as the temperature inside the passenger compartment varies. If the thermostatic switch should fail in the open position, there will be no electrical current to the clutch and, therefore, no cooling. If the switch should fail in the closed position, the compressor will operate continuously. Continuous compressor operation will possibly result in the evaporator freezing up. Erratic operation of the thermostat will result in wide variations in the discharge air temperature from the evaporator outlet. Should the power element lose its charge, the switch will remain in the open position and there will be no cooling.

Checking for Proper Thermostat Operation. Use the following procedures when checking the thermostat operation:

1. Install the manifold gauge set. Set up the car as described under *Performance Testing the System.*

2. Moving the temperature control lever should result in a definite change in the suction pressure and cycling of the compressor clutch.

3. If the compressor continues to operate regardless of where the thermostat lever is set, it is an indication that the switch contacts are fused together, which will allow the evaporator to freeze up. Replace the thermostatic switch.

4. If the compressor does not operate regardless of where the thermostat lever is set, it is an indication of a lost power element charge, provided

of course that there is electrical power at the switch. A loss of power element charge results in no operation of the compressor and no cooling. Switch replacement is necessary.

Adjustment of the Thermostatic Switch. If the preceding checks are made and the switch seems to be operating properly, adjustment may be necessary. Use the following steps in making the adjustment.

1. Set the car up as outlined under *Performance Testing the System*.

2. The suction side of the system should pull down to the readings indicated in the performance chart (Table 8-4). Check the listing indicated under the ambient temperature at the time the switch is being adjusted.

3. Remove the faceplate assembly by removing the retaining screws.

4. Loosen the retaining screws and remove the thermostatic switch. Next, remove the nonmetal end plate from the switch and locate the switch adjustment screw.

5. If the low-side pressure is found to be lower than that prescribed for the end of the cycle, turn the adjusting screw a part of a turn in the clockwise direction (see Figure 8-22).

6. If the low-side pressure is higher than that prescribed for the end of the cycle, turn the adjusting screw counterclockwise a part of a turn for adjustment.

7. Reassemble the switch. Install the switch on the faceplate. Install the faceplate assembly on the evaporator. Be sure that the sensing tube is

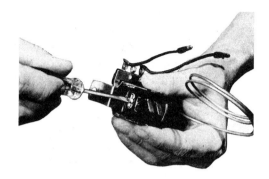

FIGURE 8-22. Thermostatic switch adjustment. *Courtesy of AC Delco/General Motors Corp.*

replaced in the proper place on the evaporator.

8. Check the performance of the system. If more adjustment is indicated, repeat steps 3 through 7 until the prescribed low-side pressure is reached.

NOTE: Do not attempt to run a performance test with the faceplate and switch removed from the evaporator assembly. If this is attempted, false readings will be the result.

SYSTEM FLUSHING

When the system has been contaminated by being left open or because metal chips from compressor bearings have been circulated through the system, it must be flushed to remove the contaminants. Use the following steps to flush the system:

1. Install the gauges on the system and purge the refrigerant from the system.

2. Remove the compressor.

3. Remove the valves, receiver–drier, or desiccant from the accumulator; make the necessary connections to connect the lines when the components have been removed, except for the compressor fittings.

4. Connect the flushing device where the compressor was removed. The flushing device may be a hand pump or an electric motor-driven pump used to circulate R-11 through the system.

5. Fill the system with R-11 and circulate it through the system and components for several minutes to remove the contaminants.

6. Disconnect the flushing device.

7. Blow R-12 through the system to remove as much of the R-11 as possible.

   NOTE: Use caution to prevent personal injury from the R-11 leaving the system. Place a rag or other covering over the opening where the R-11 will leave the system.

8. Clean the components that were previously removed to get rid of the contaminants.

9. Replace these components in the system.

10. Reinstall the compressor or install a new compressor as required. If the original compressor is to be used, make certain that oil contaminants have been removed and a new charge of oil installed.

11. Evacuate the system for at least 15 min after the greatest vacuum possible has been obtained.

12. Pressurize the system with R-12.

13. Evacuate the system again and recharge the system with R-12.

14. Check operation of the unit.

REVIEW QUESTIONS

1. What happens to R-12 when subjected to an open flame?

2. What could possibly happen to a refrigerant cylinder that is exposed to extremely high temperature?

3. What is the maximum temperature to which an R-12 cylinder should be heated?

4. Is it good practice to heat an R-12 cylinder with a torch?

5. What will a heavy concentration of refrigerant in a closed room do?

6. Name two types of service valves used on automotive air-conditioning systems.

7. What causes the core to unseat in a Schrader valve?

8. Why are there two different sizes of Schrader valves on GM cars?

9. Where is the compound gauge used in automotive air conditioning?

10. How is the pressure gauge graduated?

11. What is the center manifold connection used for?

12. When making tests, how are the gauge manifold hand valves positioned?

13. What should always be done when connecting the gauge set to the system?

14. For what is the second compound gauge mounted on the manifold set used?

15. What must be done to the system before accurate tests can be made?

16. What happens to the refrigerant when foreign materials enter the system?

17. What should be done to the refrigeration system before leak testing?

18. Name the two types of leak detectors in common use.

19. Why should the fumes from a burnt refrigerant not be breathed?

20. Where is the best place to check a fitting for an R-12 leak?

21. Do refrigeration compressors burn oil?

22. Does oil circulate through the system with the refrigerant?

23. Is it necessary to check the oil level in every service procedure?

24. Should refrigerant be pumped with a vacuum pump?

25. What should be done to a system that has been left open to the atmosphere?

26. How warm should the pan of water be that is used in speeding up the can method of charging a system?

27. What does the performance testing procedure indicate to the service technician?

28. What ambient conditions will affect the system operating pressure?

29. Why is a backup wrench recommended when tightening a fitting?

30. How far should the hose be pushed on the fitting?

Generally, when a car is brought to the shop for repairs on the air-conditioning unit, the complaint will be "no cooling" or "insufficient cooling." The first step is to find out why the unit is not operating as it should.

When normal maintenance, service procedures, and performance testing procedures are followed as described in Chapter 8, a great many of the air-conditioning systems will operate with satisfactory nozzle outlet air temperatures, and the system will be functioning with the proper pressures as shown in Table 8-4.

The need for a more detailed diagnosis is indicated when the nozzle outlet air temperature and the refrigerant system operating pressures are found to be abnormal. (The variation in temperature and humidity should be taken into consideration.)

PROBLEM DIAGNOSIS PREREQUISITES

Due to the different construction and operating variations that exist from one type of unit to another, no single uniform or standard diagnosis procedure is applicable to all types of units. There are, however, three basic prerequisites that make up the total diagnosis of the problem:

1. Determining that the system has an adequate, but not excessive, charge of refrigerant.

2. Determining whether or not the system is controlled by a cycling clutch type compressor or by an evaporator pressure control valve.

3. Performing an operational check of the air-distribution system, consisting of the blower motor, vacuum lines, switches, hoses, and air ducts, to make sure that all of them are func-

9

System Diagnosis and Troubleshooting Procedures

tioning properly before attempting a diagnosis procedure for faulty components of the refrigeration system.

The following is a brief description of the symptoms that each refrigeration system component will give when a malfunctioning condition is present.

EVAPORATOR

When the evaporator is the defective component, the problem will be noticed by an inadequate supply of cool air to the passenger compartment. An evaporator core that is partially clogged with dirt, a cracked case, or a leaking seal will generally be the problem.

COMPRESSOR

A malfunctioning compressor will present itself in one of four ways: noise, seizure, leakage, or low suction and discharge pressures.

A compressor that produces resonance noises should not cause any alarm; however, an irregular noise or rattles are a good indication that there is probably loose or broken parts inside the compressor.

To check for a seized compressor, de-energize the magnetic clutch; then see if the compressor can be rotated by hand. If rotation is impossible, the compressor is seized. Perform the false compressor seizure check as outlined in Chapter 10 before removing the compressor for repairs. If the compressor is not seized, check to see that electricity is supplied to the clutch terminals.

A leaky shaft seal will allow the refrigerant to escape out of the system

and cause the unit to malfunction. The shaft seal can be checked with a leak detector.

A low discharge pressure may be due to a leaking internal compressor seal or a restriction in the compressor. It can also be occurring because of a low refrigerant charge or a restriction in another part of the system. These conditions should be checked before proper servicing of the compressor can be accomplished.

CONDENSER

There are two ways that a condenser can malfunction: a leak or a restriction. A leak will allow the refrigerant to escape from the system, causing it to malfunction. The leak must be found and repaired before recharging the system. A restricted condenser will cause a high compressor discharge pressure. When a partial restriction is present, there will probably be a small amount of frost at the outlet of the restriction, or at least the pipe will be cooler at the outlet than at the inlet of the restriction. If the airflow through the condenser is restricted, a high compressor discharge pressure will be indicated on the gauge. When the condenser is operating properly, the condenser outlet pipe will be cooler than the inlet pipe.

RECEIVER–DEHYDRATOR

These units may fail because of a restriction inside the unit itself. A restriction at the inlet will be indicated by a higher than normal compressor discharge pressure. Restrictions located at the outlet will be indicated by a lower than normal compressor discharge pressure accompanied by a loss in cooling capacity. A cool or cold receiver–dehydrator outlet is indicative of a restricted receiver-dehydrator.

USE OF THE SIGHT GLASS FOR SYSTEM DIAGNOSIS

When the ambient temperature is 70°F or higher, the sight glass may be used to determine whether or not the system has sufficient refrigerant. After the system has operated for about 5 min, the appearance of slow-moving bubbles in the sight glass is an indication that there is a shortage of refrigerant in the system. On a cool day, however, a continuous stream of bubbles may appear in the sight glass. This is considered to be normal operation. If the sight glass is normally clear and satisfactory operation of the system occurs, occasional bubbles do not necessarily indicate a shortage of refrigerant.

If there is a constant foaming or a broken column of liquid in the sight glass, partially block the flow of air over the condenser and observe the sight glass. If the glass clears and there is a satisfactory performance, the charge is considered to be within the proper range.

In all cases where a continuous shortage of refrigerant is indicated, an additional amount of refrigerant should be added to the system in ¼-lb increments until the sight glass clears. An additional charge of refrigerant of ½ to 1 lb should be added as a reserve. However, in no case should more than 1 lb be added to the system to prevent overcharging the unit.

The procedure outlined next can be used to quickly determine if the system is low on refrigerant. This check can be made quickly, thus aiding in system diagnosis by pinpointing the problem to the amount of charge in the system, and by eliminating the refrigerant charge from the complete system checkout procedure.

Sight Glass Quick Check Procedure. The following checks must be made in an ambient temperature of 70°F or higher. Start the engine and let it run at a fast idle. Complete the following steps:

1. Set the controls for maximum cooling with the blower on high speed.

2. If bubbles appear in the sight glass, the system is low on refrigerant. Locate the leak with a leak detector. Repair the leak, if any, and recharge the system with the proper amount of refrigerant. If foaming continues, check for a restriction in the refrigerant system between the condenser and the sight glass.

3. If there are no bubbles (the sight glass is clear), the system is either fully charged or completely empty of refrigerant. Feel the high- and low-pressure pipes at the compressor. The high-pressure pipe should be warm; the low-pressure pipe should be cold.

4. If there is no appreciable temperature difference noted on the pipes at the compressor, the system is empty or almost empty of refrigerant. Turn off the engine. Put ½ lb of refrigerant in the system. If the system will not accept the refrigerant, start the engine and draw the ½ lb into the system through the low-side service valve. Check the system for a leak.

5. If there is a difference in temperature noted on the compressor pipes when checked as in step 4, proceed as follows:

    (a) Even though a temperature difference is noted, there is a possibility that the system is overcharged. An overcharged system will result in poor cooling during low-speed operation because of the higher-than-normal head pressure. An overcharge is easily checked by stopping the compressor while observing the sight glass.

    (b) If the refrigerant foams and then settles away from the sight glass in less than 45 seconds, it can be assumed that the system is properly charged. Continue checking out the system using the performance checks for the proper type of system as outlined in the remainder of this chapter.

    (c) If the refrigerant in the sight glass remains clear for more than 45 seconds before foaming begins and settling away follows, the system is overcharged. Verify with a performance check for the proper type of system.

THERMOSTATIC EXPANSION VALVE (TXV)

Thermostatic expansion valve failures are usually indicated by low suction and discharge pressures, along with insufficient cooling in the passenger compartment. This failure is usually due to the loss of power element charge, which results in the closing of the valve. A clogged expansion valve inlet screen will also produce these same symptoms, with less frequent occurrence. A clogged inlet screen is due to contaminants in the system.

ORIFICE TUBE (CCOT)

A clogged orifice tube will produce the same symptoms as a faulty expansion valve as listed previously.

SUCTION THROTTLING (POA) VALVE

Should the POA valve become defective, it may cause the suction pressure to be either high or low, depending on the type of failure, and result in a higher-than-normal evaporator discharge air temperature. No adjustment can be made to the POA valve. When a faulty valve is found, it must be replaced.

NOTE: Moisture in the system can cause either the POA or the TXV valve to freeze up and malfunction. Before replacement of the valve, turn the system off for a few minutes to allow it to defrost and repeat the performance test.

REFRIGERANT LINE RESTRICTIONS

Any restrictions in the refrigerant lines will be indicated by the following conditions:

1. *Suction line restriction:* A restriction in the suction line will result in a lower than normal suction pressure, a low discharge pressure, accompanied with little or no cooling.

2. *Discharge line restriction:* Any restriction in the discharge line will

usually cause the pressure relief valve in the compressor to open, relieving the pressure in the compressor.

3. *Liquid line restriction:* Any restriction in the liquid line will result in a lower-than-normal suction and discharge pressure, accompanied with little or no cooling.

INITIAL SYSTEM CHECKS

Before a full performance diagnosis test is attempted, certain checks should be made to verify the following conditions:

1. Check for proper compressor belt installation and tension.
2. Verify the proper clutch coil terminal connector installation.
3. Check the condenser for air block-age due to foreign material in the fins.
4. Check for loose pipe fittings on all components, and for broken, burst, or a cut refrigerant hose.
5. Check for proper compressor clutch engagement.
6. Check for proper air duct hose connections.

After completing these steps, install the pressure gauge manifold on the unit. Place thermometers in the discharge air nozzles and conduct a diagnosis test according to the type of system being worked on, as indicated in the following pages of this chapter.

GAUGE MANIFOLD INSTALLATION

The first step in diagnosing troubles in an air-conditioning unit is to install the gauge manifold set on the unit. The first steps performed are general perfor-

mance tests for refrigerant flow and refrigerant charge in the system. These conditions are all determined from the readings indicated on the gauges.

To install the manifold set on the unit, stop the engine and perform the following steps:

1. Remove the protector caps from the service valve ports on the system.
2. Connect the high-side manifold hose to the high-side service valve port on the compressor or the muffler. The high-side service valve is in the line leading from the compressor to the condenser. Tighten this connection.
3. Connect the low-side manifold hose to the low-side service valve port on the compressor, the POA valve, or the accumulator. Tighten this connection.
4. Loosen the center hose from the storage connection.
5. If service valves are used rather than Schrader valves, crack the stem from the backseat about one and a half turns to open the valve service port.
6. Purge the high-side hose by cracking the high-side manifold hand valve and allowing the refrigerant to escape from the center hose for 3 to 5 seconds to purge the air from the hoses. Close the high-side manifold hand valve.
7. Purge the low-side hose by cracking the low-side manifold hand valve and allowing the refrigerant to escape through the center hose for 3 to 5 seconds to purge the air from the hoses. Close the low-side manifold hand valve.

The manifold gauge set is now installed and ready to use (see Figure 9-1).

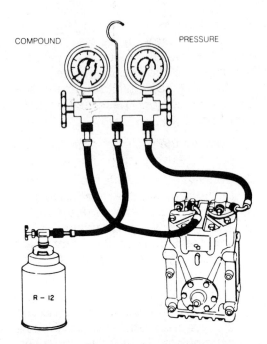

COMPOUND   PRESSURE

R – 12

FIGURE 9-1. Manifold gauge set installation.

SYSTEM DIAGNOSIS PROCEDURES

Cycling Clutch Compressor and Thermostatic Expansion Valve System. Follow the step-by-step procedures listed in Chart 9-1.

POA Valve, VIR, or EEVIR Systems. Follow the step-by-step procedures listed in Chart 9-2.

Cycling Clutch Compressor Using a Pressure Cycling Switch, Expansion Tube, and Accumulator System. Follow the step-by-step procedures listed in Chart 9-3.

GM Compressor Electrical Circuit Equipped with a Thermal Limiter and Superheat Switch System. Follow the step-by-step procedures listed in Chart 9-4.

GM Compressors. Follow the step-by-step procedures listed in Chart 9-5.

Chrysler Evaporator Pressure Regulator Valve System. Proper testing of the EPR valve requires three gauges, the regular manifold gauge set plus an auxiliary compound gauge, discussed earlier. The gauges are connected as shown in Figure 9-2.

1. The regular low-side gauge is connected to the system where the suction line enters the compressor. It will indicate the evaporator outlet pressure before the EPR valve.

2. The auxiliary low-side gauge is connected to a service fitting on the compressor head. It will indicate the pressure after the EPR valve.

3. The regular manifold high-pressure gauge is connected to the service fitting normally found on the compressor muffler. It will indicate the compressor discharge pressure.

Operate the engine at 1300 rpm (800 for Imperial) for a period of 10 to 15 min with the air-conditioning controls set for maximum cooling with the hood and windows open to stabilize the refrigeration system.

Normal Operation. With an ambient temperature of 75°F, the reading on the high-pressure gauge should be in the range from 185 to 205 psi. The low-pressure gauge reading should be in the range from 22 to 30 psi. The auxiliary gauge should indicate a pressure of 15 psi or less at the compressor inlet. If the pressure indicated on the auxiliary gauge will not drop to 15 psi, increase the engine speed to 2000 rpm (1700 for Imperial). When the ambient temperature

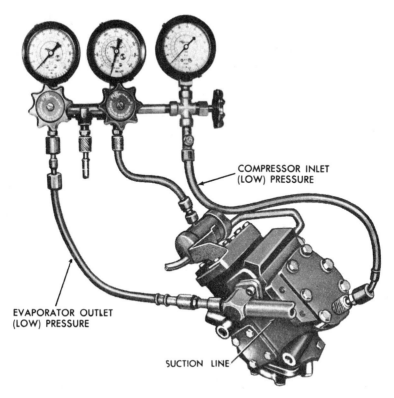

FIGURE 9-2.   Gauge connections for testing Chrysler EPR and ETR systems.
Courtesy of AC Delco/General Motors Corp.

is higher, 85° to 90°F, the evaporator pressure may be around 35 to 37 psi and the compressor inlet pressure only 1 to 4 psi lower.

EPR Stuck Open. All three pressure gauges will indicate a lower-than-normal pressure for their particular reading.

EPR Stuck Closed. The suction pressure will be above normal, the compressor discharge pressure lower than normal, and the compressor inlet pressure may be zero or indicate a vacuum.

NOTE: If the EPR valve screen is plugged, the test results will be the same as if the valve is stuck closed.

Chrysler Evaporator Temperature Regulator (ETR) Valve System. The ETR valve diagnosis with the pressure gauges is the same as that for the EPR valve discussed previously (see Figure 9-2). However, test indications of a valve stuck open or closed may be caused by an electrical or thermal switch malfunction. Therefore, the diagnosis for the ETR valve could include the following steps:

1. Check for the proper contact of the thermal switch capillary tube with the evaporator fins.

2. Check for electrical power to the thermal switch.

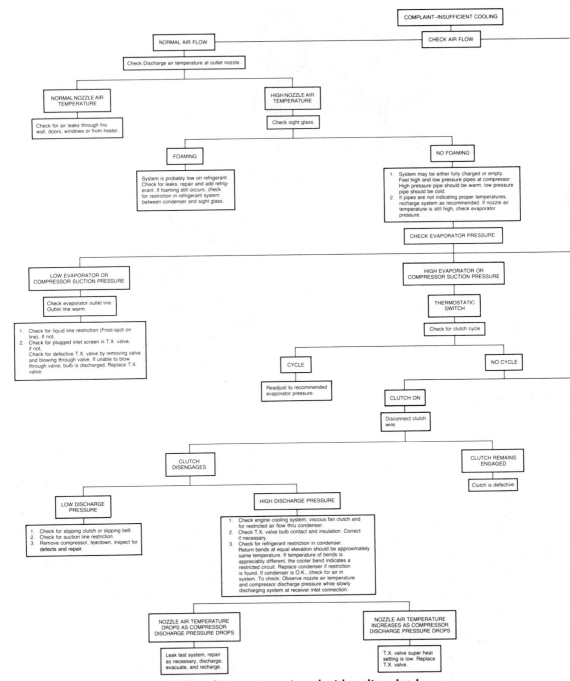

CHART 9-1.   Diagnosis procedure for system equipped with cycling clutch compressor and thermostatic expansion valve. *Courtesy of AC Delco/ General Motors Corp.*

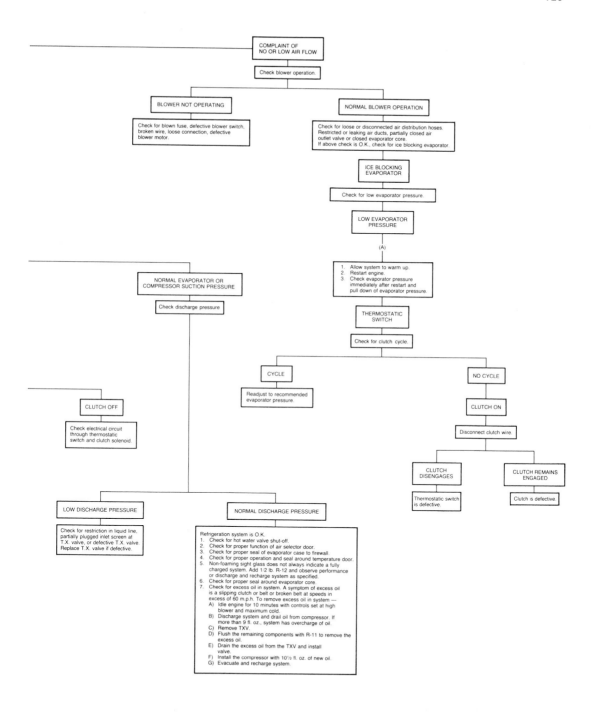

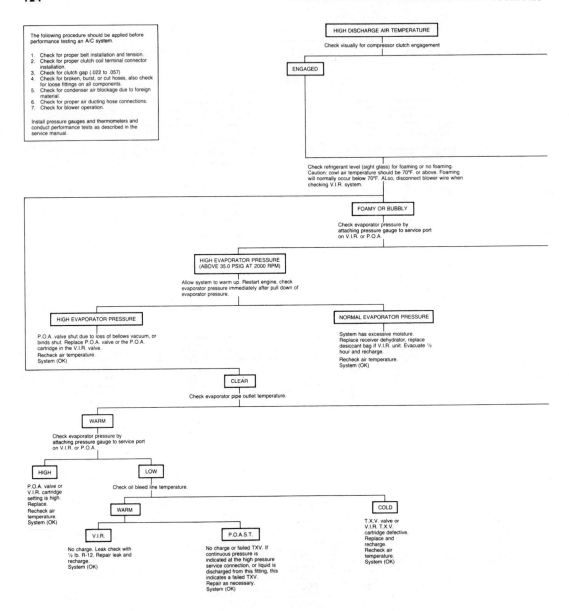

CHART 9-2. Diagnosis procedure for system equipped with POA valve, VIR, or EEVIR. *Courtesy of AC Delco/General Motors Corp.*

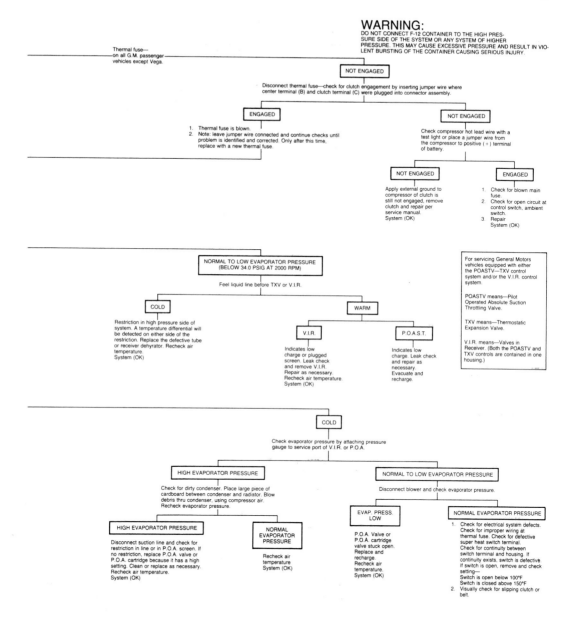

WARNING:
DO NOT CONNECT F-12 CONTAINER TO THE HIGH PRES-
SURE SIDE OF THE SYSTEM OR ANY SYSTEM OF HIGHER
PRESSURE. THIS MAY CAUSE EXCESSIVE PRESSURE AND RESULT IN VIO-
LENT BURSTING OF THE CONTAINER CAUSING SERIOUS INJURY.

Thermal fuse—
on all G.M. passenger
vehicles except Vega.

NOT ENGAGED

Disconnect thermal fuse—check for clutch engagement by inserting jumper wire where
center terminal (B) and clutch terminal (C) were plugged into connector assembly.

ENGAGED

1. Thermal fuse is blown.
2. Note: leave jumper wire connected and continue checks until
   problem is identified and corrected. Only after this time,
   replace with a new thermal fuse.

NOT ENGAGED

Check compressor hot lead wire with a
test light or place a jumper wire from
the compressor to positive (+) terminal
of battery.

NOT ENGAGED

Apply external ground to
compressor of clutch is
still not engaged, remove
clutch and repair per
service manual.
System (OK)

ENGAGED

1. Check for blown main
   fuse.
2. Check for open circuit at
   control switch, ambient
   switch.
3. Repair
   System (OK)

NORMAL TO LOW EVAPORATOR PRESSURE
(BELOW 34.0 PSIG AT 2000 RPM)

Feel liquid line before TXV or V.I.R.

COLD

Restriction in high pressure side of
system. A temperature differential will
be detected on either side of the
restriction. Replace the defective tube
or receiver dehyrator. Recheck air
temperature.
System (OK)

WARM

V.I.R.

Indicates low
charge or plugged
screen. Leak check
and remove V.I.R.
Repair as necessary.
Recheck air temperature.
System (OK)

P.O.A.S.T.

Indicates low
charge. Leak check
and repair as
necessary.
Evacuate and
recharge.

For servicing General Motors
vehicles equipped with either
the POASTV—TXV control
system and/or the V.I.R. control
system.

POASTV means—Pilot
Operated Absolute Suction
Throttling Valve.

TXV means—Thermostatic
Expansion Valve.

V.I.R. means—Valves in
Receiver. (Both the POASTV and
TXV controls are contained in one
housing.)

COLD

Check evaporator pressure by attaching pressure
gauge to service port of V.I.R. or P.O.A.

HIGH EVAPORATOR PRESSURE

Check for dirty condenser. Place large piece of
cardboard between condenser and radiator. Blow
debris thru condenser, using compressor air.
Recheck evaporator pressure.

HIGH EVAPORATOR PRESSURE

Disconnect suction line and check for
restriction in line or in P.O.A. screen. If
no restriction, replace P.O.A. valve or
P.O.A. cartridge because it has a high
setting. Clean or replace as necessary.
Recheck air temperature.
System (OK)

NORMAL
EVAPORATOR
PRESSURE

Recheck air
temperature
System (OK)

NORMAL TO LOW EVAPORATOR PRESSURE

Disconnect blower and check evaporator pressure.

EVAP. PRESS.
LOW

P.O.A. Valve or
P.O.A. cartridge
valve stuck open.
Replace and
recharge.
Recheck air
temperature.
System (OK)

NORMAL EVAPORATOR PRESSURE

1. Check for electrical system defects.
   Check for improper wiring at
   thermal fuse. Check for defective
   super heat switch terminal.
   Check for continuity between
   switch terminal and housing. If
   continuity exists, switch is defective.
   If switch is open, remove and check
   setting—
   Switch is open below 100°F
   Switch is closed above 150°F
2. Visually check for slipping clutch or
   belt.

**INSUFFICIENT COOLING —
A/C SYSTEMS WITH CYCLING CLUTCH —
EXPANSION TUBE (PRESSURE SENSING)**

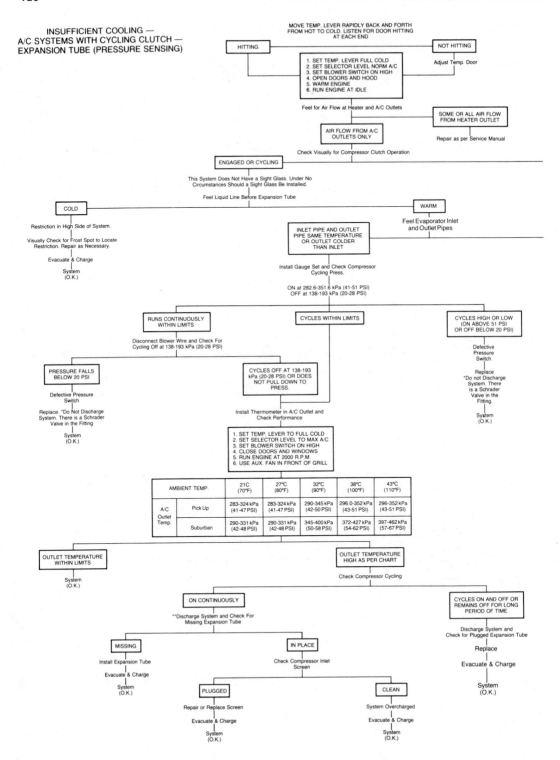

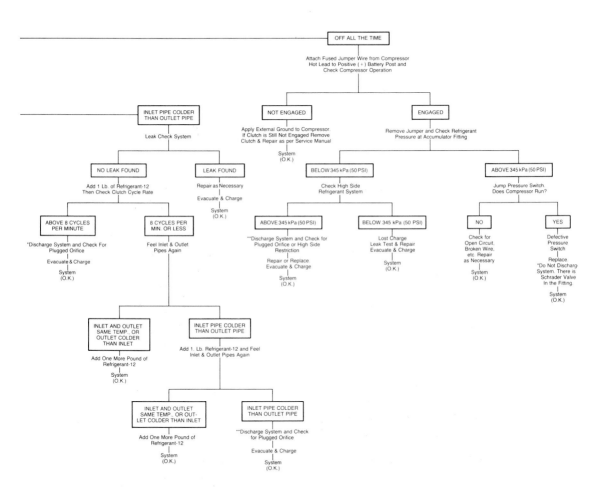

CHART 9-3. Diagnosis procedure for system equipped with pressure cycling switch, expansion tube (CCOT). *Courtesy of AC Delco/General Motors Corp.*

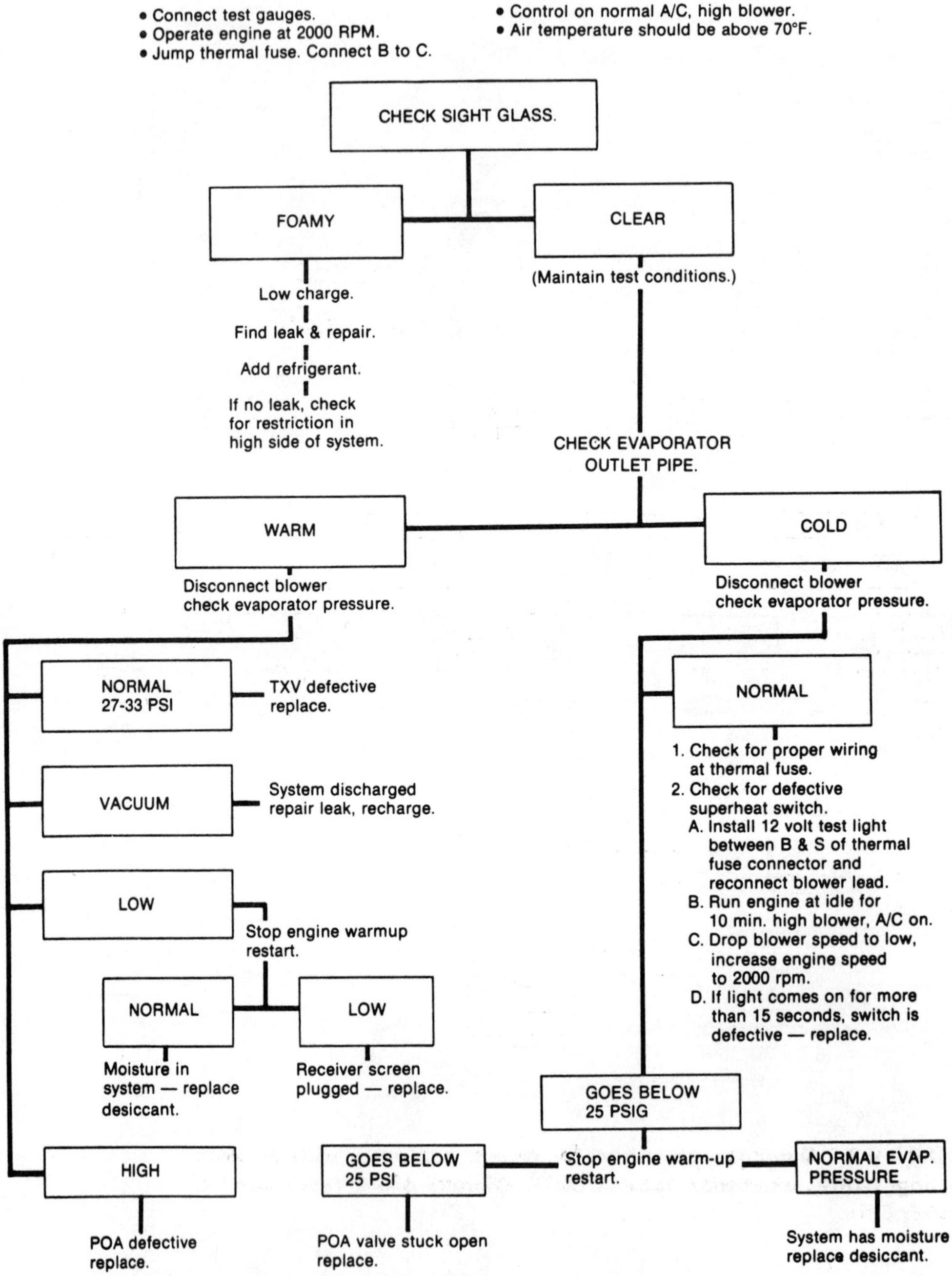

- Connect test gauges.
- Operate engine at 2000 RPM.
- Jump thermal fuse. Connect B to C.

- Control on normal A/C, high blower.
- Air temperature should be above 70°F.

CHECK SIGHT GLASS.

FOAMY

CLEAR

Low charge.

Find leak & repair.

Add refrigerant.

If no leak, check
for restriction in
high side of system.

(Maintain test conditions.)

CHECK EVAPORATOR
OUTLET PIPE.

WARM

COLD

Disconnect blower
check evaporator pressure.

Disconnect blower
check evaporator pressure.

NORMAL
27-33 PSI

TXV defective
replace.

NORMAL

1. Check for proper wiring
   at thermal fuse.
2. Check for defective
   superheat switch.
   A. Install 12 volt test light
      between B & S of thermal
      fuse connector and
      reconnect blower lead.
   B. Run engine at idle for
      10 min. high blower, A/C on.
   C. Drop blower speed to low,
      increase engine speed
      to 2000 rpm.
   D. If light comes on for more
      than 15 seconds, switch is
      defective — replace.

VACUUM

System discharged
repair leak, recharge.

LOW

Stop engine warmup
restart.

NORMAL

LOW

Moisture in
system — replace
desiccant.

Receiver screen
plugged — replace.

GOES BELOW
25 PSIG

HIGH

GOES BELOW
25 PSI

Stop engine warm-up
restart.

NORMAL EVAP.
PRESSURE

POA defective
replace.

POA valve stuck open
replace.

System has moisture
replace desiccant.

CHART 9-4. Diagnosis procedure, GM compressor equipped with thermal limiter and superheat switch. *Courtesy of AC Delco / General Motors Corp.*

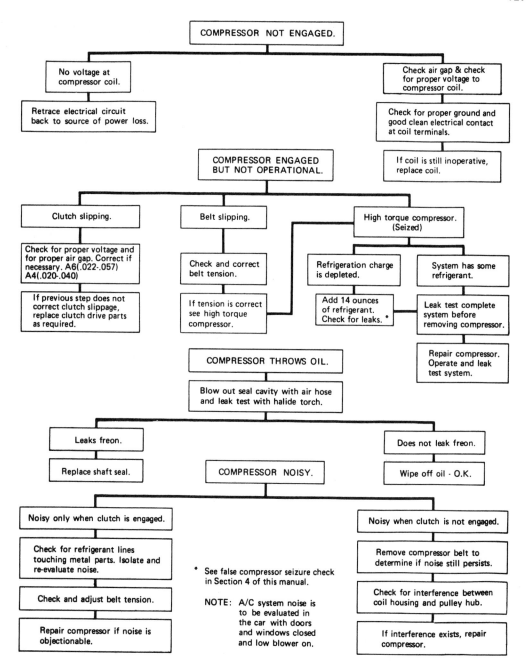

CHART 9-5. Diagnosis procedure, GM compressor. *Courtesy of AC Delco / General Motors Corp.*

3. Check for electrical power out of the switch when the evaporator is very cold (15 psi or less on the auxiliary gauge).

4. Check for electrical power to the ETR solenoid when the auxiliary gauge reading is 15 psi or below.

5. When there is electrical power to the ETR solenoid, the auxiliary gauge pressure reading should drop to zero or into a vacuum.

Otherwise, the ETR valve is not functioning.

Air-Distribution Portion of the GM System. The air-distribution (airflow) portion of General Motors air-conditioning systems operate essentially the same on all current models. However, there are several variations in the electrical and vacuum operating circuits for different makes and years of production models. These variables would be very difficult to cover in detail.

For all practical purposes, the diagnostician should understand the normal position of all air doors and the resulting airflow distribution that should be anticipated for each of the variations encountered with each change of the dash control selector and temperature lever. These conditions are shown in Figure 9-3 through 9-8 for some model GM units.

An operational check of the air-distribution components can be made by operating the air-conditioning system in each of the different selector and temperature lever positions. Should the desired results not be obtained, it will be necessary to determine whether a problem exists in the electrical or vacuum circuits. It is essential to make this operational check and correct any difficulties

before diagnosing for troubles in the refrigeration system portion of the air-conditioning unit.

Figures 9-9 through 9-20 show and describe the electrical and vacuum circuits that are functional for each position of the dash control selector and temperature levers on some model GM automobiles.

It should be noted that in most 1971 and later-model GM cars, the blower motor is operating when the ignition switch is in the on position, even when the selector lever is in the off position. Some installations also have a provision that prevents the blower motor from operating until the engine coolant temperature reaches approximately 120°F.

Selector Lever in the Off Position. With the selector lever in the OFF position, the blower motor operates at low speed regardless of the fan switch position, and the vacuum-operated doors are positioned as follows (see Figure 9-3):

1. Outside air: full open to the outside air.

2. Upper mode: open to the heat mode; closed to the A/C mode.

3. Lower mode: open to the heat mode; closed to the A/C mode.

4. Slave: in the airflow stream (actuated by the lower mode door).

5. Defroster: closed to the defroster outlets; fully open to the heater outlet.

The temperature door is controlled by the temperature lever.

Temperature Lever in The Maximum Cold Position. With the temperature lever in the MAXIMUM COLD position (see Figure 9-3), the temperature door is positioned so that the outside air from the

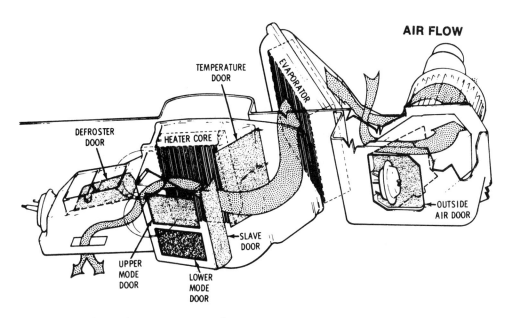

FIGURE 9-3. **Selector lever OFF, temp. lever max. COLD.** *Courtesy of AC Delco / General Motors Corp.*

evaporator bypasses the heater core and is directed to the heater outlet. The discharge air temperature may be regulated by moving the temperature lever to the right. As the temperature lever is moved to the right, a cable connected from the control lever to the temperature door moves the door into the airstream. Thus, by diverting some or all of the air from the evaporator through the heater core, the temperature in the passenger compartment is controlled, giving maximum comfort.

Selector Lever in the Air Conditioning Position. With the selector lever in the AIR CONDITIONING position, the blower speed is controlled by the fan speed switch unless the temperature lever is in the MAXIMUM COLD position, and the vacuum-operated doors are positioned as follows (see Figure 9-4):

1. Outside air: See Temperature Lever.
2. Upper mode: closed to the heat mode; open to the A/C mode.
3. Lower mode: closed to the heat mode; open to the A/C mode.
4. Slave: out of the airstream (actuated by the lower mode door).
5. Defroster: closed to defroster outlets.

Temperature Lever in the Maximum Cold Position. With the temperature lever in the extreme left, MAXIMUM COLD position (see Figure 9-4), the outside door opens to the recirculate air position and the blower motor operates at high speed. The air being discharged from the air-conditioning outlets is approximately 80% air from the inside of the car (recirculated air) and 20% outside air. The outside air door never fully closes to the outside air.

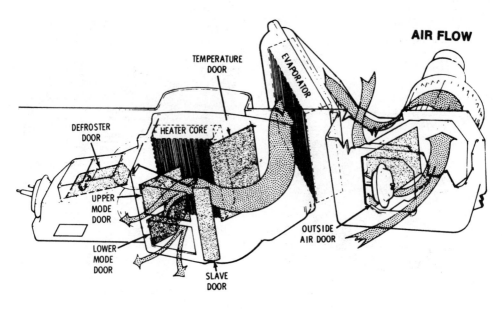

AIR FLOW

TEMPERATURE
DOOR

EVAPORATOR

DEFROSTER
DOOR

HEATER CORE

UPPER
MODE
DOOR

OUTSIDE
AIR DOOR

LOWER
MODE
DOOR

SLAVE
DOOR

FIGURE 9-4.   Selector lever AIR COND, temp. lever max. COLD. *Courtesy of
AC Delco / General Motors Corp.*

The temperature door is positioned so that the conditioned air from the evaporator core bypasses the heater core, allowing the maximum amount of cold air to be discharged from the outlets. By moving the selector lever to the right about ½ in., to the detent position, the speed of the blower motor is controlled by the fan speed switch, and the outside air door returns to the outside air position, completely sealing to recirculate the air. Continuing to move the temperature lever to the right from this position will move the temperature door so that some or all of the air is directed through the heater core, depending on how far the lever is moved, to provide passenger comfort.

Selector Lever in the Vent Position. With the selector lever in the VENT position (see Figure 9-5), the vacuum-operated doors are positioned as follows:

1. Outside air: fully open to the outside air.

2. Upper mode: open to the heat mode; closed to the A/C mode.

3. Lower mode: closed to the heat mode; open to the A/C mode.

4. Slave: out of the airflow stream (actuated by the lower mode door).

5. Defroster: closed to the defroster outlets; fully open to the heater outlet.

Air is being directed out of both the A/C and heater outlets to provide bilevel ventilation.

Temperature Lever in the Centered Position. With the temperature lever positioned near the center of the control panel (see Figure 9-5), the temperature door is positioned so that some of the air from the evaporator is directed through the heater core as shown. This air then mixes with the air that bypasses the heater core.

The airflow through the heater core may be regulated by moving the temperature lever, which regulates the discharge air temperature.

Selector Lever in the Heater Position. With the selector lever in the HEAT position (see Figure 9-6), the vacuum-operated doors are positioned as follows:

1. Outside air: fully open to the outside air.
2. Upper mode: open to the heat mode; closed to the A/C mode.
3. Lower mode: open to the heat mode; closed to the A/C mode.
4. Slave: in the airflow stream (actuated by the lower mode door).
5. Defroster: partially open.

The air is being directed out of the heater outlets, with a small amount being di-rected on the windshield from the defrost outlets.

Temperature Lever in the Maximum Heat Position. With the temperature lever in the MAXIMUM HEAT position (see Figure 9-6), all the air from the evapora-tor is being directed through the heater core for maximum heating. The airflow through the heater core may be regu-lated by moving the temperature lever, which regulates the discharge air tem-perature.

Selector Lever in The De-Fog Posi-tion. With the selector lever in the DE-FOG position (see Figure 9-7), the vac-uum-operated doors are positioned as follows:

1. Outside air: fully open to the outside air.
2. Upper mode: open to the heat mode; closed to the A/C mode.

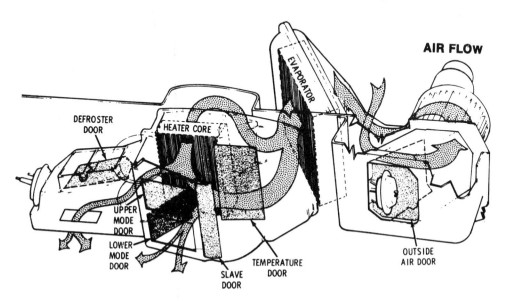

FIGURE 9-5. Selector lever VENT, temp. lever CENTERED. *Courtesy of AC Delco / General Motors Corp.*

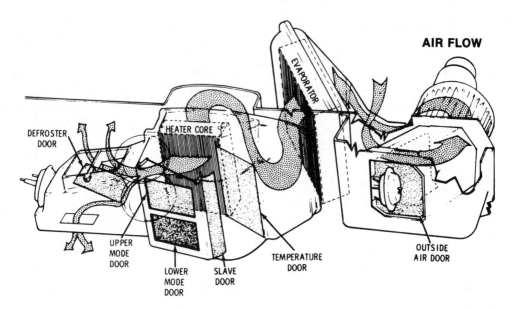

FIGURE 9-6. **Selector lever HEATER, temp. lever max. HOT.** *Courtesy of AC Delco / General Motors Corp.*

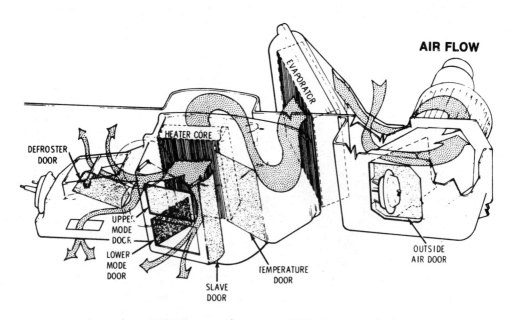

FIGURE 9-7. **Selector lever DEFOG, temp. lever max. HOT.** *Courtesy of AC Delco / General Motors Corp.*

3. Lower mode: closed to the heat mode; open to the A/C mode.

4. Slave: out of the airstream (actuated by the lower mode door).

5. Defroster: partially open.

The air is being directed out of all the outlets (A/C, heater, and defroster) to provide trilevel ventilation.

Selector Lever in the De-Ice Position. With the selector lever in the DE-ICE position (see Figure 9-8), the vacuum-operated doors are positioned as follows:

1. Outside air: fully open to the outside air.

2. Upper mode: open to the heat mode; closed to the A/C mode.

3. Lower mode: open to the heat mode; closed to the A/C mode.

4. Slave: in the air stream.

5. Defroster: fully open.

Most of the air is being directed to the windshield from the defroster outlets, with some air being directed out of the heater outlet.

GM Electrical Circuit and Vacuum System. The following pages describe the electrical and vacuum circuits that are functional for each position of the dash control selector and temperature levers in the typical GM cars.

It should be noted that in most 1971 and later-model GM cars the blower motor is operating when the ignition is in the run position, even if the selector lever is in the off position. Some installations also have a provision that prevents the blower motor from operating until the engine coolant temperature reaches approximately 120°F.

Selector Lever in the Off Position. With the engine running and the selector lever in the OFF position, electrical cur-

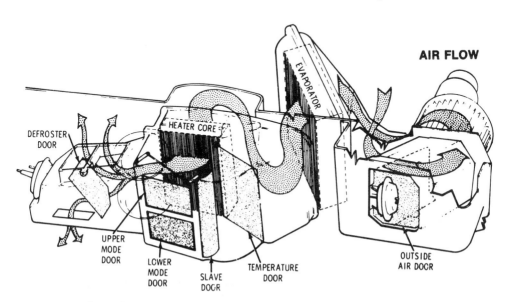

FIGURE 9-8. **Selector lever De-Ice, temp. lever max. HOT.** *Courtesy of AC Delco/General Motors Corp.*

rent is directed from the ignition switch to the heater—A/C fuse in the fuse block. From the fuse block, the current is directed to the coil in the delay relay (see Figure 9-9). The delay relay coil circuit is completed through the closed engine thermo switch. The engine thermo switch closes when the engine coolant temperature reaches approximately 120°F.

The electrical current is then directed through the closed points to the resistor block, through all the resistors, through the normally closed HI blower relay points to the blower motor. The blower motor is operating at low speed.

With the selector lever in the OFF position (see Figure 9-10), vacuum is being directed to the selector valve; however, all ports on the valve are either vented or sealed.

Temperature Lever in the Maximum Cold Position. The vacuum from the reserve tank is directed to the number 3 port of the temperature lever valve. With the temperature lever in the MAXIMUM COLD position, vacuum is directed from port 3 to ports 1 and 2 (see Figure 9-10).

From port 2 of the temperature lever valve, vacuum is directed to port 4 of the selector lever valve, where it is sealed. From port 1 of the temperature lever valve, vacuum is directed to the hot water valve, to close the valve and shut

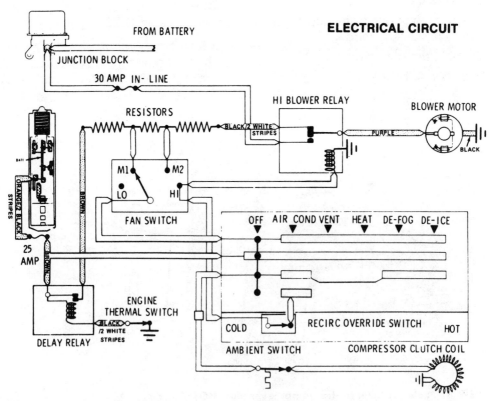

FIGURE 9-9. Selector lever OFF. *Courtesy of AC Delco/General Motors Corp.*

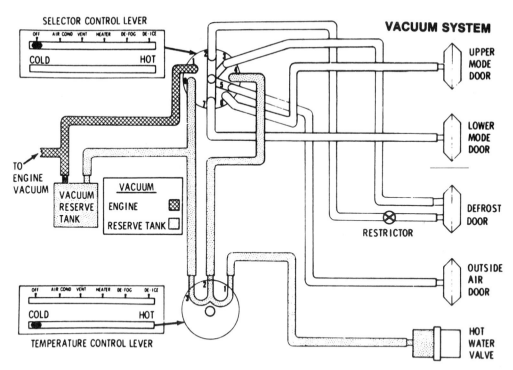

FIGURE 9-10.   Selector lever OFF, temp. lever max. COLD. *Courtesy of AC Delco / General Motors Corp.*

off any circulation of engine coolant through the heater core.

Selector Lever in the Air Conditioning Position. Electrical current is directed from the ignition switch to the fuse block, and then to the control. With the selector lever in the AIR CONDITIONING position (see Figure 9-11), current is directed through the contacts in the switch to the other three contact bars.

From the upper contact bar, current is directed to the fan switch. With the fan switch in the M2 position, as shown, current is then directed through the resistor on the right, through the normally closed HI blower relay points to the blower motor. The blower motor is oper-

ating at medium two (M2) speed. Medium one (M1) is obtained by adding another resistor in series with the blower motor.

With the fan speed switch in the LO position, the feed circuit from the control is opened at the switch. Low speed is then obtained in the same manner as when the selector lever is in the OFF position.

When the fan speed switch is in the HI position, electrical current from the control is being directed through the fan speed switch to the HI blower relay, energizing the coil. With the coil energized, the lower set of points in the relay closes, and the current from the junction block is directed through a 30-ampere in-line fuse to the lower points in the HI blower relay. Current is then directed through the relay points to operate the blower motor at high speed.

From the control panel, electrical current is directed to the ambient switch. If the ambient temperature is above approximately 32°F, the ambient switch is closed and the compressor clutch is energized.

Also from the control, current is directed to the recirc override switch. With the temperature lever in the MAXIMUM COLD position, the recirc override switch is closed and the current is directed to the HI terminal of the fan speed switch. The current is then directed to the HI blower

relay coil, and the blower motor will operate at high speed.

When the selector lever is in the AIR CONDITIONING position (see Figure 9-12), vacuum is directed from the vacuum reserve tank to port 9, where it is directed to ports 7 and 6 on the selector lever valve. The engine vacuum is sealed at port 1 on the valve. All diaphragms, except the defroster door diaphragm, have vacuum applied.

Temperature Lever in The Maximum Cold Position. When the temperature control is in the MAXIMUM COLD position (see Figure 9-12), vacuum from the

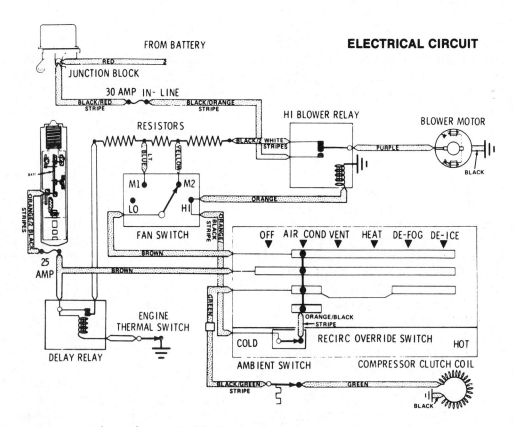

FIGURE 9-11. Selector lever **AIR COND.** *Courtesy of AC Delco/General Motors Corp.*

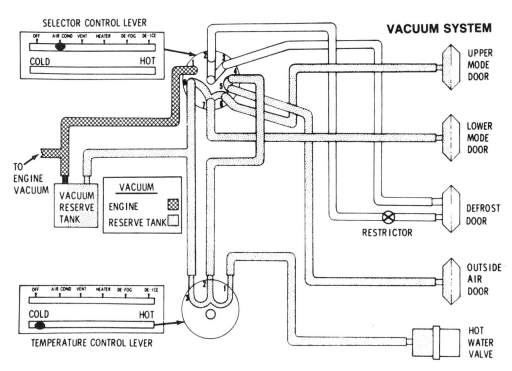

FIGURE 9-12.   Selector lever AIR COND, temp. lever max. COLD. *Courtesy of AC Delco / General Motors Corp.*

reserve tank is directed from port 3 to ports 2 and 1 of the temperature lever valve. Port 2 directs vacuum to port 4 of the selector lever valve. With the selector lever in the AIR CONDITIONING position, port 4 of the selector lever is connected to port 5, which moves the outside air door to the recirculate position. Vacuum is being applied to the hot water valve from port 1, which shuts off the engine coolant circulation through the heater core.

As the temperature lever is moved to the right approximately ½ in. (to detent), port 2 is vented, which vents port 4 at the selector lever valve. This allows the outside air door to move to the outside air position, closing to recirculate the air.

When the temperature lever is moved approximately ¾ in. from the MAXIMUM COLD position, toward the MAXIMUM HOT position, port 1 is also vented, which allows the hot water valve to open.

Selector Lever in the Vent Position. Electrical current is directed from the ignition switch to the fuse block and then to the control. When the selector lever is in the VENT position (see Figure 9-13), the only electrical connection through the control is to the fan switch to operate the blower motor. The electrical current is directed through the control to the fan switch.

LO blower speed is obtained the same as low speed with the selector lever

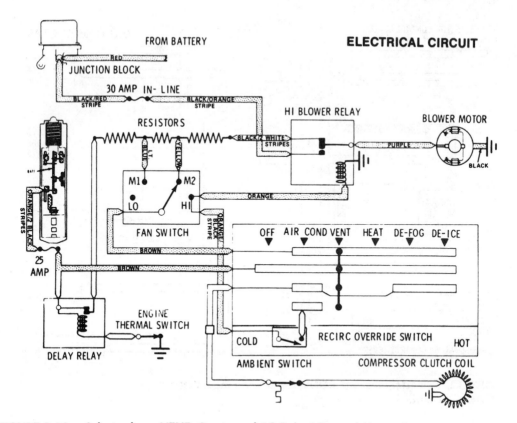

FIGURE 9-13.   Selector lever VENT. *Courtesy of AC Delco / General Motors Corp.*

in the OFF position. The engine coolant temperature must be at least 120°F to close the engine thermo switch and energize the delay relay coil.

M1 and M2 blower speeds are obtained in the manner shown with the selector lever in the AIR CONDITIONING position.

HI blower speed is obtained by energizing the HI blower relay, which directs electrical current from the junction block, through the set of closed points, and directly to the blower motor.

With the selector lever set to the VENT position (see Figure 9-14), vacuum is directed from the vacuum reserve tank

to port 9 of the selector lever. Port 9 is connected to port 7, which directs vacuum to the lower-mode door diaphragm and opens the door to the A/C mode. All other ports are either vented or sealed.

Temperature Lever in The Maximum Cold Position. With the temperature lever in the MAXIMUM COLD position (see Figure 9-14), vacuum is directed from the vacuum reserve tank to port 3 on the temperature lever valve. Vacuum is also directed to port 1 to close the hot water valve. With the hot water valve closed, the engine coolant cannot circulate through the heater core.

Selector Lever in the Heat Position. In this position (see Figure 9-15), electrical current is directed from the ignition switch to the fuse block and then to the control. With the selector lever in the HEAT position, the only electrical connection through the control is to the fan switch to operate the blower motor.

The electrical current is directed through the control to the fan switch.

LO blower speed is obtained the same as low speed with the selector lever in the off position. The engine coolant temperature must be at least 120°F to close the engine thermo switch in order to energize the delay relay coil.

M1 and M2 blower speeds are obtained in the same manner as shown with

the selector lever in the air-conditioning position.

HI blower speed is obtained by energizing the HI blower relay, which directs electrical current from the junction block, through the closed set of points, and directly to the blower motor.

With the selector lever in the HEAT position (see Figure 9-16), the engine vacuum is directed to port 1 of the selector valve. Vacuum is then directed from port 1 to port 2, which applies the vacuum to the lower port of the defroster door diaphragm to partially open the defroster door. All other ports are vented or sealed.

Temperature Lever in the Maximum Hot Position. With the temperature lever

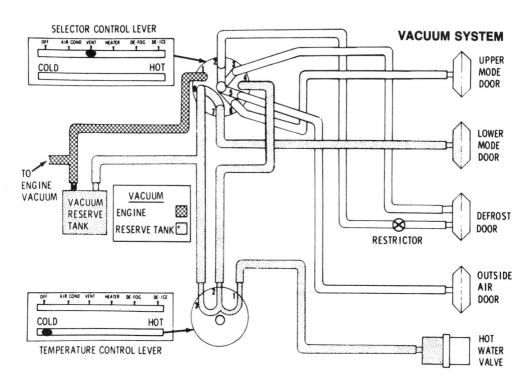

FIGURE 9-14. Selector lever VENT, temp. lever max. COLD. *Courtesy of AC Delco / General Motors Corp.*

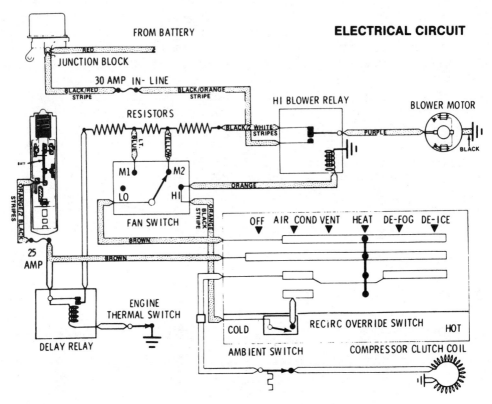

FIGURE 9-15. **Selector lever HEAT.** *Courtesy of AC Delco/General Motors Corp.*

in the MAXIMUM HOT position (see Figure 9-16), vacuum from the reserve tank is directed to port 3 of the temperature lever valve where it is sealed. Ports 1 and 2 are vented, allowing the hot water valve to open and admit the engine coolant to the heater core for heating.

Selector Lever in the De-Fog Position. The electrical current is directed from the ignition switch to the fuse block, then to the control. With the selector lever in the DE-FOG position (see Figure 9-17), electrical connection is made through the control to the fan switch to operate the blower motor and the air-conditioning

compressor clutch coil circuit. The blower motor will operate at the speed selected by the fan switch.

The compressor will operate in the DE-FOG position if the ambient temperature is above approximately 32°F to close the ambient switch.

With the selector lever placed in the DE-FOG position (see Figure 9-18), the engine vacuum is directed to port 1 of the selector valve. Vacuum is then directed from port 1 to port 2, which applies vacuum to the lower port of the defroster door diaphragm to partially open the defrost door.

Vacuum from the vacuum reserve tank is directed to port 9 of the selector

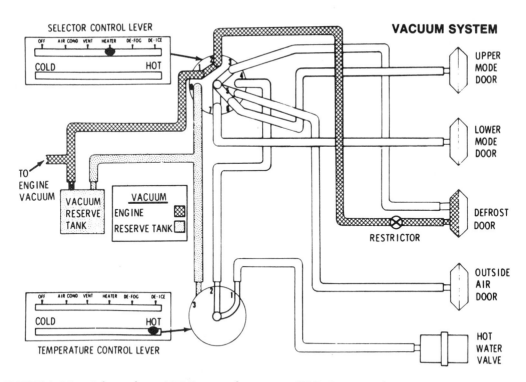

FIGURE 9-16. Selector lever HEAT, temp. lever max. HOT. *Courtesy of AC Delco / General Motors Corp.*

lever valve. Port 9 is connected to port 7, which directs vacuum to the lower-mode door diaphragm and opens the door to the A/C mode.

Temperature Lever in the Maximum Hot Position. With the temperature lever in the MAXIMUM HOT position (see Figure 9-18), vacuum from the reserve tank is directed to port 3 of the temperature lever valve, where it is sealed. Ports 1 and 2 are vented, allowing the hot water valve to open and the engine coolant to circulate through the heater core for heating.

Selector Lever in the De-Ice Position. With the selector lever in the DE-ICE position (see Figure 9-19), electrical connection is made through the control to the fan switch to operate the fan motor and to the air-conditioning compressor clutch coil circuit. The blower motor will operate at the speed selected on the fan switch. The compressor will operate in the DE-ICE position if the ambient air temperature is above approximately 32°F to close the ambient switch.

With the selector lever in the DE-ICE position (see Figure 9-20), the vacuum from the engine is directed to the number 1 port on the selector valve. The vacuum is then directed from port 1 to port 2 which applies the vacuum to the lower port of the defroster door diaphragm to partially open the defrost door.

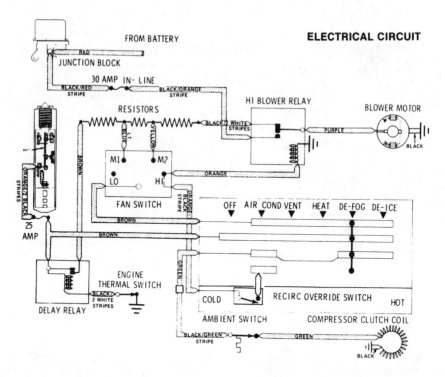

FIGURE 9-17. Selector lever DEFOG. *Courtesy of AC Delco / General Motors Corp.*

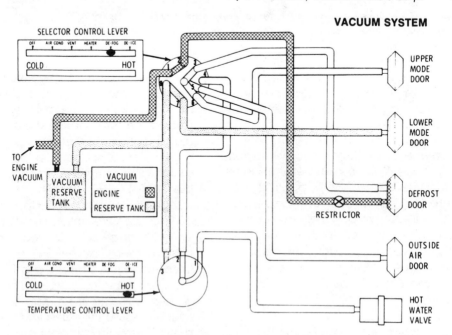

FIGURE 9-18.   Selector lever DEFOG, temp. lever max. HOT. *Courtesy of AC Delco / General Motors Corp.*

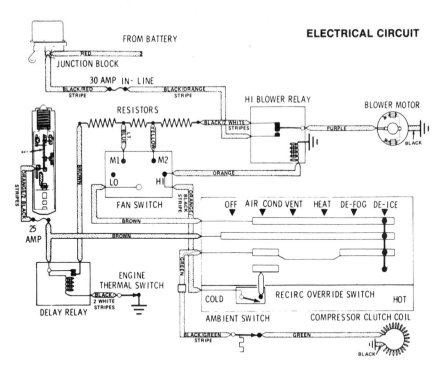

FIGURE 9-19. **Selector lever De-Ice.** *Courtesy of AC Delco / General Motors Corp.*

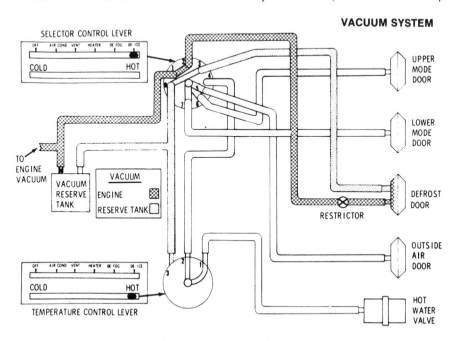

FIGURE 9-20. **Selector lever De-Ice, temp. lever max. HOT.** *Courtesy of AC Delco / General Motors Corp.*

The vacuum from the reserve tank is directed to port 9, where it is directed to port 3. From port 3, the vacuum is directed to the other port of the defroster door diaphragm to completely open the door. All the other ports are vented.

Temperature Lever in the Maximum Hot Position. With the temperature lever in the MAXIMUM HOT position (see Figure 9-20), vacuum from the reserve tank is directed to port 3 of the temperature lever valve and is sealed there. Ports 1 and 2 are vented, allowing the hot water valve to open and the engine coolant to circulate through the heater core for heating the passenger compartment.

REVIEW QUESTIONS

1. What are the most common complaints about automotive air-conditioning units?

2. What is needed when abnormal air temperatures and refrigerant pressures are found?

3. What component is at fault when an inadequate supply of cool air to the passenger compartment is experienced?

4. Should compressors that make a resonance noise always be changed?

5. List two ways that a condenser can malfunction.

6. How can a restriction in a refrigerant line be found?

7. Under normal conditions, will the condenser inlet pipe be warmer than the outlet pipe?

8. What does a cool or cold outlet of a receiver–dehydrater indicate?

9. What is the lowest ambient temperature at which the sight glass is useful in checking the refrigerant charge in a system?

10. What is the recommended maximum amount of refrigerant to be added to a system?

11. When feeling the high and low pressure at the compressor on a fully charged system, what should the temperatures be?

12. What will be the result of an overcharged system at low-speed operation?

13. What is usually indicated by a low suction and low discharge pressure in a system using a TXV?

14. What will always be accompanied by a defective POA or STV?

15. What is the first step in diagnosing troubles in an air-conditioning unit?

The procedure for removing, replacing, and servicing the refrigeration system components of an air-conditioning system are very similar for all models. We will attempt to make the following procedures as general as possible so that the ideas presented will be applicable to all types of systems.

PREPARING THE SYSTEM FOR COMPONENT PARTS REPLACEMENT

Air conditioning, when the basic principles are understood, is fairly simple to perform service procedures on. However, certain practices, procedures, and precautions should be followed when performing these service procedures. Failure to do so may result in injury to the service technician and/or the equipment itself. Because of this, it is recommended that the information presented in the previous chapters be studied and thoroughly understood before attempting to perform these operations.

Cleanliness of the refrigeration system cannot be overemphasized. Use plugs or caps to close the system to prevent dirt and moisture from entering the system when it is open to the atmosphere. Keep the work area clean and follow the component parts manufacturer recommendations when replacing them.

When removing or replacing any component that requires opening the refrigeration system to the atmosphere, perform the following operations in the sequence given:

1. Purge the system by discharging the refrigerant to the atmosphere through an exhaust removal system.

2. Remove and either repair or replace the defective component.

10

Procedures for System Component Repair and Replacement

147

3. Evacuate, recharge the system with refrigerant, and check the operation of the system.

CAUTION: Always wear protective goggles when working on refrigeration systems. Also, precautions should be taken to prevent being overcome by carbon monoxide fumes from the car's exhaust.

CONTAMINANTS IN THE SYSTEM

When contaminants are found in the system, they must be removed before it is placed back into operation. When the compressor has had a mechanical failure, the following operations should be performed:

1. Purge the system of refrigerant.
2. Remove the defective compressor.
3. Remove the receiver–dehydrator, VIR screen, desiccant bag or the accumulator dehydrator, and expansion tube and discard these components.
4. Flush the condenser to remove any foreign material that may have gotten into it from the defective compressor.
5. Disconnect either the refrigerant line at the evaporator core inlet or the line connected to the expansion device. Inspect the expansion tube or the inlet screen of the expansion device for any foreign material. Should the expansion tube or the inlet screen be plugged, replace it. Reconnect the refrigerant line to the evaporator core or the expansion device.
6. Install the replacement compressor.
7. Add the required amount of oil to the system as recommended by the system manufacturer.

8. Evacuate, recharge, and check the operation of the system.

PROCEDURE FOLLOWING A COLLISION

The air-conditioning unit on a car that has been in an accident should be checked as soon as possible and any needed repairs made to prevent contaminants from entering the refrigeration system. The longer the amount of time the unit is exposed to the atmosphere, the more contaminants will enter the system. Since every case will be different, it is almost impossible to establish any hard and fast procedures to follow in every instance. The exercise of good judgment will determine what steps are required in each specific case.

The procedure presented next is a guide for inspecting a car, equipped with an air-conditioning unit, that has been in an accident:

1. Remove the compressor drive belt. It may need to be cut off.
2. Inspect the condenser, expansion device, compressor, mounting brackets, refrigerant lines, and all the controls to determine the amount and extent of the damage.
   (a) Because of the type of construction of the condenser, no welding, brazing, or soldering should be attempted on it. If the refrigerant tubing has been damaged in any way, the condenser should be replaced. The fins may be straightened with a fin comb when they are not too badly damaged.
   (b) The VIR or the accumulator should be inspected for any

type of damage, such as cracks and deep dents. When there is no apparent damage, the VIR should be disassembled, cleaned, with a suitable solvent, thoroughly dried, and a new bag of desiccant installed. The accumulator dehydrator should be replaced if the refrigerant system has been open to the atmosphere.

(c) Inspect the compressor for any visible external damage, especially the clutch plate and hub assembly. Measure the clutch air gap because the shaft may have been damaged or struck in the accident.

(d) Check the operation of the clutch pulley and the clutch drive. Also, check them for damage.

(e) Inspect the evaporator for damage, even if it must be removed and replaced.

(f) Inspect the connecting refrigerant lines for damage. Repair or replace as required.

(g) Inspect all the controls and the connecting wiring for damage. Repair or replace any damaged components.

3. Connect the charging station to the unit.

4. Purge the refrigerant from the system.

5. Remove the compressor from the mounts and remove the oil test plug.

6. Pour the oil from the compressor into a clean glass container and inspect it for any contaminants, such as dirt or metal particles. If contaminants are found, the compressor must be rebuilt or replaced as required. In

addition, the expansion tube, VIR desiccant bag, receiver–dehydrator, or the accumulator dehydrator should be replaced as applicable. The remainder of the system should be flushed with a recommended solution.

7. When the oil is found to be clean, replace it with the proper type as recommended by the unit manufacturer.

NOTE: When the system components have been replaced or flushed, charge the compressor with the full recommended charge of oil. When there have been no repairs to the system, do not replace the oil with more than was drained from the compressor.

8. Charge the compressor with refrigerant up to the container pressure, and leak test the seal before installing it back on the car.

9. Reinstall the compressor. Evacuate the system according to the evacuation procedure discussed previously.

10. Charge the system up to the same pressure as the refrigerant container.

11. Leak test the complete system. Pay particular attention to the areas where any damage has occurred.

12. Complete the charging procedure and check the operation of the system.

ORIFICE TUBE REMOVAL

The orifice tube is an expansion device used by at least two original equipment manufacturers at this time: General Motors and Ford Motor Company. It is placed in the refrigerant liquid line at the inlet of the evaporator.

Ford Motor Company Orifice Tube. The procedures used to remove and replace the Ford Motor Company orifice tube are listed next:

1. Purge the refrigerant from the system. Disconnect the jumper tube from the liquid refrigerant line. Pour a small amount of oil into the liquid line to lubricate the orifice tube and the O-rings. Install the orifice removal tool, using the Motorcraft No. YT-1008 tool or its equivalent (see Figure 10-1).

2. While holding the T-handle of the orifice tube remover tool, turn the nut down against the liquid line until the orifice tube is removed from the pipe. Should the orifice tube be broken inside the pipe, it must be removed. Use the extractor tool Motorcraft No. YT-1009 or its equivalent.

3. To remove the broken orifice tube, insert the screw end of the extractor tool into the liquid line and screw the threaded end of the extractor tool into the brass tube in the center

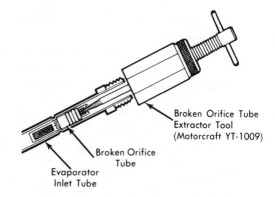

FIGURE 10-2.   Removing broken orifice tube. *Courtesy of Ford Motor Co.*

of the orifice tube. Turn the nut down against the liquid line and remove the broken orifice tube (see Figure 10-2).

4. Dip the new orifice tube into clean refrigerant oil to lubricate the O-rings. Place the orifice tube onto the removal tool. Install the orifice tube into the inlet pipe until the orifice tube seats at the dimple (see Figure 10-3).

5. Remove the extractor tool and reverse the procedure for removing the

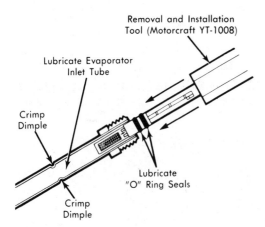

FIGURE 10-1.   Removing orifice tube. *Courtesy of Ford Motor Co.*

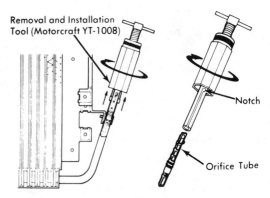

FIGURE 10-3.   Installing orifice tube. *Courtesy of Ford Motor Co.*

orifice tube to complete the installation process.

6. Recharge the system with refrigerant and check the operation of the unit.

General Motors Orifice Tube. The procedures used to remove and replace the GM orifice tube are listed next:

1. Discharge the refrigerant from the system. Disconnect the liquid refrigerant line at the evaporator inlet. To remove the orifice tube, it is recommended that the remover tool J26549-C or its equivalent be used.

2. If difficulty is encountered during the removal of the orifice tube, the residue must be removed from inside the tube. The use of a heat gun will facilitate the removal of this residue. A hair dryer will also work fairly well. Apply the heat to the inlet pipe about ¼ in. from the dimples. Do not overheat the pipe.

   NOTE: If there is a pressure switch near the orifice tube location, remove the switch before heating the inlet pipe to avoid possible damage to the switch.

3. While applying the heat, insert the orifice tube removal tool J26549-C or its equivalent by using a turning motion to loosen the orifice tube and pull it from the inlet pipe.

4. Clean out the inside of the pipe where the orifice tube belongs and add 1 oz of clean refrigeration oil to the system. Dip the new O-rings in clean refrigeration oil and insert them into the inlet pipe. Next, install the orifice tube with the shorter screen into the inlet pipe first.

5. Reverse the removal procedure described above. Recharge the system with refrigerant and check the unit operation.

FALSE COMPRESSOR SEIZURE

There may be some slipping or broken compressor drive belts and/or scored clutch surfaces may occur on initial start-up of an air-conditioning unit that has been in storage for a long period of time, or even if the compressor has not been operated for a long period of time. Normally, this condition would indicate that the compressor would need overhauling. However, this is not always the proper procedure.

During long periods of nonoperation of the unit, temperature changes cause the refrigerant in the compressor to expand and contract. During this period of expansion and contraction, the lubricating oil that coats the polished surfaces migrates from these areas. Without the lubricating oil on these surfaces, they tend to become dry and "ring" together, and appear to be seized.

Use the following check-out procedure before overhauling the compressor to determine if it is actually seized. With a clutch hub holding tool, rock the compressor in the direction opposite to the normal rotation. If the compressor becomes loose during this procedure, rotate it at least three more turns in the counterclockwise direction. Start the engine and operate the compressor for at least 1 min before stopping operation.

This procedure will not loosen a compressor that is actually frozen, but it should be attempted before overhauling a compressor that has been idle for one month or more.

GM 6-CYLINDER AXIAL COMPRESSOR SERVICING PROCEDURES

During service operations on these compressors, remove only the components that are necessary to perform a preliminary diagnosis. Then remove only those components that are in need of service. For information relative to the parts nomenclature and location, refer to Figures 10-4 and 10-5.

Four service operations may be performed on the GM 6-cylinder compressor:

1. Replace the complete compressor assembly.
2. Replace the clutch plate and hub, pulley and clutch coil, and housing assemblies.

3. Replace the shaft seal.
4. Overhaul the compressor using a new cylinder and shaft assembly. (It is usually more economical to replace compressors that are rebuilt at a rebuilding plant than field rebuilt, and we will omit complete rebuilding in this text.)

Some of the compressor service operations can be performed without disturbing the internal components or completely removing the unit from the car engine, if there is enough room. Some of these operations are replacement of the clutch plate and hub assembly, the pulley and bearing assembly, the pulley bearing, and the clutch coil and housing assembly after the clutch and pulley

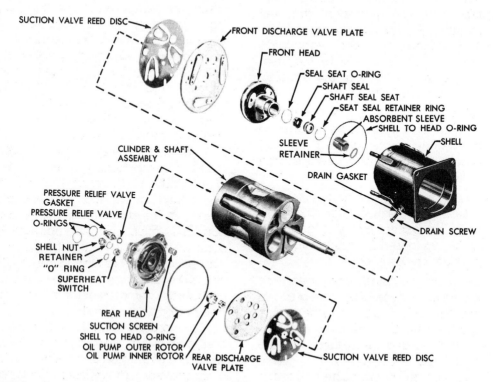

FIGURE 10-4. Compressor disassembly. *Courtesy of AC Delco/General Motors Corp.*

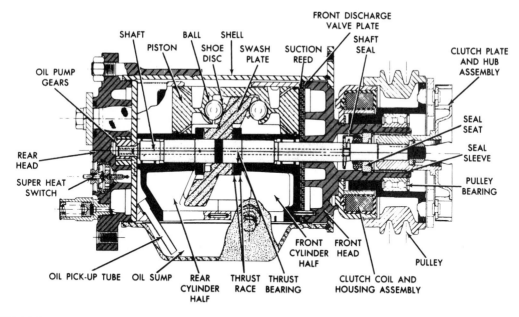

FIGURE 10-5.   GM 6-cylinder compressor—internal. *Courtesy of AC Delco/ General Motors Corp.*

parts have been removed. In some cases it has been found that the compressor shaft seal can be replaced on the car by removing the clutch plate and hub assembly to gain access to the seal parts, however, the refrigerant must be purged from the system before seal replacement is attempted.

The disassembly and reassembly of the compressor components must be performed on a clean work bench. The work area, tools, and parts must be kept clean at all times. Use parts trays for all parts being removed, as well as the replacement parts.

Even though some of the service operations can be performed without removal of the compressor from the car, the operations described here are based on bench overhaul procedures with the compressor removed from the car.

NOTE: When the compressor is removed from the engine for servicing, the amount of oil left in the compressor should be drained and measured. This oil should be replaced with clean, dry oil after the servicing operations are complete.

When a compressor mechanical failure has occurred or when foreign material is found inside the system, the following operations must be completed:

1. Remove the compressor from the car for a complete overhaul or replacement with a new compressor.

2. Replace the receiver-dehydrator, the accumulator-dehydrator, or replace the desiccant bag and clean the VIR assemblies.

3. Clean the lines and the condenser with an approved solvent.

4. Clean or replace the expansion valve inlet screen.

5. Add the necessary amount of oil to the system to compensate for that which was lost during the compressor servicing procedures from the condenser, receiver–dehydrator, or the accumulator.

Replacement of the Compressor. The following procedures are recommended for compressor replacement:

1. Purge the refrigerant from the system.

2. Remove the clutch wire connector from the compressor.

3. Remove the bolts and plates that are holding the suction and discharge lines to the rear head. Disconnect both lines from the compressor and plug the openings in both the lines and the compressor ports in the rear head.

4. Remove the mounting bolts and remove the compressor from the engine compartment.

   NOTE: Do not rotate the compressor shaft. Keep the compressor positioned so that the oil sump is downward.

5. If a new or rebuilt compressor is being installed, the pulley assembly, clutch coil housing, the clutch plate, and drive hub assembly must be taken from the old compressor and installed on the replacement.

6. If the original compressor is being reinstalled, replace the oil with the proper amount.

7. Remove and discard the old O-rings from the compressor. Install the new O-rings.

8. Install the compressor and adjust the compressor drive belt tension to the

recommended service manual specifications.

9. Lubricate the O-rings with clean refrigeration oil and attach the suction and discharge lines and the retaining plate to the compressor. Torque the bolts to 20 to 25 ft-lb.

Replacement of the Clutch Drive Plate and Hub, Pulley, Clutch Coil, and Housing Assemblies. The procedures used in the replacement of these components are listed next (see Figures 10-6 and 10-7):

1. Purge the refrigerant from the system.

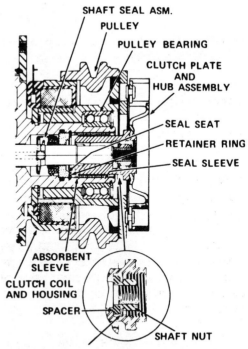

FIGURE 10-6. **Cross section of clutch assembly.** *Courtesy of AC Delco / General Motors Corp.*

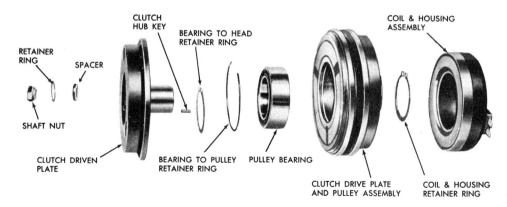

FIGURE 10-7. Magnetic clutch and pulley assembly. *Courtesy of AC Delco/General Motors Corp.*

2. Remove the compressor from the engine compartment.

3. Firmly clamp the compressor holding fixture in a vise; attach the compressor to the fixture.

4. Hold the hub of the clutch drive plate with the spanner wrench. Using a thin-walled 9/16-in. socket and a 3/8-in. drive ratchet, remove the shaft nut (see Figure 10-8).

5. Remove the hub and drive plate retainer ring, using No. 21 Truarc pliers. Remove the spacer (see Figure 10-9).

6. Screw the threaded hub puller onto the hub. Hold the body of the hub puller with a wrench, tighten the center screw of the hub puller, and lift off the clutch drive plate and the drive key (see Figure 10-10).

FIGURE 10-8. Removing shaft nut. *Courtesy of AC Delco/General Motors Corp.*

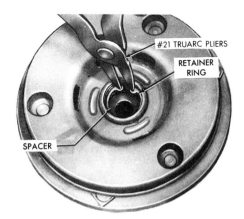

FIGURE 10-9. Removing retainer ring and spacer. *Courtesy of AC Delco/General Motors Corp.*

FIGURE 10-10. Removing hub plate and drive assembly. *Courtesy of AC Delco / General Motors Corp.*

7. Using the No. 26 Truarc pliers, remove the bearing to head retainer ring (see Figure 10-11).

8. Place the puller pilot on the hub of the front head and remove the pulley assembly by using the pulley puller (see Figure 10-12).

   CAUTION: Do not jar the compressor shaft to prevent damage to the internal parts. Always use the proper tools.

9. Remove the bearing to pulley retaining ring with a small screw driver (see Figure 10-13).

10. Drive out the bearing, using the proper bearing remover and handle (see Figure 10-14).

FIGURE 10-11. Removing pulley retaining ring. *Courtesy of AC Delco/General Motors Corp.*

FIGURE 10-12. Removing pulley and drive plate with puller tool. *Courtesy of AC Delco/ General Motors Corp.*

FIGURE 10-13. Removing pulley bearing retaining ring. *Courtesy of AC Delco / General Motors Corp.*

11. Mark the position of the clutch coil and housing assembly in relationship to their position on the compressor housing. Remove the coil housing

retainer ring using the No. 26 Truarc pliers. Lift off the coil and housing assembly (see Figure 10-15).

12. Examine the coil for loose or bent terminals and for cracked insulation. Check the current draw; it should be 3.2 A at 12 V. The resistance should be 3.85 ohms at room temperature.

13. Reassemble the coil and housing assembly by reversing the procedure for disassembly. Be sure that the coil and housing marks line up with those on the compressor.

14. Drive the new bearing into the pulley assembly with the proper bearing installer and handle. The bearing installer will ride on the outer race of the bearing (see Figure 10-16).

15. Lock the bearing into place with the bearing to pulley retainer ring.

16. Press or tap the pulley assembly onto the hub of the front head using the installer handle. The bearing installer

FIGURE 10-14. Removing bearing from pulley assembly. *Courtesy of AC Delco / General Motors Corp.*

FIGURE 10-15. Removing or installing coil housing retaining ring. *Courtesy of AC Delco / General Motors Corp.*

FIGURE 10-16.   Installing bearing to pulley assembly. *Courtesy of AC Delco / General Motors Corp.*

FIGURE 10-17.   Installing pulley and bearing assembly. *Courtesy of AC Delco / General Motors Corp.*

will ride on the inner race of the bearing (see Figure 10-17).

17. Check the pulley for binding or roughness. The pulley should rotate freely.

18. Lock the pulley assembly into position with the bearing to head retainer ring (flat side of the retainer ring should face downward) using the No. 26 Truarc pliers.

19. Install the square drive key into the keyway of the clutch driver hub.

20. Clean the frictional surface of the clutch plate and pulley assembly.

21. Place the clutch plate and hub assembly on the compressor shaft, aligning the shaft keyway with the key in the hub (see Figure 10-18).

NOTE: The drive key is made with a small curvature to help hold it in

place during the assembly procedure.

CAUTION: To prevent compressor damage, do not drive or pound on the hub or shaft. This could misposi-

CLUTCH DRIVE PLATE

WOODRUFF KEY

KEY WAY
IN SHAFT

FIGURE 10-18.   Positioning clutch drive plate on shaft. *Courtesy of AC Delco / General Motors Corp.*

tion the axial plate on the shaft, resulting in compressor damage.

22. Place the spacer on the hub. Thread the clutch plate and hub assembly onto the end of the compressor shaft (see Figure 10-19).

23. Hold the hex head bolt and turn the tool body several turns to press the hub partially onto the shaft. Remove the clutch plate and hub assembly installer and spacer.

24. Check alignment of the drive key with the keyway in the shaft. When the alignment is correct, replace the installer tool and continue to press the hub onto the shaft until there is approximately a 3/32-in. air gap between the frictional surfaces of the pulley and clutch plate.

25. Remove the installer tool and spacer.

26. Install the hub spacer.

27. Using the snap ring pliers, Truarc No. 21, install the hub retainer ring with

FIGURE 10-19. Installing clutch plate and hub assembly. *Courtesy of AC Delco / General Motors Corp.*

the flat side of the ring facing the spacer (see Figure 10-11).

28. Install a new shaft locknut with the small diameter boss of the nut against the hub spacer, using a thin-wall 9/16-in. socket. Hold the clutch hub with the spanner wrench and tighten the nut to 15 ft-lb torque, using a 0 to 25 ft-lb torque wrench. The air gap between the frictional surfaces of the pulley and clutch plate should now be approximately 0.022 to 0.057 in.

Leak Testing the Compressor Shaft Seal. A compressor shaft seal should not be replaced because of an oil line on the hood liner and the fender. The seal is designed to leak a small amount of oil for lubrication purposes. Change the shaft seal only when a leak is detected by the following procedures:

1. Be certain that there is a sufficient amount of refrigerant in the system. This can be done by feeling the suction line at the compressor or the orifice tube at the evaporator. Cooling of either of these lines indicates that there is sufficient refrigerant in the system for leak testing.

2. Turn off the engine.

3. Blow off the compressor clutch area with compressed air. Blow out the clutch vent holes to completely remove all refrigerant and oil accumulations.

4. Allow the car to sit idle for 5 min without operating the compressor.

5. Rotate the compressor drive plate by hand until one of the vent holes is at the lower side of the drive plate. Using a leak detector, sense through the vent hole at the lower side of the clutch plate only.

Some compressor shaft seal leaks may be due to the mispositioning of the axial plate on the compressor shaft. A mispositioned axial plate may be due to improper procedures used during the pulley and drive plate removal, pounding, collisions, or from dropping the compressor.

If the axial plate is mispositioned, the carbon face of the seal assembly may not touch the seal seat, resulting in damage to the rear thrust races and bearing.

If there appears to be an insufficient amount of air gap between the drive and driven plates, dislocation of the shaft should be suspected. If the carbon seal is not touching the seal seat, it will not be possible to completely evacuate the system.

To determine if the axial plate is properly positioned on the shaft, remove the clutch drive plate and measure the distance between the front head extension and the flat shoulder on the shaft (see Figure 10-20). To measure this distance, use a wire gauge. The clearance should be between 0.026 and 0.075 in. If the shaft is pushed back in the axial plate as indicated by a measurement of greater than 0.075 in., disassemble the compressor and replace the shaft and cylinder assembly or replace the complete compressor.

Replacing the Shaft Seal. The following procedures are recommended when replacing a shaft seal in a 6-cylinder GM compressor, with the exception noted (see Figures 10-21 and 10-22):

NOTE: Contrary to the art work shown here, it is not necessary to disassemble the pulley assembly when replacing the GM compressor shaft seal.

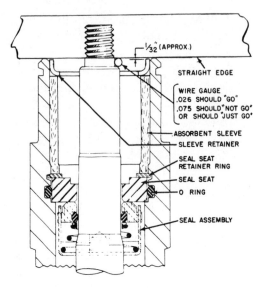

FIGURE 10-20. Checking shaft position. *Courtesy of AC Delco/General Motors Corp.*

1. Remove the compressor from the car.
2. Remove the clutch drive plate and hub assembly.
3. If the compresor is equipped with an absorbent sleeve in the neck, pry out the sleeve retainer and remove the sleeve.
4. Thoroughly clean the area inside the compressor neck surrounding the

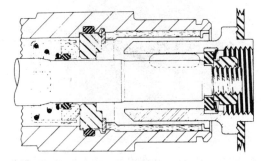

FIGURE 10-21. Shaft seal assembly. *Courtesy of AC Delco/General Motors Corp.*

FIGURE 10-22. Kit required in shaft seal replacement. *Courtesy of AC Delco/General Motors Corp.*

shaft and the exposed portion of the seal seat to remove any foreign material that may be there. This step is absolutely necessary to prevent such material from getting into the compressor. Remove the seal seat retaining ring, using the No. 23 Truarc pliers (see Figure 10-23).

5. Remove the seal seat using the seal seat remover and installer tool. Grasp the flange of the shaft seal with the tool and pull straight up and out (see Figure 10-24).

NOTE: Cast-iron seal seats may be found in GM vehicles up to and including the 1968 models. Later models and all replacement seal kits have the ceramic seal seat shown in Figure 10-22.

6. To use the seal remover and installer tool, insert the tool into the neck of the front head, press downward, and turn the tool clockwise to engage the tabs of the shaft seal; then gently but firmly pull straight out (see Figure 10-25).

7. Remove the seal seat O-ring from inside the neck of the front head using the O-ring remover (see Figure 10-26).

FIGURE 10-23. Removing and installing shaft seal seat retainer. *Courtesy of AC Delco/General Motors Corp.*

FIGURE 10-24. Removing ceramic seal seat. *Courtesy of AC Delco/General Motors Corp.*

FIGURE 10-25. Removing and installing shaft seal. *Courtesy of AC Delco / General Motors Corp.*

8. Check the inside of the compressor neck again and check the compressor shaft for damage. Be sure that these areas are perfectly clean and free of any burrs before installing the new parts.

9. Coat the compressor shaft and the O-ring with clean refrigeration oil. Place the O-ring installer in the bottom of the front head assembly (see Figure 10-27). Slide the O-ring into place, using the handle of the O-ring removing tool, until it bottoms out. Remove the O-ring installer tool with the removal tongs (see Figure 10-28).

10. Coat the new O-ring and seal face with clean refrigeration oil. Carefully mount the seal assembly on the shaft seal installer tool by engaging the tabs of the seal with the tongs of the tool.

FIGURE 10-26. Removing seal seat O-ring.
Courtesy of AC Delco / General Motors Corp.

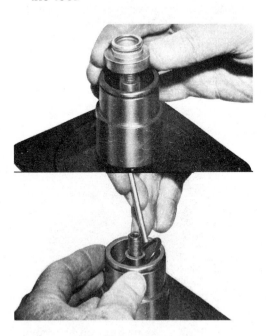

FIGURE 10-27. Installing seal seat O-ring.
Courtesy of AC Delco / General Motors Corp.

FIGURE 10-28. Removing O-ring installer.
Courtesy of AC Delco / General Motors Corp.

11. Place the seal protector over the end of the compressor shaft and carefully slide the new seal assembly onto the shaft. Gently twist the tool clockwise while pushing the seal assembly down the shaft until the seal assembly engages the flats on the shaft and is seated in place. Disengage the tool by pressing downward and twisting the tool counterclockwise (see Figure 10-25).

12. Coat the seal face of the new ceramic seal seat with clean 525 viscosity refrigeration oil. Mount the seal seat on the seal seat installer and remover and install it in the neck of the compressor, take care not to dislodge the seal seat and O-ring. Be sure that the seal makes a good seal with the O-ring (see Figure 10-29).

13. Install the new seal seat retainer ring with the flat side against the seal seat using the Truarc No. 23 pliers. Remove the seal protector from the end of the shaft. Push the snap ring into the groove with the snap ring installing sleeve (see Figure 10-30).

14. Install the new absorbent sleeve by rolling the material into the cylinder,

FIGURE 10-29. Installing ceramic seal seat.
Courtesy of AC Delco / General Motors Corp.

FIGURE 10-30. Installing seal seat snap ring. *Courtesy of AC Delco / General Motors Corp.*

overlapping the ends, and slipping it into the compressor neck with the overlap at the top of the compressor. Using a small screwdriver or similar instrument, carefully spread the sleeve so that in its final position the ends butt together at the top vertical centerline. Install the new sleeve retainer so that its flange face will be against the front end of the sleeve. Using the snap ring installing sleeve, press and tap with a mallet, setting the retainer and sleeve into place, until the outer edge of the sleeve retainer is recessed approximately $1/32$ in. from the face of the compressor neck.

15. Install the clutch drive plate and hub assembly.

16. Evacuate and recharge the system with refrigerant.

17. Check the system for proper operation.

Compressor External Leak Test. The following procedures are recommended when externally leak testing a compressor:

1. Install the leak test fixture on the rear head of the compressor (see Figure 10-31).

2. Attach the center hose of the gauge manifold set to a refrigerant cylinder standing in the upright position. Open the cyclinder valve.

3. Connect the gauge set to the air-conditioning unit as described earlier.

   NOTE: The compressor suction port has a large internal opening; the discharge port has a small opening into the compressor.

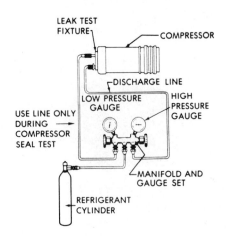

FIGURE 10-31. Leak testing shaft seal and seal O-ring (6 cyl.). *Courtesy of AC Delco/ General Motors Corp.*

4. Open all the valves to allow refrigerant vapor to enter the compressor.

5. Check for leaks at the pressure relief valve, compressor shell to cylinder joint, compressor front seal, oil charge port, and the compressor shaft seal. After the test is complete, shut off the gauge manifold hand valves.

6. If an external leak is detected, perform the necessary corrective measures and recheck for leaks to make certain that the leak has been repaired.

7. Loosen the manifold gauge hose connections at the system service valves and allow the vapor to escape from the compressor.

8. Disconnect both gauge adapters from the test fixture.

9. Rotate the complete compressor assembly (not the crankshaft or drive plate hub) slowly for several revolutions to distribute the oil to all the cylinder and piston areas.

10. Install a shaft nut on the compressor crankshaft if the drive plate and clutch assembly are not already installed.

11. Using a boxed end wrench or a socket and handle, rotate the compressor by hand several turns to ensure piston assembly to cylinder wall lubrication.

Superheat Switch Repair and Replacement. The following steps are recommended when performing these operations:

1. Completely purge the refrigerant from the air-conditioning system.

2. After purging the system, remove the superheat switch retainer ring, using the snap ring pliers.

3. Remove the superheat switch from the rear head by pulling at the terminal housing groove with a pair of pliers.

4. Remove the O-ring from the switch cavity in the rear head.

5. Recheck the superheat switch for closed contacts. Replace as necessary (see Figure 10-32).

6. Check the superheat switch cavity and O-ring groove in the rear head for dirt or any foreign material. Be sure that the area is clean before installing the new O-ring. Lubricate the O-ring with No. 525 viscosity refrigeration oil before installing it in the groove. Install the new O-ring in the groove in the rear head of the compressor. The new O-ring is part of the new switch kit.

7. Lubricate the superheat switch housing with No. 525 viscosity refrigeration oil and insert the switch carefully into the cavity until the switch bottoms out. The seal seat remover and installer may be used to install the switch.

8. Install the superheat switch retainer ring, using the snap ring pliers, with the high point of the curved sides next to the switch housing. Be sure that the retainer ring is properly seated in the snap ring groove.

9. Check for electrical continuity between the switch housing and the rear head. Also, check for continuity between the switch terminal and the switch housing to be sure that the contacts are open.

10. Evacuate and recharge the system with refrigerant according to the following special charging procedure.

Special Charging Procedure. Use the following steps during the special charging procedure:

NOTE: To prevent the possibility of blowing out the new thermal fuse during the evacuation process, when charging, or when making an analysis of the system, disconnect the connector plug from the thermal fuse and install a jumper wire between the center terminal B and the clutch lead terminal C of the connector plug.

1. Leak test the entire refrigeration part of the system using the normal procedures.

2. After the system is charged and operating properly, remove the jumper wire from the connector and reconnect the thermal fuse.

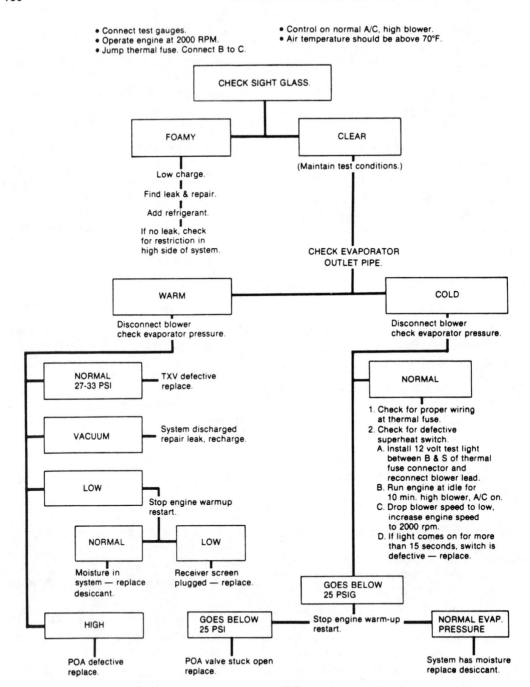

FIGURE 10-32. Diagnosis of GM compressor equipped with thermal limiter and superheat switch. *Courtesy of AC Delco / General Motors Corp.*

GM 4-CYLINDER RADIAL COMPRESSOR SERVICING PROCEDURES

During the servicing of any compressor, it is essential that steps be taken to prevent dirt or any foreign material from entering the compressor or any of the refrigeration system. Clean tools, a clean workbench, and a clean work area are very important for proper service to the unit. The compressor connection areas and the exterior of the compressor should be cleaned off prior to attempting any "on vehicle" repairs or before removing the compressor for workbench repairs.

The parts must be kept clean at all times and any parts that are to be reused should be cleaned with an approved cleaning solvent and dried with compressed air. When cloth shop towels are to be used, they must be of the nonlint-producing type (see Figure 10-33).

When a compressor is removed from the car for repairs, the oil remaining in the compressor should be drained through the compressor suction and discharge ports and measured. This amount of new oil must be replaced in the compressor before it is placed back into service on the car. For the proper oil charge, refer to Table 10-1.

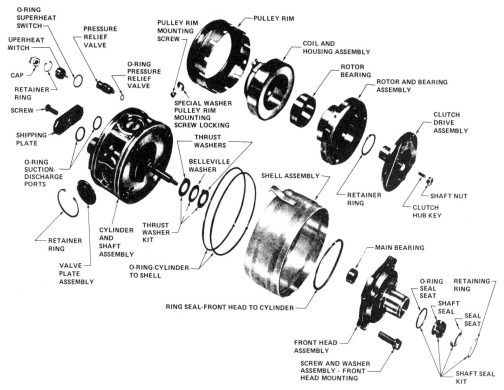

FIGURE 10-33. GM 4-cylinder compressor—internal. *Courtesy of AC Delco / General Motors Corp.*

TABLE 10-1.   Oil Change Procedure

Unit	Add Oil
Condenser	1 fluid ounce
Evaporator	3 fluid ounces
EE-VIR	1 fluid ounce

Compressor Condition	Amount of Oil Drained from Compressor	Amount of Oil to Install
Replacing compressor with a new compressor	More than: 4 fl oz in A-6 ½ fl oz in R-4	*Drain new compressor, refill with new oil (same amount as drained from old compressor except see Note)
	Less than: 4 fl oz in A-6 ½ fl oz in R-4	**Drain new compressor. Install new oil in new compressor: 6 fl oz in A-6 3 fl oz in R-4
Replacing compressor with a service rebuilt compressor	More than: 4 fl oz in A-6 ½ fl oz in R-4	*Same as above plus an additional fluid ounce (more oil is retained in a drained compressor than one that has been rebuilt)
	Less than: 4 fl oz in A-6 ½ fl oz in R-4	**Same as above plus an additional fluid ounce
Unable to run compressor being replaced, prior to removal from car	More than: 1½ fl oz in A-6 ½ fl oz in R-4 and system appears to have lost little or no oil	*Same as above
	Less than: 1½ fl oz in A-6 ½ fl oz in R-4 or system appears to have lost major amount of oil	**Same as above
Contaminated oil drained from system	Any amount	Drain as much oil as possible from system. Flush system with refrigerant-11. Replace drier desiccant and install new 525 viscosity oil in new compressor: A-6 comp: 10½ fl oz R-4 comp: 6 fl oz

Courtesy of AC Delco/General Motors Corp.

Note: For A-6 only: If the amount of oil drained is 8 fl oz or more, an overcharge of oil should be suspected. Flush the system with refrigerant-11, replace drier desiccant, and install new compressor with total compressor oil charge, 10½ fl oz.

If for any reason the R-4 compressor air-conditioning hose assembly is removed from the compressor, great care must be taken to ensure that the hose plate is fully seated onto the compressor during the reinstallation. Should the plate be cocked and the retainer bolt driven, metal flanges in the O-ring cavities could damage the seal surface of the compressor. New O-rings should be used on reassembly.

Minor Repair Procedures. Some service operations can be performed without disturbing the internal components of the compressor or without completely removing the compressor from the vehicle or discharging the system. Some of these operations are replacement of the clutch drive plate and hub assembly, clutch rotor and bearing assembly, and clutch coil and pulley rim where "on vehicle" room is available.

Major Compressor Repair Procedures. When doing major compressor repairs, the refrigerant must be purged from the system. Anytime the system is opened to the atmosphere, it must be evacuated when the repairs are completed. Some of the major repairs that can be performed while the compressor is still on the car are shaft seal replacement, replacement of the pressure relief valve and the rear head switches. Refer to the section *Evacuation and Charging Procedures.*

The service operations given in the following procedures are for on the bench compressor overhaul. When performing those operations that are possible to perform while the compressor is on the vehicle, the procedures are essentially the same. The procedures are basically in the order of normal sequence of removal for the accessible components.

NOTE: When it is necessary to adjust the compressor belt tension, *do not* pry on the compressor shell. Lift at the square hole on the compressor mounting bracket.

It is recommended that the compressor holding fixture be used for all work-

bench procedures to keep the compressor assembly off the workbench and to help prevent any possible dirt or other contaminants entering the system or getting on the parts (see Figures 10-34 and 10-35). The compressor holding fixture may be clamped into a vise with the shaft end of the compressor in any desired position to facilitate servicing.

Servicing the Compressor Clutch Plate and Hub Assembly. When removing these components, the following steps are recommended:

1. Attach the compressor to the holding fixture (see Figure 10-34) and clamp the fixture in a vise.

2. Prevent the clutch hub from turning by using the clutch hub holding tool. Remove and discard the shaft nut using a thin-wall socket (see Figure 10-35).

3. Thread the clutch plate and hub assembly remover onto the hub. Hold the body of the tool with a wrench and turn the center screw into the

FIGURE 10-34. Installing holding fixture.
Courtesy of AC Delco/General Motors Corp.

FIGURE 10-35. Removing shaft lock nut.
Courtesy of AC Delco / General Motors Corp.

remover tool and remove the clutch plate and hub assembly (see Figure 10-36).

4. Remove the shaft key.

The following steps are recommended when installing the compressor clutch plate and hub assembly:

1. Install the shaft key into the hub groove. Allow the key to project approximately $\frac{3}{16}$ in. out of the keyway (see Figure 10-37). The shaft key is slightly curved to provide a small interference fit in the key groove, to permit key projection without falling out.

2. Be certain that the frictional surface of the clutch plate and clutch rotor are clean before installing the clutch plate and hub assembly onto the compressor.

3. Align the shaft key with the keyway and assemble the clutch plate and hub assembly on the compressor shaft.

CAUTION: To prevent internal compressor damage, do not drive or pound on the clutch hub or the shaft.

4. Place the spacer bearing on the hub and insert the end of the clutch plate and hub assembly installer through the spacer bearing and

FIGURE 10-36. Removing clutch plate and hub assembly. *Courtesy of AC Delco / General Motors Corp.*

FIGURE 10-37. Installing shaft key. *Courtesy of AC Delco / General Motors Corp.*

FIGURE 10-38. Installing clutch plate and hub assembly. *Courtesy of AC Delco / General Motors Corp.*

thread the tool onto the end of the compressor shaft (see Figure 10-38).

5. Hold the hex head bolt with a wrench and turn the tool body to press the hub onto the shaft until there is an air gap of 0.020 to 0.040 in. between the frictional surfaces of the clutch plate and the clutch rotor. Remove the installer tool and the spacer bearing.

6. Install a new shaft nut with the small-diameter boss of the nut against the crankshaft shoulder using a special thin-wall socket tool. Hold the clutch plate and hub assembly with the clutch hub holding tool and tighten to 8 to 12 ft-lb of torque.

Compressor Shaft Seal Assembly Replacement. When removing a compressor shaft seal, the following steps are recommended:

1. Purge the refrigerant from the system. Remove the clutch plate and hub assembly as described under *Compressor Clutch Plate and Hub Assembly.*

2. Remove the shaft seal retainer ring, using No. 23 snap ring pliers.

3. Thoroughly clean the inside of the compressor neck area surrounding the shaft seal, seal seat, and shaft to remove all lint and foreign material before attempting to remove the seal seat.

4. Insert the seal seat remover and installer tool over the shaft and into the recessed area of the seal seat, and tighten the tool, turning the adjustment clockwise to tighten and securely engage the knurled tangs of the tool with the seal seat. Remove the seal seat with a twisting and pulling motion. Discard the old seat (see Figure 10-39).

FIGURE 10-39. Removing seal seat. *Courtesy of AC Delco / General Motors Corp.*

5. Insert the seal remover and installer tool over the shaft and engage the shaft seal by pressing downward on the tool to overcome the shaft seal spring pressure. Turn the tool clockwise to engage the seal assembly tabs with the tangs of the tool (see Figure 10-40).

6. Remove the seal seat O-ring from the compressor neck using the removal tool. Discard the old O-ring.

When installing a new compressor shaft seal, the following steps are recommended:

1. Inspect the inside of the compressor neck and shaft area for any lint or dirt or any other type of foreign material. Be certain that these areas are perfectly clean before installing the new seal parts. Be sure that the seal remover and installer, seal protector, and O-ring installer are clean internally and externally. The seal seat O-ring, shaft seal, and seal seat should be dipped in clean 525 viscosity refrigeration oil and not handled any more than is absolutely necessary, particularly the mating surfaces. Any dirt or lint on the sealing surfaces could cause a leak or seal damage.

2. Place the O-ring installer in the bottom of the front head assembly (see Figure 10-41). Slide the O-ring into place, using the handle of the removing tool, until it is bottomed out (see Figure 10-42). Remove the O-ring installer tool and the tangs (see Figure 10-43).

3. Dip the new O-ring and seal face in 525 viscosity refrigeration oil and carefully engage the shaft seal assembly with the locking tangs of the seal remover and installer.

FIGURE 10-40. Removing shaft seal. *Courtesy of AC Delco/General Motors Corp.*

FIGURE 10-41. Installing O-ring installer. *Courtesy of AC Delco/General Motors Corp.*

FIGURE 10-42.   Installing seal seat O-ring.
Courtesy of AC Delco / General Motors Corp.

FIGURE 10-43.   Removing O-ring installer.
Courtesy of AC Delco / General Motors Corp.

4. Install the shaft seal protector over the end of the compressor shaft, and slide the shaft seal onto the compressor shaft. Slowly turn the tool in a clockwise direction while applying a light pressure until the seal engages the flats of the compressor shaft and can be seated into place. Rotate the seal remover counterclockwise to disengage it from the seal tabs and remove the tool.

5. Attach the ceramic seal seat to the seal remover and installer, and dip the ceramic seat into clean 525 viscosity refrigeration oil to coat the seal face and outer surface. Carefully install the seat over the compressor shaft and seal protector. Push the seat into place with a rotary motion. Remove the shaft seal protector.

6. Install the new seal seat retainer ring with No. 23 snap ring pliers and snap ring installing sleeve.

7. Leak test the compressor as described under *Compressor Leak Testing* and correct any leaks that are found.

8. Reinstall the clutch plate and hub assembly as described under *Compressor Clutch Plate and Hub Assembly.*

NOTE: For the clutch using an inertia ring, refer to the appropriate instructions.

Servicing the Clutch Rotor and Bearing Assembly. When removing the rotor and bearing assembly, the following steps are recommended:

1. Remove the clutch plate and hub assembly as described under *Compressor Clutch Plate and Hub Assembly.*

2. Remove the rotor and bearing assembly retaining ring using No. 24 snap ring pliers (see Figure 10-44). Mark the location of the clutch coil terminals. If the clutch rotor and/or bearing only are being replaced, bend the lock washers away from the pulley rim mounting screws and remove the six mounting screws and special lock washers before proceeding with step 3. Discard the special lock washers.

3. Install the rotor and bearing puller guide over the end of the compressor shaft and seat on the front head of the compressor (see Figure 10-45).

4. Install the rotor and bearing puller down into the rotor until the puller arms engage the recessed edge of the rotor hub. Hold the puller and arms in place and tighten the puller screw against the puller guide to

FIGURE 10-45.   Installing rotor and bearing puller guide. *Courtesy of AC Delco/General Motors Corp.*

FIGURE 10-44.   Removing bearing retaining ring. *Courtesy of AC Delco/General Motors Corp.*

remove the clutch rotor and assembly parts (see Figure 10-46). If the pulley rim mounting screws and washers were removed, only the clutch rotor and bearing assembly will be removed for replacement.

The clutch coil and housing assembly are pressed onto the front head of the compressor with an interference fit and cannot be removed unless the pulley rim mounting screws are left securely in place. The pulley rim pulls the coil and housing assembly off with the total clutch rotor and pulley rim assembly (see Figure 10-47).

Replacing the Clutch Rotor Bearing. Use the following steps when removing and replacing the clutch rotor bearing:

1. Perform the *Removal of Rotor Bearing Assembly* instructions and re-

FIGURE 10-46. Installing rotor and bearing puller. *Courtesy of AC Delco/General Motors Corp.*

FIGURE 10-48. Removing clutch rotor bearing. *Courtesy of AC Delco/General Motors Corp.*

move the pulley rim mounting screws as described in step 2.

2. Place the rotor and bearing assembly on blocks and drive the bearing out of the rotor hub with the rotor

bearing remover and rotor assembly installer (see Figure 10-48). It will not be necessary to remove the staking at the rear of the rotor hub to remove the bearing (see Figure 10-49). However, the staking must be removed before the new bearing can be installed.

Use the following steps when installing a rotor bearing:

FIGURE 10-47. Clutch coil and housing assembly. *Courtesy of AC Delco/General Motors Corp.*

FIGURE 10-49. Bearings stake locations. *Courtesy of AC Delco/General Motors Corp.*

1. Place the rotor and bearing assembly face down on a clean, flat, and firm surface (see Figure 10-50).

2. Align the new bearing squarely with the hub bore, and using the pulley and bearing installer with a universal handle, drive the bearing fully into the hub. The tool will apply force to the outer race of the bearing.

3. Stake the bearing into place with a 45° angle punch, but do not stake too deeply (0.045 to 0.055 in.) and possibly distort the outer race of the bearing (see Figure 7-49). Use new stake locations 120° apart. Do not use old stake locations.

Rotor and Bearing Assembly Installation. The following steps are recommended when performing this procedure:

1. The recommended method is to press the rotor and bearing assembly onto the front head of the compressor

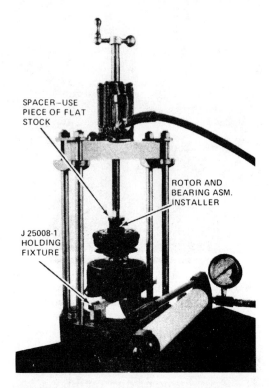

FIGURE 10-51. **Installing rotor and bearing assembly.** *Courtesy of AC Delco/General Motors Corp.*

FIGURE 10-50. **Installing clutch rotor bearing.** *Courtesy of AC Delco/General Motors Corp.*

using the rotor and bearing installer tool (see Figure 10-51). The installer tool will apply force to the inner race of the bearing when installing the assembly onto the front head. The alternate method is to reassemble the rotor and bearing assembly to the front head of the compressor using the rotor bearing remover and rotor assembly installer. With the installer assembled with the universal handle (see Figure 10-52), force will be applied to the inner race of the bearing and face of the rotor when installing the assembly on the front head of the compressor.

FIGURE 10-52. Alternate installation of 4-cylinder rotor and bearing assembly. *Courtesy of AC Delco/General Motors Corp.*

2. Install the rotor and bearing retainer ring using No. 24 snap ring pliers.

3. Assemble and fully seat the pulley rim to the clutch rotor and bearing assembly, using Loctite 601 or equivalent on the screw threads and using new lock washers (see Figure 10-51). Do not torque the mounting screws to the final limits until the pulley rim is checked to be rotating in line.

4. Tighten the pulley rim mounting screws to a 100 in.-lb torque and lock the screw heads in place as shown in Figure 10-51.

5. Install the clutch plate and hub assembly as described under *Compressor Clutch Plate and Hub Assembly.*

Replacing the Clutch Coil and Pulley Rim. The following steps are recom-

mended when removing these components:

1. Perform the *Compressor Clutch Rotor and Bearing Assembly Replacement* procedures, but do not loosen or remove the pulley rim mounting screws until the clutch rotor, coil, and pulley rim assembly have been removed from the front head in step 2.

2. Remove the pulley rim mounting screws and slide the pulley rim off the rotor and hub assembly. The pulley rim and clutch coil are replaceable at this point.

The following steps are recommended when installing the clutch coil and pulley rim:

1. Assemble the clutch coil, pulley rim, and clutch rotor and bearing assembly, using Loctite 601 or equivalent on the screw threads (see Figure 10-47). Use new lock washers, but do not lock the screw heads in place.

2. Place the assembly on the neck of the front head and seat it into place using the rotor bearing remover and rotor assembly installer (see Figure 10-51). Before fully seating the assembly onto the front head, be sure that the clutch coil terminals are in the proper location in relation to the compressor and that the three protrusions on the rear of the clutch coil align with the locator holes in the front head.

3. Install the rotor and bearing assembly retaining ring and reassemble the clutch plate and hub assembly.

4. Rotate the pulley rim and the rotor to make certain that the pulley rim is rotating in line. Make any adjustments needed. Tighten the pulley rim mounting screws to 100 in.-lb torque and lock the screw heads in place.

Replacement Compressor Oil Charge.
The amount of oil that should be added
to a replacement compressor is dependent on the amount of oil that was in
the original compressor. The amount of
oil being replaced will also depend on
what other components, if any, were also
being replaced in the system. (For the
exact amount of oil to be installed in a
replacement compressor, refer to Table
10-1.)

System Performance Evaluation. When
the system performance, efficiency, and
proper oil charge are in doubt and the
system must be evaluated accurately, it
should be purged and flushed with R-11,
properly evacuated, and recharged with
the proper amount of R-12, and the exact
amount of clean refrigeration oil added
to the compressor as recommended by
the manufacturer before performing any
other checks on the system.

**Clutch Coil and Pulley Rim Replace-
ment on Compressors Having an Inertia
Ring.** Some of the General Motors R-4
compressors will have an inertia ring
either bolted on or welded on the pulley
rim. Special service procedures are required on compressors equipped with
the inertia ring. The procedure used will
be determined by whether the inertia
ring is welded on or bolted on.

Bolted-on Inertia Ring. Use the following steps when replacing an inertia ring:

1. Loosen the compressor drive belt
   and rotate the compressor pulley as
   required to locate one screw and lock
   washer mounted through a mounting
   hole of the pulley rim, rather than a
   mounting notch screw location (see
   Figure 10-53). *Do not* remove the

MOUNTING HOLES (3)

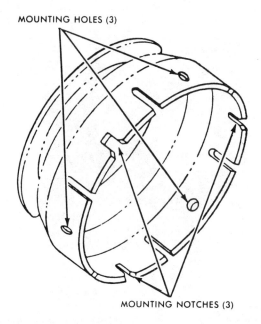

MOUNTING NOTCHES (3)

**FIGURE 10-53. R-4 pulley rim mounting
location detail.** *Courtesy of AC Delco / General
Motors Corp.*

drive belt unless it is absolutely necessary.

NOTE: For identification purposes,
washers locked over the edge of the
pulley rim at the mounting hole locations will not usually dimple down in
the center like the indentation of the
lockover at a mounting notch screw
location.

2. Remove the three mounting screws
   and lock washers at the pulley rim
   mounting hole locations. The pulley
   rim mounting holes are located 120°
   apart radially around the rim or
   every other mounting screw location.
   Do not remove the screws in the
   mounting notches.

3. Temporarily make a trial fit of the
   inertia ring to the pulley rim. If any

portion of the sheer edge of the pulley rim prevents installation of the inertia ring, the raised edge may be filed off to remove the excess material to aid in the installation. *Do not* use unnecessary force or cock the inertia ring when making the installation of the inertia ring over the pulley rim that would cause distortion or stress.

4. Assemble the inertia ring onto the pulley rim; be careful to align the inertia ring mounting holes in the pulley rim. If the inertia ring must be rotated on the pulley rim for centering the mounting holes and cannot be moved by hand, use a drift punch or blunt tool and a hammer to carefully tap the inertia ring at a clearance notch to move the ring into position (see Figure 10-53).

5. Install a special lock washer onto each $\frac{1}{4}$-28 $\times$ $\frac{17}{32}$ in. mounting screw.

6. Apply a coat of Loctite 601 or its equivalent to the screw threads of each mounting screw and to the threads of the mounting holes in the clutch rotor. Wet the threads thoroughly to ensure complete thread coverage.

7. Install the screws into the mounting holes and tighten finger tight. Torque each screw to 100 in.-lb of torque.

8. Lock the screws into place by flattening the special washer against the two sides of the hex head of the screw using vise grip pliers and one portion of the lock washer bent down over the edge of the inertia ring slot (see Figure 10-53). *Do not* move the screw heads from the torqued position. Locking of the screws must be similar to the production forming of the lock

washer in order to effectively retain the screw.

9. Retighten the compressor drive belt to the proper tension.

10. Check the operation of the system.

Welded Inertia Ring and Pulley Rim Assembly. A new pulley rim and inertia ring kit is required.

1. Loosen the compressor mounting bracket and remove the drive belt.

2. Remove the clutch hub and drive plate assembly as described in *R-4 Compressor Clutch Plate and Hub Assembly* removal procedure.

3. To remove the clutch hub as an assembly, perform steps 1 through 4 of the *R-4 Compressor Clutch Rotor and/or Bearing Removal Procedures,* but do not loosen or remove the pulley rim mounting screws, so as to remove the clutch rotor and bearing, clutch coil, pulley rim, and inertia ring as a total assembly.

4. Remove all six pulley rim mounting screws and lock washers from the assembly and discard them.

5. Separate the pulley rim and the inertia ring from the rotor and bearing assembly.

6. Inspect the drive surfaces of the rotor and drive plate to make certain that they are still in good condition. Replace as required.

7. Assemble a new pulley rim over the clutch coil and mount the pulley rim onto the rotor and bearing assembly, using the short notch mounting location (see Figure 7-53). The mounting notches are located 120° apart radially around the pulley rim.

8. Assemble the three new lock washers on the three new ¼-28 × ⁵⁄₁₆ in. mounting screws and apply Loctite 601 or its equivalent to the entire threaded surface of the mounting screws and in the mounting hole in the rotor. Assemble the three screws into the short notch mounting hole locations and tighten finger tight.

9. Align the pulley rim so that the bottom of the rim notches touch the mounting screws at all three locations. Also, center the drilled holes in the pulley rim with the remaining mounting hole threads in the rotor. When the rim is positioned properly, tighten the three mounting screws to 110 in.-lb of torque.

10. Temporarily make a trial fit of the inertia ring to the pulley rim. If any portion of the sheared edge of the pulley rim prevents the installation of the inertia ring, the raised edge may be filed off to remove the excess metal to aid in the installation. *Do not use unnecessary force or cock the ring in the assembly operation of the inertia ring over the pulley rim that would cause undue stress or distortion.*

11. Assemble the inertia ring onto the pulley rim being careful to align the inertia ring mounting holes with the mounting holes in the pulley rim. If the inertia ring cannot be moved by hand and must be rotated for centering the mounting holes, use a drift punch or blunt tool and a hammer to carefully tap at one of the large clearance notches in the inertia ring to rotate the inertia ring into position (see Figure 10-54).

12. Install the special lock washers onto the ¼ × ¹⁷⁄₃₂ in. mounting screws and apply Loctite 601 or its equivalent to the total screw threads and the

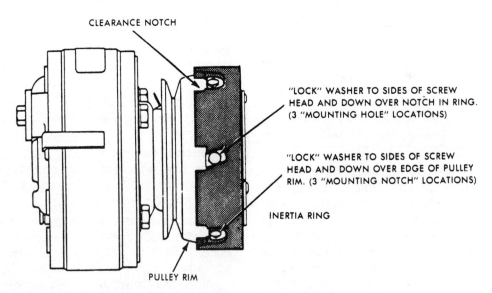

CLEARANCE NOTCH

"LOCK" WASHER TO SIDES OF SCREW HEAD AND DOWN OVER NOTCH IN RING. (3 "MOUNTING HOLE" LOCATIONS)

"LOCK" WASHER TO SIDES OF SCREW HEAD AND DOWN OVER EDGE OF PULLEY RIM. (3 "MOUNTING NOTCH" LOCATIONS)

INERTIA RING

PULLEY RIM

FIGURE 10-54. R-4 pulley rim and inertia ring mounting detail. *Courtesy of AC Delco/General Motors Corp.*

threads of the mounting holes in the rotor.

13. Install the screws and washers into the mounting holes in the rotor and tighten them finger tight. When all the screws are in place, torque each screw to 100 in.-lb of torque.

14. Using the rotor and bearing assembly installer No. 15-9349, install the pulley, clutch coil, rotor, and bearing assembly onto the front head of the compressor. Be sure to locate the clutch coil terminals in the proper position.

15. Spin the rotor and bearing assembly to determine if the pulley runs in line. If not, the mounting screws must be loosened and the parts aligned.

16. When all the mounting screws are torqued in place, lock all the mounting screws in position by flattening the special washers against two opposite sides of the hex head screw, using vise grip pliers. Form a portion of the lock washer down over the pulley rim or over the inertia ring slot to secure the screws in place. *Do not* move the screws from the torqued position (see Figure 10-54).

17. Install the clutch hub and drive plate assembly as described in *R-4 Compressor Clutch Plate and Hub Assembly Replacement Procedures.*

18. Install the compressor drive belt and adjust it to the proper tension.

19. Check the air-conditioning unit for proper operation.

Compressor Leak Test. When making an external leak test on the compressor, use the following steps:

1. Install the leak test fixture on the rear head of the compressor (see Figure 10-55).

2. Attach the center hose of the manifold gauge set to a refrigerant cylinder standing in the upright position. Open the cylinder valve.

3. Connect the HIGH and LOW pressure hoses from the gauge set to the corresponding fittings on the test fixture, using the gauge adapters.

NOTE: The suction port of the compressor has a large internal opening. The discharge port has a small internal opening to the compressor.

4. Open the LOW side gauge manifold hand valve, the HIGH side manifold hand valve, and the refrigerant cylinder hand valve and allow refrigerant vapor into the compressor.

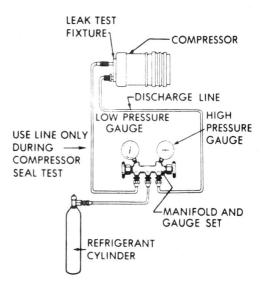

FIGURE 10-55. Leak testing shaft seal and seal O-ring (4 cyl.). *Courtesy of AC Delco/ General Motors Corp.*

5. Using a leak detector, check for leaks at the pressure relief valve, compressor shell to cylinder, compressor front head seal, rear head seal, the oil charge port, and the compressor shaft seal. After leak testing, shut off the hand valves on the manifold gauge set and the refrigerant cylinder.

6. If an external leak is located, perform the necessary steps to correct the leak and retest to be sure that the leak has been repaired.

7. Loosen the gauge hoses at the test fixture and allow the refrigerant vapor to escape from the hoses and the compressor.

8. Disconnect both gauge adapters from the test fixture.

9. Rotate the complete compressor assembly, not the compressor crankshaft or the drive plate hub, slowly for several turns to distribute the oil to all the cylinder and piston areas.

10. Install a shaft nut on the compressor crankshaft if the drive plate and clutch assembly are not installed.

11. Using a box-end wrench or a socket and handle, rotate the compressor crankshaft, or the clutch drive plate on the crankshaft, several turns to ensure piston assembly to cylinder wall lubrication.

When performing the internal compressor leak test, use the following steps:

1. Connect the manifold gauge set HIGH side line to the test fixture HIGH side connector (see Figure 10-56).

2. Attach an adapter to the suction or LOW pressure port of the test fixture plate to open the Schrader-type valve.

NOTE: The oil will drain out of the compresor suction port adapter if the compressor is positioned with the port downward.

3. Attach the compressor to the holding fixture. Clamp the fixture in a vise so that the compressor can be turned manually with a wrench.

4. Using a wrench, rotate the compressor crankshaft, or the drive plate hub, 10 complete revolutions at a speed of approximately one revolution per second.

NOTE: Turning the compressor at less than one revolution per second can result in a lower pump-up pressure and disqualify a good pumping compressor.

5. Observe the reading on the HIGH side pressure gauge at the completion of the tenth revolution of the compressor. The pressure reading for a good pumping compressor should be 45 psi or above for the R-4 compressor. A pressure reading of less than 45 psi for the R-4 would indicate one or more suction and/or discharge valves leaking, an internal leak, or an inoperative valve, and the compressor should be disassembled and checked for the cause. Make the necessary repairs, reassemble, and repeat the pump-up test. Externally leak test (see Figure 10-55).

6. When the compressor pump-up test is completed, release the air pressure from the HIGH side and remove the gauge adapter test plates.

7. Tilt the compressor and drain the oil out through the suction and discharge plates.

8. Allow the compressor to drain for about 10 min; then charge with the

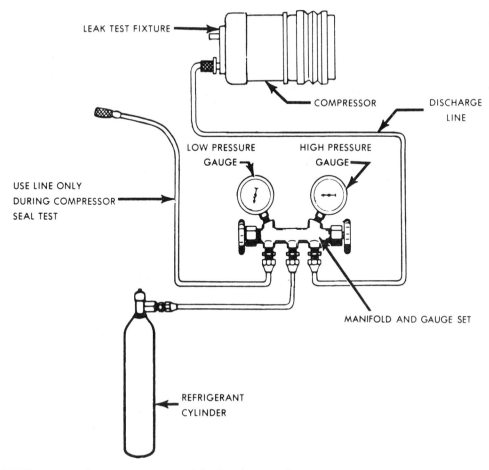

FIGURE 10-56. Compressor internal leak test (4 cyl.). *Courtesy of AC Delco/General Motors Corp.*

proper amount of oil. The oil may be poured into the suction port.

NOTE: If more assembly or processing is needed, a shipping plate or test fixture should be installed to keep out the dirt, air, and moisture until the compressor is installed on the car.

EEVIR (Evaporator-Equalized Valves-in-Receiver. Because of the space limitation and the possibility of foreign material

entering the system, it is recommended that the complete VIR unit be removed from the car for service (see Figure 10-57). When it is necessary to replace the expansion valve or the POA valve capsules, the desiccant bag should also be changed.

When replacing the VIR assembly, the following steps are recommended for its removal:

1.   Disconnect the battery ground cable.

FIGURE 10-57. Evaporator and VIR instal-lation. *Courtesy of AC Delco/General Motors Corp.*

2. Purge the refrigerant from the system.

3. Remove the radiator supply tank if necessary.

4. Clean the surface dirt from the exterior of the VIR assembly and all the line connections. Blow any loose dirt away with compressed air.

5. Disconnect the compressor inlet line, the oil bleed line, and the condenser outlet line at the VIR assembly. Cap or plug all the open connections immediately upon opening.

6. Loosen the evaporator inlet and outlet connections. Remove the VIR mounting clamp screw and remove the clamp from the assembly. Slide the VIR assembly off the evaporator outlet line first and then off the evaporator inlet line.

7. Remove and discard all the old O-rings.

NOTE: All the line openings and connections should be plugged or sealed to prevent the entry of dirt and moisture into the system.

When installing the VIR assembly, the following steps are recommended:

NOTE: When connecting the refrigerant lines, be sure to use new O-rings, coated with clean, clear refrigeration oil.

1. Lubricate all VIR assembly connection O-rings with clean and clear refrigeration oil and install the O-rings onto the connecting lines.

   CAUTION: When making all connections, use care to prevent nicking the O-rings and cross threading the connecting threads.

2. Remove the plugs from the evaporator inlet and outlet tube openings of the VIR assembly. Assemble the VIR assembly onto the evaporator inlet tube first, and then onto the outlet tube. When the assembly is in the proper position, install the VIR mounting clamp. Tighten the evaporator inlet connection to 18 ft-lb of torque and the evaporator outlet connection to 30 ft-lb of torque.

3. Remove the plug from the liquid bleed line connection opening of the VIR assembly. Connect and tighten the liquid bleed line connection to the VIR assembly to 6 ft-lb of torque.

4. Remove the plug from the liquid line connection opening in the VIR assembly. Connect and tighten the condenser line connection to the VIR assembly to 12 ft-lb of torque.

5. Remove the plug from the compressor line connection opening to the VIR assembly. Connect and tighten the compressor line connection to 30 ft-lb of torque.

6. Reinstall the radiator supply tank if removed previously.

7. Connect the battery ground cable.

8. Evacuate, charge the system with refrigerant, and check the operation of the unit.

Expansion Valve Capsule and Moisture Indicator Replacement. When these components are to be replaced, use the following steps in the removal process:

1. Remove the EEVIR assembly as outlined previously. Mark the housing and the inlet connector shell for correct installation.

2. Loosen and remove all the screws that mount the inlet connector shell assembly to the valve housing. Remove the inlet connector shell assembly. Discard the shell to housing O-ring. Place the shell assembly in a location where the sealing surface of the flange will not be damaged.

   CAUTION: All the pressure must be released and the expansion valve freed in its cavity before removing the capsule retaining screw and washer assembly in step 6. Now perform steps 3 through 6.

3. Clean the top area of the valve housing of any dirt that may be dislodged from the bottom flange of the inlet connector shell assembly during removal. Blow away any loose dirt with compressed air.

4. Loosen the expansion valve and the POA valve capsule retaining screws. Remove one screw and washer only partially (three turns). Completely remove the other screw and washer assembly (see Figure 10-58).

5. Attach the expansion valve removal tool to the tapered groove projection

FIGURE 10-58. Removing expansion valve capsule. *Courtesy of AC Delco / General Motors Corp.*

on the diaphragm end of the expansion valve.

6. Position the handle of the removal tool over the partially removed retaining screw and press down on the tool handle to lift and free the expansion valve in its cavity. Allow any entrapped refrigerant to escape before proceeding to step 7.

7. When the expansion valve becomes free, remove the removal tool, the retaining screw, the washer assembly, and remove the expansion valve capsule.

8. Using the O-ring removal tool, remove the O-ring from the expansion valve cavity. Wipe the expansion valve cavity clean with a clean lint-free cloth if any residue is present.

9. Remove the moisture indicator from the expansion valve.

Use the following steps when installing the expansion valve and moisture indicator:

1. To install the moisture indicator, place it on a clean, flat, firm surface. Align the lower end of the expansion valve with the inside of the sleeve. Insert the end of the capsule and force it straight down until the sleeve is fully seated.

   NOTE: If the moisture indicator should become cocked on the valve, it may be distorted or damaged.

2. Lubricate the expansion valve O-rings and the valve cavity in the housing with clean refrigeration oil.

   NOTE: On the EEVIR, use only the center (the large) and lower (small) O-rings. On the early VIR units with the silver TXV capsule, install an upper O-ring as shown in Figure 10-59.

3. Install the new O-ring in the valve cavity. Carefully install the new expansion valve capsule in the valve cavity and press it into position by hand.

4. Reinstall the two valve retaining screw and washer assemblies and tighten to 5 to 7 ft-lb of torque.

5. Clean the entire bottom flange surface of the inlet connector shell assembly free of all dirt. Inspect the O-ring sealing area of the flange for any scratches that could result in a leak.

6. Apply clean refrigeration oil to the new valve housing to inlet connector shell assembly O-ring.

7. Position the inlet connector shell assembly over the valve housing and install the mounting screws. Tighten to 7 to 12 ft-lb of torque.

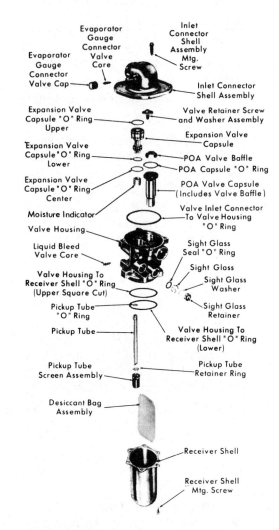

FIGURE 10-59. Components of VIR assembly. *Courtesy of AC Delco/General Motors Corp.*

8. Replace the desiccant bag as outlined under *Desiccant Bag Replacement.*

9. Reinstall the VIR assembly as outlined under *VIR Assembly: Installation.*

POA Valve Capsule Replacement. When replacing the POA valve, use the following steps during the removal process:

1. Remove the VIR assembly as outlined under *VIR Assembly: Removal.* Be sure to mark the housing and inlet connection shell so that it can be assembled properly for installation.

2. Loosen and remove all the screws that mount the inlet connector shell assembly to the valve housing. Remove the inlet connector shell assembly. Discard the shell to housing O-ring. Place the shell assembly in a location where the sealing surface of the flange will not be damaged.

3. Clean the top area of the valve housing of any dirt dislodged from the bottom flange of the inlet connector shell assembly during removal. Blow away any dirt with compressed air.

4. Loosen the expansion valve and the POA valve retaining screw and washer assemblies, and partially remove one screw and washer assembly three turns. Remove the other screw and washer assemblies entirely (see Figure 10-60).

WARNING: Even though only the POA valve is being replaced, all the refrigerant pressure must be released and the expansion valve freed in its cavity before removing the capsule retaining screw and washer assembly in step 6 below. For personal safety and to ensure that the pressure in the receiver and the inlet side of the expansion valve is released, perform steps 1 through 4 of *Desiccant Bag Replacement* before re-

FIGURE 10-60. Servicing POA capsule. *Courtesy of AC Delco/General Motors Corp.*

moving the retainer screw and washer.

5. Insert the POA valve remover tool into the valve baffle of the POA valve so that the edge of the tool clears the edge of the POA valve capsule (see Figure 10-60).

CAUTION: Position the fulcrum heal of the removal tool away from the O-ring sealing area to prevent damaging the O-ring groove of the valve housing.

6. Keep the tool firmly engaged with the valve baffle while pressing down on the handle of the removal tool to free the capsule in the cavity.

7. When the POA valve capsule breaks free, remove the tool, the retaining screw, and washer assembly, and remove the POA valve capsule.

8. Wipe the POA valve cavity and the mounting recess clean, using a clean, lint-free cloth.

When installing the POA valve, use the following steps:

1. Lubricate the new POA valve capsule and O-ring and the POA valve cavity mounting flange recess area with clean refrigeration oil.

2. Carefully install the POA valve capsule in the valve cavity. Press it into position by hand.

3. Reinstall the two capsule retaining screw and washer assemblies and tighten to 7 to 12 ft-lb of torque.

4. Clean the entire bottom flange surface of the inlet connector shell assembly clear of all dirt. Inspect the O-ring sealing area of the flange for any scratches that could result in a leak.

5. Apply clean refrigeration oil to the new valve housing to inlet connector shell assembly O-ring.

   NOTE: The service-only POA valve filter may be installed to protect the POA valve from foreign material circulating in the refrigeration system (see Figure 10-60). It is recommended if the system has been exposed to contamination, such as accident damage, or in high-humidity areas. Install the filter over the valve capsules onto the housing before installing the inlet shell. It is also recommended that the filter screen be changed or cleaned anytime the VIR assembly is opened for service.

6. Position the inlet connector shell assembly over the valve housing and install the mounting screws. Tighten the screws to 5 to 7 ft-lb of torque.

7. Complete the *Desiccant Bag Replacement* procedure.

8. Reinstall the VIR assembly as described under *VIR Assembly Replacement: Installation.*

VIR Housing Replacement. When replacing the VIR housing, use the following steps:

1. Remove the VIR assembly as described under *VIR Assembly Replacement: Removal.*

2. Loosen and remove all the screws that hold the inlet connector shell to the valve housing. Discard the shell to housing O-ring. Place the shell assembly in a location where the sealing surface of the flange will not be damaged.

   WARNING: All the refrigerant pressure must be relieved and the expansion valve freed in its cavity before removing the capsule retaining screw and washer assembly in step 6. Perform steps 3 through 6 as indicated.

3. Clean the top area of the valve housing of any dirt that was dislodged from the bottom flange of the inlet connector shell during removal.

4. Remove one of the two capsule retaining screw and washer assemblies. Loosen the other screw and washer assembly and partially back off three turns.

5. Using the remover tool, lift the expansion valve capsule free in its cavity (see Figure 10-58).

6. Remove the retaining screw and washer assembly and the expansion valve capsule. Remove and discard the three expansion valve O-rings (two from the expansion valve cap-

sule and one from the expansion valve cavity in the valve housing).

7. Using the remover tool, lift the POA valve capsule free in its cavity and remove the capsule (see Figure 10-60). Remove and discard the POA valve capsule O-ring.

8. Remove the receiver shell mounting screws and remove the shell. Discard the receiver shell to valve housing O-ring and desiccant bag. Clean the receiver shell and pickup screen as required before reassembling.

9. Using a small screwdriver blade, or similar tool, raise each tang of the pickup tube retainer ring a little at a time, moving around the retainer ring in a circular manner until the retainer ring is free of the valve housing opening (see Figure 10-61).

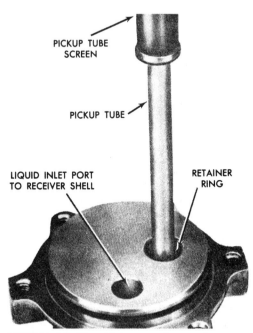

PICKUP TUBE SCREEN

PICKUP TUBE

LIQUID INLET PORT TO RECEIVER SHELL

RETAINER RING

FIGURE 10-61. Pick-up tube and screen.
Courtesy of AC Delco/General Motors Corp.

10. Remove the pickup tube and discard the pickup tube retainer and O-ring.

When installing the VIR housing, use the following steps:

1. Reassemble the VIR using the new valve housing and all new O-rings.

   NOTE: The new valve housing contains the liquid bleed valve-core and sight glass assembly. These parts are factory assembled into the housing and torqued into place. Check to make sure that the new valve assembly is free of lint and dirt in all the cavities and connections. Clean with a solvent if necessary and blow dry with compressed air.

2. Place the new valve housing upside down on a clean flat surface. Install a new O-ring and pickup tube retainer on the pickup tube. Lubricate the O-ring with clean refrigeration oil.

3. Install the pickup tube into the valve housing. Be sure that the tube is bottomed in the opening and the tool vertically in line before seating the tube and retainer in place. Visually check the seating of the retainer tangs to see that no tang was fractured during the installation process (see Figure 10-62).

4. Lubricate the top of the POA valve capsule cavity of the valve housing and the new POA valve capsule O-ring with clean refrigeration oil. Install the POA valve in its cavity in the valve housing. Push into place with the thumb or hand.

5. Lubricate the expansion valve cavity of the valve housing and the new expansion valve capsule and O-rings

FIGURE 10-62. Installing pick-up tube assembly. *Courtesy of AC Delco / General Motors Corp.*

with clean refrigeration oil. Install the center O-ring in the expansion valve capsule cavity of the valve housing.

6. Install the expansion valve capsule and thumb or hand press into position. Install both capsule retaining screw and washer assemblies and torque to 7 to 12 ft-lb of torque.

7. Lubricate the inlet connector shell assembly to valve housing O-ring with clean refrigeration oil and install it in the valve housing O-ring groove.

8. Install the inlet connector shell in the proper alignment and torque the

mounting screws to 5 to 7 ft-lb of torque.

9. Lubricate the valve housing to receiver shell O-ring with clean refrigeration oil and install it in the valve housing O-ring groove.

10. Lubricate the inner top surface of the receiver shell with clean refrigeration oil and install the pickup tube screen to the pickup tube.

11. Unpack the new desiccant bag and immediately place the bag in the receiver shell and install the receiver shell to the valve housing. Torque the mounting screws to 5 to 7 ft-lb of torque.

12. Reinstall the VIR assembly as outlined under *VIR Assembly Replacement: Installation.*

Desiccant Bag Replacement. When replacing the desiccant bag, use the following steps during the removal process:

1. Remove the VIR assembly as outlined under *VIR Assembly Replacement: Removal.*

   WARNING: Do not remove the receiver shell to housing screws entirely until step 3:

2. Loosen the screws that hold the receiver shell to the housing. Loosen these screws about three turns. Do not completely remove the screws.

3. Hold the VIR valve housing and push the lower end of the receiver shell to break the seal to the housing.

   NOTE: If the receiver shell should stick and be difficult to remove, use a flat-blade screwdriver and carefully pry between the shell mounting flange and the condenser line connection to free the shell.

4. Remove the receiver shell mounting screws and remove the shell, clearing the liquid pickup tube and filter screen (see Figure 10-63).

5. Discard the old bag of desiccant and the valve housing to receiver O-rings. Wash the liquid pickup tube filter screen and the interior of the receiver with a cleaning solvent as required, and blow dry with compressed air.

When replacing the desiccant bag, use the following steps during the installation process:

1. Lubricate the new valve housing to receiver O-rings with clean refrigeration oil and install the O-rings in the valve housing grooves.

2. Add a film of oil to the top of the receiver shell to aid in the assembly process. Reassemble the filter screen

to the liquid pickup tube. Be sure that the screen is all the way onto the tube.

3. Add 1 oz of new refrigeration oil and a new bag of desiccant to the receiver shell, and assemble the shell to the valve housing. Tighten the shell mounting screws to 5 to 6 ft-lb of torque.

4. Reinstall the VIR assembly as outlined under *VIR Assembly Replacement: Installation.*

Liquid Bleed Line Valve Core (VIR System) Replacement. When replacing the liquid bleed line valve core, use the following steps for the removal procedure:

1. Remove the VIR assembly as outlined under *VIR Assembly Replacement: Removal.*

2. Remove the valve core with the special tool as shown in Figure 10-64.

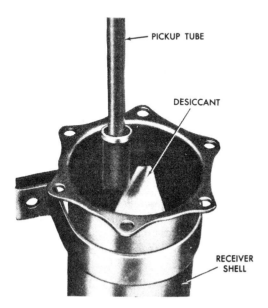

FIGURE 10-63.   Desiccant bag replacement.
Courtesy of AC Delco/General Motors Corp.

FIGURE 10-64.   Liquid bleed line core. *Courtesy of AC Delco/General Motors Corp.*

When installing the liquid line bleed valve core, use the following procedure:

1. Install the new valve core. Turn the core inward until the core threads just start to tighten. Note the position of the valve core tool and rotate the tool an additional travel of 180° to approximately 24 to 36 oz-in. of torque.

    NOTE: Be sure to use the correct valve core; it is not identical to the gauge cores nor is it identical to the valve cores used in automobile tires.

2. Reinstall the VIR assembly as outlined under *VIR Assembly Replacement: Installation*.

CHRYSLER COMPRESSOR SERVICE PROCEDURES

When working on Chrysler units, use the following procedures for proper service:

Compressor Replacement. When replacing a Chrysler compressor, use the following steps for proper removal:

1. Purge the refrigerant from the system.

2. Measure and record the oil level so the oil level in the replacement or repaired compressor can be adjusted to the exact level as that in the compressor removed from the car.

3. Disconnect the suction and discharge lines from the compressor.

    CAUTION: Plug or cap all the refrigerant lines as soon as they are disconnected to keep moisture and dirt out of the system.

4. Disconnect the magnetic clutch-to-control unit wire.

5. Loosen and remove the compressor drive belts.

6. Remove the compressor to bracket attaching bolts and remove the compressor from the car.

When installing a Chrysler compressor on the car, use the following steps:

1. Install the compressor to the bracket and tighten the attaching bolts.

2. Install the compressor belts and adjust to the proper tension.

3. Connect the magnetic clutch-to-control-unit wire.

4. Remove the caps or plugs and connect the suction line to the suction fitting, and connect the discharge line to the discharge fitting.

    CAUTION: When replacing the compressor assembly, the crankshaft should be rotated by hand at least two revolutions to clear any oil accumulation from the compressor head before the clutch is energized to avoid damage to the compressor reed valves.

5. Evacuate, recharge the system, and check the unit operation.

Clutch and Pulley Assembly Replacement. Various types of magnetic clutch assemblies are used on Chrysler systems, all of which use a stationary electromagnet attached to the compressor. Since the electromagnet does not rotate, the collector rings and brushes are eliminated.

When replacing the clutch and pulley assembly, use the following steps during the removal procedure:

1. Loosen and remove the compressor drive belts. Disconnect the clutch field

wire at the connector. Note the location of the coil lead wire so that the coil can be reinstalled in the same position.

2. Remove the special locking bolt and the washer from the compressor crankshaft at the front center of the clutch (see Figure 10-65).

3. Insert a ⅝-11 × 2½ cap screw into the threaded portion of the hub assembly.

4. Support the clutch with one hand; then tighten the cap screw until the clutch is removed from the crankshaft (see Figure 10-66).

5. Remove the three hexagonal head screws attaching the clutch field assembly to the compressor and lift off the assembly.

When installing the clutch and pulley assembly, use the following steps during the procedure:

1. Install the clutch field coil assembly on the base of the compressor bear-

FIGURE 10-65.   Removing pulley retaining bolt. *Courtesy of AC Delco / General Motors Corp.*

FIGURE 10-66.   Removing clutch and pulley. *Courtesy of AC Delco/General Motors Corp.*

ing housing. Make certain that the coil assembly is positioned so that the lead wire points to the left of the compressor as viewed from the front of the car. Install the three mounting screws and tighten to 17 in.-lb of torque.

2. Insert the Woodruff key in the crankshaft keyway.

3. Install the clutch assembly on the crankshaft.

4. Install the washer and a new self-locking bolt. Hold the clutch to keep it from turning with a spanner wrench placed in the holes in the front bumper plate. Tighten the bolt to 20 ft-lb of torque.

5. Connect the clutch coil field wire to the terminal.

6. Install the compressor drive belts and adjust to the proper tension.

Shaft Seal Assembly Replacement. The shaft seal may be replaced while the compressor is still on the car, provided that there is enough space, or with the compressor removed and placed on a workbench.

Special care should be taken when installing a new seal in a compressor while it is mounted on the engine. By adequately lubricating the rotating seal assembly prior to its installation on the compressor shaft, the carbon ring will be kept from falling out of place.

To aid in the replacement of the seal, the compressor should be placed on its back after removal from the car. Use the following steps when removing the compressor from the car:

1. Purge the refrigerant from the system.

2. Remove the compressor drive belt; remove the clutch, coil, and drive key.

3. Remove the five compressor crankshaft bearing housing bolts.

4. Remove the bearing housing from the crankshaft, using two screwdrivers inserted into the slots provided for this purpose. Pry the housing from the compressor case (see Figure 10-67).

FIGURE 10-67. Removing crank shaft housing. *Courtesy of AC Delco/General Motors Corp.*

FIGURE 10-68. Removing seal. *Courtesy of AC Delco/General Motors Corp.*

5. Position the seal remover behind the seal drive ring and attach sleeve (see Figure 10-68).

6. Remove the seal assembly by lifting the tool straight up. Do not scratch or burr the crankshaft or seal plate cover face.

7. Support the crankshaft bearing housing in the upright position on a workbench; use a screwdriver or other tool to tap the seal seat down and out of the housing. Discard this seal seat and its O-ring (see Figure 10-69).

8. Remove and discard the O-ring on the outer diameter of the crankshaft bearing housing (see Figure 10-70). Thoroughly clean this housing and make certain that the seal recess, compressor shaft, and housing face on the compressor are completely

FIGURE 10-69. **Removing seal seat.** *Courtesy of AC Delco / General Motors Corp.*

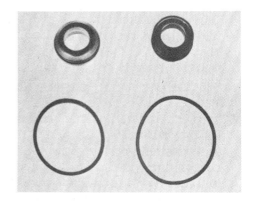

FIGURE 10-71. **Seal kit.** *Courtesy of AC Delco / General Motors Corp.*

clean before installing the new seal assembly.

When installing the new seal, use the following steps during the procedure:

1. Install all the new seal parts (see Figure 10-71) that are furnished in the seal kit. Lubricate all the new seal parts with refrigeration oil before installation.

2. Install the new O-ring in the proper groove on the outer diameter of the crankcase bearing housing.

3. Position the new seal assembly (with the O-ring in place) in the recess of the housing with the machine face upward so that this face will be toward the carbon face of the seal when the housing is installed (see Figure 10-72).

FIGURE 10-70. **Removing housing O-ring.** *Courtesy of AC Delco / General Motors Corp.*

FIGURE 10-72. **Positioning seal seat in bearing housing.** *Courtesy of AC Delco / General Motors Corp.*

4. Using the fingers, press the seal seat fully into the recess of the bearing housing. Wipe the seal seat clean with a lint-free cloth and relubricate with refrigeration oil (see Figure 10-73).

5. Lubricate the compressor shaft with refrigeration oil; position the new seal assembly on the shaft with the carbon ring outward. Do not attempt to seat the seal in the recess; it will be seated when the bearing housing is installed (see Figure 10-74).

CAUTION: Use care not to touch the sealing face of the seal with the fingers.

6. Lubricate the mating surfaces of the seal and seal seat, O-ring seating surface in the compressor recess, and the O-ring with clean refrigeration oil. Position the bearing housing on the shaft with the bolt holes aligned with the bolt holes in the compressor, and press the assembly straight in until it is seated on the compressor face (see Figure 10-75).

FIGURE 10-74. Installing seal. *Courtesy of AC Delco/General Motors Corp.*

7. Install the bolts in the bearing housing flange bolt holes. Tighten all five bolts evenly to 10 to 13 ft-lb of torque.

8. Install the clutch coil assembly on the compressor with the coil lead in the same position as it was before it was removed; tighten the coil mounting screws to 17 in-lb of torque.

FIGURE 10-73. Installing seal seat. *Courtesy of AC Delco/General Motors Corp.*

FIGURE 10-75. Installing bearing housing. *Courtesy of AC Delco/General Motors Corp.*

9. Install the Woodruff key in the compressor crankshaft slot, align the keyway in the clutch assembly with the key on the shaft, and slide the clutch into place on the shaft (see Figure 10-76).

10. Install the washer and a new self-locking bolt in the end of the compressor shaft. Hold the clutch stationary with a spanner wrench and tighten the shaft bolt to 20 ft-lb of torque.

11. Tighten all bolts on the compressor brackets after the compressor has been replaced on the car. Tighten the compressor drive belts to their specific tension.

12. Evacuate and recharge the system with refrigerant.

13. Leak test the compressor shaft seal.

ETR or EPR Valve Replacement. When replacing either of these valves, use the following steps during the removal procedure:

1. Purge the refrigerant from the system.

FIGURE 10-76. Installing clutch and pulley assembly. *Courtesy of AC Delco/General Motors Corp.*

FIGURE 10-77. Removing and installing EPR valve. *Courtesy of AC Delco/General Motors Corp.*

2. Remove the electrical wire from the ETR valve.

3. Remove the two EPR valve suction line fitting bolts, the fitting which also contains the compressor suction screen, spring, and the gasket.

4. Remove the valve and O-ring from the compressor using the EPR remover and installer tool by rotating the valve counterclockwise slightly (see Figure 10-77).

CAUTION: Do not handle the EPR or ETR valve more than necessary. The valve should be inspected externally and wiped clean with a lint-free cloth. Place the valve in a plastic bag until installation time.

When installing the ETR or the EPR valve, use the following steps in the procedure:

1. Install a new O-ring on the valve.

2. Lubricate the O-ring with clean refrigeration oil and install the valve in the compressor using the installer

tool while rotating the valve counter-clockwise.

3. Install the compressor suction screen in the valve suction line fitting.

4. Install the suction line fitting gasket, spring, and fitting, and tighten the attaching bolts to 8 to 14 ft-lb of torque.

5. Install the electrical connector on the ETR valve.

TECUMSEH AND YORK COMPRESSOR SERVICE PROCEDURES

Compressor Isolation. If the compressor is equipped with stem-type service valves, it may be isolated from the system for checking the oil level, replacing the shaft seal, or the complete compressor assembly for disassembly. To isolate the compressor, proceed as follows:

1. Backseat both the high- and low-side service valves.

2. Remove the cap from the high-pressure service valve gauge port.

3. Connect the manifold gauge set to the compressor service valve gauge ports.

4. Be sure that both hand valves on the manifold gauge set are closed.

5. Front seat both the high- and low-side compressor service valves.

6. Open the high-side hand valve on the manifold gauge set one quarter-turn to allow the R-12 to escape slowly to prevent the loss of refrigeration oil. Allow the R-12 to escape until the pressure is zero on the gauge.

NOTE: If the compressor is equipped with a Schrader valve, it will be necessary to purge the complete system refrigerant

charge to perform the compressor service discussed above.

Compressor Replacement. When replacing a compressor, use the following steps during the process:

1. Isolate the compressor as discussed above.

2. Remove the suction and discharge service valves from the compressor.

3. Remove the mounting bolts from the compressor and remove the compressor from the engine.

4. Remove the clutch with the clutch removing bolt (refer to *Compressor Clutch Replacement*).

When installing the compressor, use the following steps during the process:

1. Check the oil level in the replacement compressor.

2. Install the clutch that was removed from the defective compressor on the new compressor. Tighten the retaining bolts and torque to the specified torque.

3. Mount the compressor using the specified torque for the mounting bolts. Make sure that the drive belt is properly aligned and tightened to the specified tension.

4. Secure the service valves to the compressor using the following procedure:

   (a) If the valves are of the pad type, check to see that the valve mounting surfaces on both valve and cylinder head are clean and free of nicks, gaskets, and foreign material. Use the new mounting gaskets dry. Tighten the bolts to the specified torque.

(b) If the valves are of the rotolock type, check to see that the valve mounting surfaces on both valves and the compressor are clean and that the O-ring valve mounting gasket is properly positioned and in good condition. If it is deformed, split, or broken, replace it with a new gasket. Properly align the valve to cylinder head and tighten the rotolock nuts to their torque limits as specified.

(c) Special care should be taken to prevent dirt or foreign material from entering the compressor during the installation process. The new replacement compressor should not be left unsealed to the atmosphere longer than is absolutely necessary for preparation and the actual installation.

5. With the service valves in the closed position, connect the vacuum pump to the suction and discharge gauge ports of the service valves and evacuate the system to 28 in. of vacuum for 20 min. Stop the vacuum pump and close the service valve on the compressor.

6. Turn both the service valves to the extreme counterclockwise position to connect the compressor back into the system.

7. Start the engine. Turn on the air conditioner. Run the engine at 1500 rpm to stabilize the system. Check the sight glass for the proper charge of R-12.

Clutch and Pulley Assembly Replacement. During the removal of the clutch and pulley, use the following steps.

1. Hold the clutch hub stationary with a spanner wrench tool. Remove the retaining bolt from the end of the compressor shaft with the correct socket (see Figure 10-78).

2. Thread the clutch removing bolt into the outer diameter of the clutch hub. Hold the clutch hub stationary with a spanner wrench tool. Tighten the bolt with a wrench until the clutch assembly is removed from the shaft, lift the clutch off, and remove the bolt (see Figure 10-79).

3. Take out the two bolts and remove the brush assembly (rotating coil type of clutch) or take out the four bolts and remove the coil assembly (stationary coil type of clutch).

4. Remove the Woodruff key from the shaft keyway.

During the installation of the clutch and pulley assembly, use the following steps.

1. Install the brush assembly (rotating coil type of clutch) or the coil assembly (stationary coil type of clutch) on

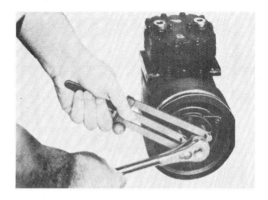

FIGURE 10-78. Removing retaining bolt.
Courtesy of AC Delco/General Motors Corp.

FIGURE 10-79. Removing clutch and pulley assembly. *Courtesy of AC Delco / General Motors Corp.*

the compressor face and tighten the bolts securely.

2. Install the Woodruff key in the shaft groove, align the keyway in the clutch assembly with the key, and slide the clutch onto the shaft (see Figure 10-80).

FIGURE 10-80. Installing clutch assembly. *Courtesy of AC Delco / General Motors Corp.*

CAUTION: If the clutch is the rotating coil type, use care not to damage the coil brushes.

3. Install the bolt and washer into the end of the compressor shaft; use a spanner wrench tool to hold the clutch assembly stationary. Tighten the bolt to 20 ft-lb of torque (see Figure 10-81).

Shaft Seal Assembly Replacement. When replacing a compressor shaft seal, use the following steps during the removal process:

1. Isolate the compressor. Refer to *Isolating the Compressor.*

2. Remove the clutch and pulley assembly. Refer to *Clutch and Pulley Assembly Replacement.*

3. On later-model compressors, remove the secondary dust shield from the shaft, using care not to mar the shaft. On all compressors, remove the six bolts holding the seal seat plate assembly onto the compressor.

4. Remove the seal seat plate and discard. There is a new one in the new seal kit.

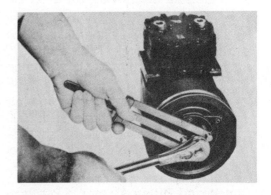

FIGURE 10-81. Installing retaining bolt. *Courtesy of AC Delco / General Motors Corp.*

5. Remove and discard the O-ring in the seal plate groove on the front of the compressor (see Figure 10-82).

   NOTE: If a flat gasket is used rather than an O-ring at this point, remove all traces of the old gasket. Make certain that the seal recess, compressor shaft, and seal plate face on the compressor are completely clean.

6. Position the seal remover behind the seal drive ring and attach the sleeve (see Figure 10-83).

When installing a new compressor shaft seal assembly, use the following steps:

1. Install all the new seal parts which are furnished in the new seal kit (see Figures 10-84 and 10-85).

   NOTE: An O-ring and several flat gaskets are furnished in each kit. Select and use the same type as that removed from the compressor.

2. Install the O-ring, or the correct flat gasket, on the seal plate face of the

FIGURE 10-83. Removing seal. *Courtesy of AC Delco / General Motors Corp.*

FIGURE 10-84. Typical Tecumseh shaft seal kit. *Courtesy of AC Delco / General Motors Corp.*

FIGURE 10-82. Removing O-ring. *Courtesy of AC Delco / General Motors Corp.*

FIGURE 10-85. Typical York shaft seal kit. *Courtesy of AC Delco / General Motors Corp.*

FIGURE 10-86.   Installing O-ring. *Courtesy of AC Delco / General Motors Corp.*

compressor (see Figure 10-86). Seat the O-ring evenly in the groove.

3. Lubricate all exposed surfaces of the shaft and seal with clean refrigeration oil. Set the seal on the shaft with the carbon ring and shoulder outward (if the carbon ring is a separate part, place it on the shaft over the seal with the face outward) (see Figure 10-87).

CAUTION: Do not touch the carbon ring with the fingers. This will possibly cause a leak.

4. Lubricate the seal seat plate with clean refrigeration oil and install the plate on the installer tool with the outer face of the plate against the shoulder of the tool (see Figure 10-88).

5. Position the plate and tool on the shaft; align the bolt holes in the plate with those in the compressor. Press the assembly straight in until the seal plate is seated on the compressor (see Figure 10-89).

6. Install all bolts in the seal plate and tighten finger tight. Remove the seal installer tool.

7. Tighten all the seal plate bolts evenly in a circular or diagonal pattern to 7 to 13 ft-lb for the York, and 6 to 10 ft-lb for the Tecumseh (see Figure 10-90).

8. Rotate the shaft by hand for 15 to 20 revolutions to seat the seal parts.

FIGURE 10-87.   Installing seal. *Courtesy of AC Delco / General Motors Corp.*

FIGURE 10-88.   Installing seal seat plate. *Courtesy of AC Delco / General Motors Corp.*

FIGURE 10-89. Aligning seal seat plate.
Courtesy of AC Delco/General Motors Corp.

9. Install the clutch brush assembly (rotating coil type of clutch) or the coil assembly (stationary coil type of clutch) on the compressor face, and tighten the mounting bolts securely.

10. Install the Woodruff key into the shaft groove, align the keyway in the clutch assembly with the keyway in

FIGURE 10-90. Tightening seal plate bolts.
Courtesy of AC Delco/General Motors Corp.

FIGURE 10-91. Installing retaining bolt.
Courtesy of AC Delco/General Motors Corp.

the shaft, and slide the clutch onto the compressor shaft.

CAUTION: If the clutch is the rotating coil type, use care not to damage the coil brushes.

11. Install the retainer bolt and washer in the end of the compressor shaft. Use a spanner wrench tool to hold the clutch assembly stationary. Tighten the bolts to 20 ft-lb of torque (see Figure 10-91).

NIPPONDENSO, CHRYSLER, AND FORD 6-CYLINDER COMPRESSOR

Replacement of the clutch coil is the only field repair that is recommended on these compressors. Use the following steps for replacement of the clutch coil:

1. Hold the clutch hub stationary with a spanner wrench and remove the shaft nut and washer. Use a 13-mm socket (see Figure 10-92).

2. Screw the clutch front plate remover into the clutch hub. Tighten the center screw, removing the front plate, clutch key, and the shims (see Figure 10-93).

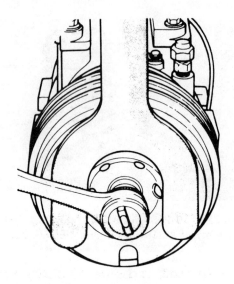

FIGURE 10-92. Removing shaft nut. *Courtesy of Ford Motor Co.*

3. Remove the pulley snap ring with the snap ring pliers. Remove the pulley from the compressor shaft. Replace the pulley bearing if it is worn or there is evidence of grease leaking

from it. On some units the front plate must be replaced when the bearing is defective (see Figure 10-94).

4. Disconnect the coil electrical wire from the terminals. Remove the snap ring with the snap ring pliers. Slide the coil off the housing. Install the new coil, making sure that the hole in the rear of the coil lines up with the pin on the compressor end housing. Replace the snap ring with the beveled side outward. Check to see that the snap ring is fully seated in the groove. Reconnect the electrical wires to the coil terminals (see Figure 10-95).

5. Install the pulley assembly on the compressor shaft. If the pulley does not fully seat, place a block of wood on the grease slinger and tap gently with a hammer. Repair any damage done to the grease slinger. Replace the snap ring in the groove, with the beveled side outward. Check to

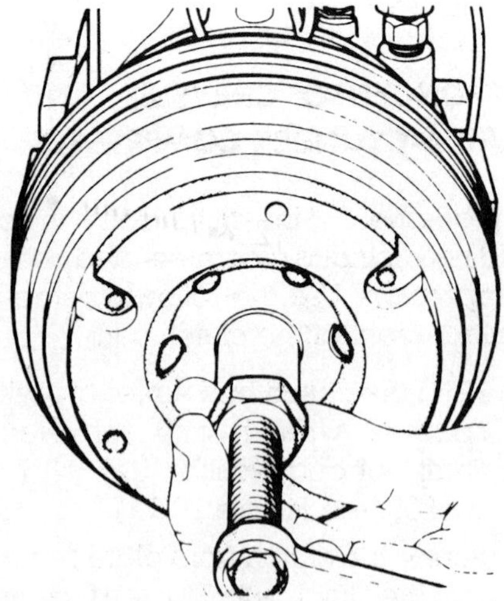

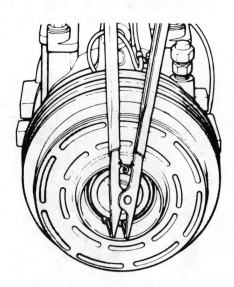

FIGURE 10-93. Removing clutch plate. *Courtesy of Ford Motor Co.*

FIGURE 10-94. Removing compressor pulley. *Courtesy of Ford Motor Co.*

be sure that the snap ring is fully seated in the groove (see Figure 10-96).

6. Install the shims, the shaft key, and the clutch front plate on the compresor shaft. Add or remove the number of shims required to maintain an air gap between the clutch plate and pulley face of 0.020 to 0.035 in. Install the lock washer and the shaft nut. Hold the clutch hub with a spanner wrench and tighten the nut to 12 ft-lb of torque. Recheck the air gap and make any adjustments required (see Figure 10-97).

SANKYO SD-5 COMPRESSOR

The Sankyo SD-5 compressors are designed for low weight and size and high capacity. They have the following features:

1. A unique wobble plate design concept.

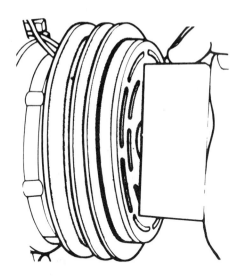

FIGURE 10-96.   Installing compressor pulley. *Courtesy of Ford Motor Co.*

2. Lightweight but strong construction.
3. A magnetic clutch engineered together with the compressor as a complete assembly for a small overall package.

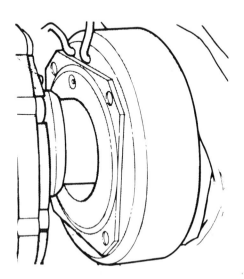

FIGURE 10-95.   Replacing clutch coil. *Courtesy of Ford Motor Co.*

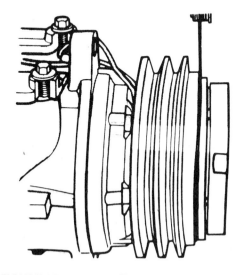

FIGURE 10-97.   Installing clutch plate. *Courtesy of Ford Motor Co.*

Lubrication. The SD-505 uses a lubrication system which reduces the oil circulation ratio (OCR) to a level of less than 2% at 1800 rpm. This lubrication system also provides oiling to the cylinder walls, piston rod assembly, main bearings, and the shaft seal. Compressor models SD-505, 507, and 510 use a centrifugal forced oiling system to assure positive lubrication to all components.

The SD-508 has a positive pressure lubrication system which uses the pressure differential between the suction intake and the cylinder block to supply refrigerant oil to the bearings. Sankyo's internal design provides proper lubrication to the cylinder walls, piston-rod assemblies, and to the shaft seal.

These compressors also use an oil deflector with the positive pressure differential lubrication system which provides oiling to the cylinder walls, piston-rod assemblies, main bearing, and to the shaft seal. Oil circulation through the refrigerant system is at a minimum.

Anti-Slug Feature. To prevent valve damage from refrigerant "liquid slugging," valve stops are designed into the cylinder block to limit the travel of the suction reeds.

Specifications. The SD-5 compressors are factory charged with Suniso No. 5GS. Only this oil or equivalent oils should be used when adding or changing oil. Equivalent oils are: Texaco Capella E and Virginia Chemicals 500 viscosity. (See Table 10-2.)

Do not add to the oil charge before installation. (See the Service section of this chapter for special applications.)

Torque. Since many of the SD-5 compressor parts are made from alumi-

TABLE 10-2. Sankyo Factory Oil Charge.

SD-505	3.4 ± 0.5 fluid ounces (100 ± 15cc)
SD-507	5 ± 1.0 fluid ounces (150 ± 30cc) −0
SD-508	6 ± 0.5 fluid ounces (175 ± 15cc)
SD-510	3.5 ± 0.5 fluid ounces (135 ± 15cc)

Courtesy of Sanden International (USA) Inc.

num alloys, exercise great care not to damage the machined surfaces. Adhere to the torque specifications by inserting cap screws to finger-tight snugness, then use a suitable torque wrench (See Table 10-3.)

Rotation Speed. Under normal operating conditions, the SD-5 compressor should operate at the specified speed for that model. (See Table 10-4.)

Refrigerant. Refrigerant-12 is the only refrigerant that can be used with Sankyo

TABLE 10-3. Sankyo Torque Specifications.

Item	Ft./Lbs.	Kg./M.
Clutch Retaining Nut	25-30	3.4-4.2
Cylinder Head Cap Screws	22-25	3.0-3.4
Service Port w O-Ring	9-12	1.2-1.7
Oil Filler Plug	6-9	0.8-1.2
Discharge Hose Fitting, ½″ flare	18-22	2.5-3.0
Suction Hose Fitting, ⅝″ flare	22-25	3.0-3.4
Drive Belt (New)	100	13.8
Drive Belt (After Run-in)	80-90	11-12.5
	In./Lbs.	**Kg/cm**
Clutch Wire Clamp Screw	35 ± 12	30 ± 10
Field Coil Retaining Cap Screws	17-23	15-20
Charge Valve Cap	58 ± 12	50 ± 10

Courtesy of Sanden International (USA) Inc.

TABLE 10-4. Sankyo Compressor Speed.

Year and Model	Constant	Downshift Short Duration
1978 and prior	500-5000	6000
1980 (SD-505)	500-6500	7500
1979/1980 (SD-507, SD-508)	500-6000	7000
1980 (SD-510-HD)	500-4000	6000

Courtesy of Sanden International (USA) Inc.

SD-5 compressors. Certain refrigerants, such as methyl chloride, deteriorate aluminum. Other types are not compatible with the proper operating temperatures and pressures.

Capacity. The capacity and power requirement standards of the SD-5 compressors are given in Table 10-5. Since the curves reflecting this data are derived with laboratory test equipment using ideal system components, in actual practice variations in system balance may alter this performance data.

Weight. The clutch weight is for standard 5.2-inch diameter, two groove, A section pulley (see Table 10-6).

Leak Standard. Most automotive air conditioning systems have some permissible loss in refrigerant. The Sankyo leak-rate specification is below the detection range of the Halide (flame type) detector and the normal sensitivity setting of most electronic shop-type leak detectors. Laboratory-type detection instruments are not recommended for field service because their sensitivity can detect even permissible refrigerant losses.

TABLE 10-5. Sankyo Compressor Capacity.

	Displacement per Revolution	Bore	Stroke	No. of Cylinders
SD-505	5.3 cubic inch (87 cc)	1.378 inches (35 mm)	.711 inches (18.07 mm)	5
SD-507	6.59 cubic inch (108 cc)	1.378 inches (35 mm)	.890 inches (22.6 mm)	5
SD-508	8.42 cubic inch (138 cc)	1.378 inches (35 mm)	1.13 inches (28.6 mm)	5
SD-510-HD	9.82 cubic inch (161 cc)	1.417 inches (36 mm)	1.248 inches (31.7 mm)	5

Courtesy of Sanden International (USA) Inc.

TABLE 10-6. Sankyo Compressor Weight.

	Compressor Lbs. (Kg.)	Clutch Lbs. (Kg.)	Assembly Lbs. (Kg.)
SD-505	7.93 (3.5)	4.19 (1.9)	11.88 (5.4)
SD-507	9.04 (4.1)	5.73 (2.6)	14.77 (6.7)
SD-508	11.24 (5.1)	5.95 (2.7)	17.19 (7.8)
SD-510-HD	10.58 (4.8)	5.18 (2.35)	15.76 (7.15)

Clutch weight is for standard 5.2-inch diameter, two-groove, A section.
Courtesy of Sanden International (USA) Inc.

Cutaway. See Figure 10-98 for a cutaway of the SD-5 compressor.

Service Procedures. A troubleshooting chart is provided in Figure 10-99. The following are specific inspection procedures:

Leak Check Procedures: In the following checks, "R" means that the compressor can be repaired, and "NR" means that the compressor is non-repairable and must be replaced.

When visually checking a system, seeping oil does not necessarily indicate leaking refrigerant. Look for the following problems:

1. Shaft seal area seeping oil. Feel under the seal area between the clutch and the compressor—R.

2. Dislocation of front housing O-ring (protruding section)—NR.

3. Oil around cylinder head (gasket, service port, or fittings)—R.

4. Oil around filler hole; O-ring—R. Stripped threads—NR.

5. Oil around crack in cylinder block—NR.

It is always good procedure to clean away all oil, grease, etc., and to blow away residual refrigerant before starting detection. Refer to system or supplier manuals for the proper techniques to be used for Halide or electronic leak detectors.

When using Halide leak detectors, any portion of the compressor, including the seals, which shows a leak indication on the flame will require leak repair.

When using electronic shop-type detectors (detectors with a minimum leak rate of ½ to 1 ounce per year) in the seal area of the compressor, set the instrument ¼ to ⅓ range above maximum sensitivity. For all other portions of the compressor, set the detector to maximum sensitivity.

When using "soap bubble" type detection, any bubbles found on any portion of the compressor indicate a leak requiring repair.

NOTE: A useful device for finding a shaft seal leak while the compressor is installed can be made by bending a 12-inch piece of ¼-inch copper tubing to a 90° angle, making about a ¾ inch leg. Insert the straight end into one of the clutch front plate holes.

Oil Check Procedures. Whenever a system component has been replaced or there is an obvious oil leak after repairs have been made, follow the steps below.

1. Determine the compressor mounting angle. Position the angle gauge (#32448) across the flat surfaces of the

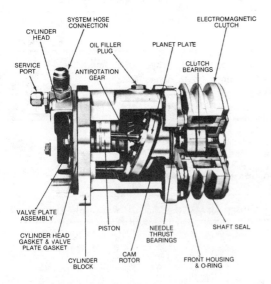

FIGURE 10-98.   Sankyo SD-5 cutaway. *Courtesy of Sanden International (USA) Inc.*

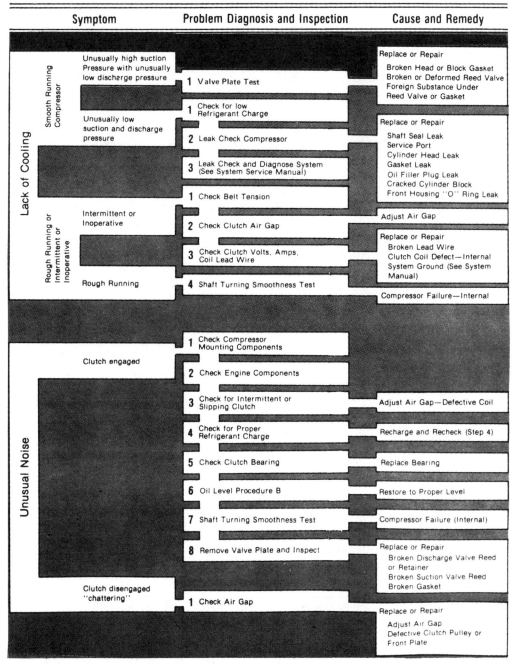

Symptom	Problem Diagnosis and Inspection	Cause and Remedy

Lack of Cooling

Smooth Running Compressor

Unusually high suction Pressure with unusually low discharge pressure — **1** Valve Plate Test — Replace or Repair: Broken Head or Block Gasket / Broken or Deformed Reed Valve / Foreign Substance Under Reed Valve or Gasket

Unusually low suction and discharge pressure — **1** Check for low Refrigerant Charge / **2** Leak Check Compressor / **3** Leak Check and Diagnose System (See System Service Manual) — Replace or Repair: Shaft Seal Leak / Service Port / Cylinder Head Leak / Gasket Leak / Oil Filler Plug Leak / Cracked Cylinder Block / Front Housing "O" Ring Leak

Rough Running or Intermittent or Inoperative

Intermittent or Inoperative — **1** Check Belt Tension / **2** Check Clutch Air Gap / **3** Check Clutch Volts, Amps, Coil Lead Wire — Adjust Air Gap / Replace or Repair: Broken Lead Wire / Clutch Coil Defect—Internal / System Ground (See System Manual)

Rough Running — **4** Shaft Turning Smoothness Test — Compressor Failure—Internal

Unusual Noise

Clutch engaged —
1 Check Compressor Mounting Components
2 Check Engine Components
3 Check for Intermittent or Slipping Clutch — Adjust Air Gap—Defective Coil
4 Check for Proper Refrigerant Charge — Recharge and Recheck (Step 4)
5 Check Clutch Bearing — Replace Bearing
6 Oil Level Procedure B — Restore to Proper Level
7 Shaft Turning Smoothness Test — Compressor Failure (Internal)
8 Remove Valve Plate and Inspect — Replace or Repair: Broken Discharge Valve Reed or Retainer / Broken Suction Valve Reed / Broken Gasket

Clutch disengaged "chattering" — **1** Check Air Gap — Replace or Repair: Adjust Air Gap / Defective Clutch Pulley or Front Plate

This chart refers specifically to the Sankyo compressor. During diagnosis follow the inspection procedures in the sequence shown until a defect is found. Then perform the repair in the Cause and Remedy Section. If this repair does not fully solve the problem, proceed to the next Inspection Step.

FIGURE 10-99. Troubleshooting chart. *Courtesy of Sanden International (USA) Inc.*

two front mounting ears. Center the bubble. Read the mounting angle to the closest degree. (This will be important in step 5.)

2. Remove the oil filler plug. Look through the oil filler plug hole and rotate the clutch front plate to position the internal parts (see Figure 10-100). When the compressor is mounted to the right (facing the clutch), center the parts as they are moving to the rear of the compressor (discharge stroke). When the compressor is mounted to the left (facing the clutch), center the parts as they are moving to the front of the compressor (suction stroke). This step is necessary to clear the dipstick of internal parts and allow its insertion to full depth.

3. Insert the dipstick to its STOP position (see Figure 10-101). The STOP is the angle near the top of the dipstick. The point of the dipstick angle must be to the left if the mounting angle is to the right. The point of the dipstick angle must be to the right if the mounting angle is to the left. The bottom surface of the angle, in either case, must be flush with the surface of the oil filler hole.

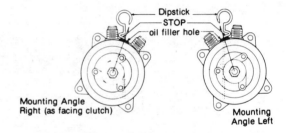

FIGURE 10-101. Mounting angle guide. *Courtesy of Sanden International (USA) Inc.*

4. Remove the dipstick and count the indicated increments of oil.

5. Determine the correct oil level for the mounting angle of the compressor (see Table 10-7).

6. If the increments read on the dipstick do not match the table, add or subtract oil to the mid-range value. For example, if the mounting angle of the SD-508 is 10° and the dipstick increment is 3, add oil in one fluid ounce increments until 7 is read on the dipstick.

TABLE 10-7. Sankyo Oil Level Table.

Mounting Angle/ Degree	Acceptable Oil Level in Increments			
	505	507	508	510
0	4-6	3-5	4-6	2-4
10	6-8	5-7	6-8	4-5
20	8-10	6-8	7-9	5-6
30	10-11	7-9	8-10	6-7
40	11-12	8-10	9-11	7-9
50	12-13	8-10	9-11	9-10
60	12-13	9-11	9-12	10-12
90	15-16	9-11	9-12	12-13

Courtesy of Sanden International (USA) Inc.

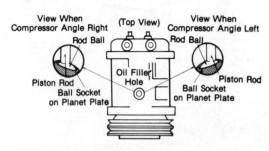

FIGURE 10-100. Positioning internal parts for oil check. *Courtesy of Sanden International (USA) Inc.*

7. Install the oil filler plug. First check to make sure that the sealing O-ring is not twisted. (The seat and O-ring must be clean.) Torque the plug to 6-9 ft. lbs. Do not overtighten the plug to stop a leak. If a leak is present, remove the plug and install a new O-ring.

In most cases it is not necessary to check the oil level as routine maintenance. However, if there is reason to suspect an incorrect oil level or it is specified in a diagnosis procedure to check the oil, follow these steps:

1. Run the compressor for ten minutes at engine idle RPM.

2. Remove all Refrigerant-12 from the system. Be careful not to lose the oil.

3. Proceed with steps 1 through 7 above.

Shaft Turning Smoothness Test (compressor installed). Use the following steps for this procedure:

1. Disconnect the refrigerant hoses.

2. Disengage the clutch.

3. Uncap the fittings.

4. Rotate the compressor using a ¾-inch socket and wrench on the shaft nut.

5. While rotating the compressor, if severe rough spots or "catches" are felt, replace the compressor.

Clutch Test. Use the following steps when testing a clutch:

1. If the field coil wire is broken, replace the field coil (see the Clutch Service section later in this chapter).

2. Check the amperage and the voltage. The amperage range requirement is 3.6 to 4.2 at 12 volts. A very high amperage reading indicates a short within the field coil. No amper-

age reading indicates an open circuit within the field coil. An intermittent or poor system ground results in lower voltage at the clutch. Check for tight fit of coil-retaining snap ring or coil-retaining screws for a good ground. Consult the systems manual to determine proper system ground. Replace the field coil for open or short circuit.

3. Check the air gap. An incorrect air gap could cause erratic engagement or disengagement and/or clutch rattle. Check the air gap with a feeler gauge for 0.016 to 0.031 inch. Adjust based on the Clutch Service section of this chapter.

4. When there is a suspected bearing noise, remove the compressor belt and disengage the clutch. Rotate the pulley by hand and listen for bearing noise. Feel for hard spots; if excessive, replace rotor pulley and clutch front plate assembly or bearing set.

Unusual Noise. When the compressor mounting components are suspected, check for:

- Loose belts—torque to 80 to 90 ft. lbs.

- Broken bracket and/or compressor mounting ear—replace broken component.

- Missing, broken, or loose bolts at the compressor and engine fixing points.

- Flush-fit all points and replace any bracket component not fitting properly. Torque bolts to the engine using the manufacturer's specifications.

- Loose or wobbling crankshaft pulley and center bolt torque and "bottoming"—repair to bracket manufacturer's specifications.

- Rough idler pulley bearing—replace if necessary.

When an engine component is suspected, check for noise in the:

- Alternator bearing
- Air pump (if so equipped)
- Water pump bearing
- Engine valves
- Timing mechanism
- Loose engine mounting bolts.

A 0-5 psig or lower suction pressure due to a low refrigerant charge can cause unusual noise. Restore refrigerant to the proper level. Retest by applying heat to the evaporator by opening the car doors to cause a higher suction pressure.

When the clutch bearing is suspected, refer to the Clutch Test procedures in the preceding section.

Insufficient oil can cause unusual noise. See the Oil Check Procedures section above.

When the valves are suspected of making noise, check for a broken or distorted reed valve or broken gasket.

Valve Plate Test: Valve plate failures (suction or discharge valve or gasket) may be determined with the compressor installed on the car.

To check for discharge or suction valve breakage, run the compressor at idling speed. The compressor will make a "clacking" sound when the valves are defective.

To check for head gasket breakage, run the compressor at idling speed. The discharge pressure will not increase to the normal condition and the suction pressure will be high.

One method of checking the discharge valve and head gasket is the pressure balancing test. Use the following steps when making this test:

1. Connect manifold gauge set to the suction and the discharge service ports.
2. Run the compressor for five minutes at idling speed and stop.
3. Measure the elapsed time that the discharge pressure takes to balance to the suction pressure; if less than two minutes, the discharge valve or the head gasket is broken.

Clutch Service. Generally, all clutch service operations should be performed on the work bench. The service operations described in this section apply to all clutches.

See Figures 10-102, 10-103, 10-104, and 10-105 for differences in belt gauge line between SD-5 compressors.

The clutches for all models include a visible counterweight on the front plate to improve the dynamic balance. The counterweight clutch fits all models which have a controlled compressor shaft keyway so that the counterweight offsets the cam angle. The clutch without the counterweight fits 1979 and prior models.

When removing the clutch, use the following steps:

1. Insert the two pins of the front plate spanner into any two threaded holes of the clutch front plate. Hold the clutch plate stationary. Remove the hex nut with a ¾-inch socket. (See Figure 10-106.)
2. Remove the clutch front plate using the puller (#32416). Align puller center bolt to the compressor shaft. Thumb-tighten the three puller bolts

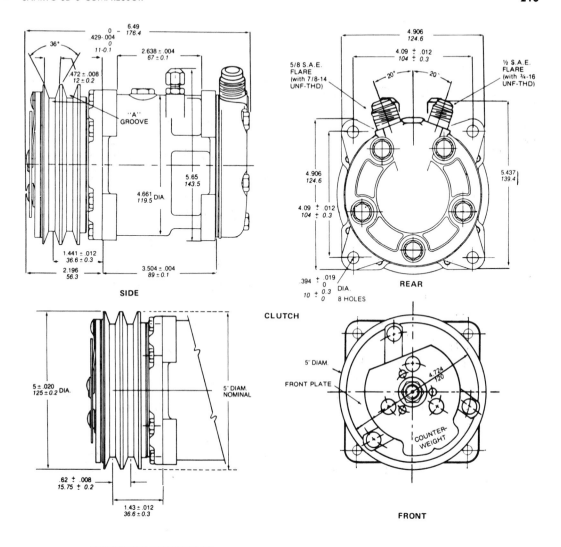

COMPRESSOR SPECIFICATIONS

Bore	1.378 in.	35mm
Stroke	0.711 in.	18.07mm
Displacement per Revolution	5.3 cu. in.	87cc
Number of Cylinders	5	5
Maximum Allowable Continuous RPM		
(Normal operating conditions)	6500	6500
Refrigerant	R-12	R-12
Oil (SUNISO 5GS or Equiv.)	3.4 fl. oz.	100cc
Weight	8.16 lb.	3.7 kg

INCHES IN REGULAR TYPE
METRIC IN ITALIC TYPE

FIGURE 10-102. **Dimensions and physical data SD-505.** *Courtesy of Sanden International (USA) Inc.*

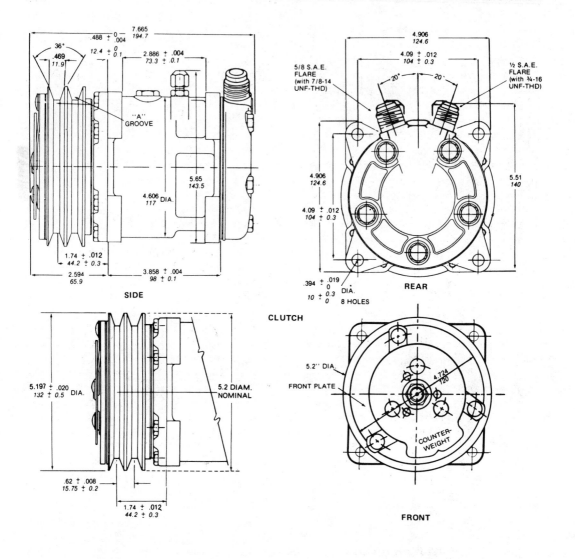

SIDE

CLUTCH

REAR

FRONT

COMPRESSOR SPECIFICATIONS

Bore	1.378 in.	*35mm*
Stroke	.890 in.	*22.6mm*
Displacement per Revolution	6.59	*108cc*
Number of Cylinders	5	*5*
Maximum Allowable Continuous RPM	6,000	*6,000*
(normal operating conditions)		
Refrigerant	R-12	*R-12*
Oil (Suniso 5GS or equiv.)	5 fl. oz.	*150cc*
Weight	9.03	*4.1 kg.*

INCHES IN REGULAR TYPE
METRIC IN ITALIC TYPE

FIGURE 10-103. Dimensions and physical data SD-507. *Courtesy of Sanden International (USA) Inc.*

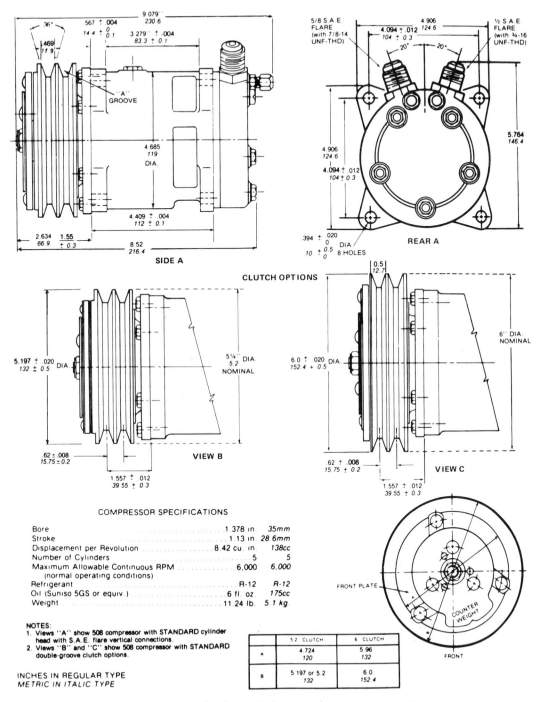

COMPRESSOR SPECIFICATIONS

Bore	1.378 in.	35mm
Stroke	1.13 in.	28.6mm
Displacement per Revolution	8.42 cu. in.	138cc
Number of Cylinders	5	5
Maximum Allowable Continuous RPM (normal operating conditions)	6,000	6,000
Refrigerant	R-12	R-12
Oil (Suniso 5GS or equiv.)	6 fl. oz.	175cc
Weight	11.24 lb.	5.1 kg.

NOTES:
1. Views "A" show 508 compressor with STANDARD cylinder head with S.A.E. flare vertical connections.
2. Views "B" and "C" show 508 compressor with STANDARD double-groove clutch options.

INCHES IN REGULAR TYPE
METRIC IN ITALIC TYPE

	5.2 CLUTCH	6 CLUTCH
A	4.724 / *120*	5.96 / *132*
B	5.197 or 5.2 / *132*	6.0 / *152.4*

FIGURE 10-104. Dimensions and physical data SD-508. *Courtesy of Sanden International (USA) Inc.*

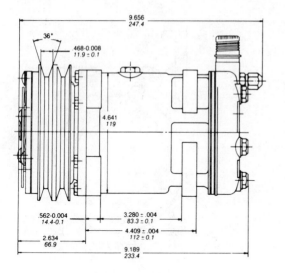

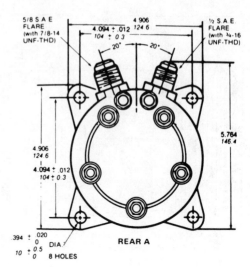

CLUTCH

REAR A

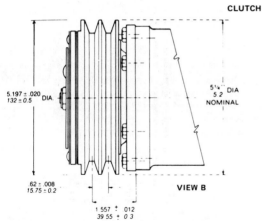

VIEW B

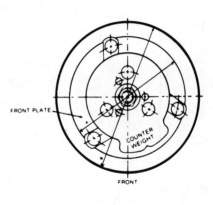

FRONT PLATE

COUNTER WEIGHT

FRONT

INCHES IN REGULAR TYPE
METRIC IN ITALIC TYPE

COMPRESSOR SPECIFICATIONS

Bore	1.417 in.	36mm
Stroke	1.248 in.	31.7mm
Displacement per Revolution	9.825 cu. in.	161cc
Number of Cylinders	5	5
Maximum Allowable Continuous RPM		
(Normal operating conditions)	4000	
Refrigerant	R-12	R-12
Oil (SUNISO 5GS or Equiv.)	4.6 fl. oz.	135cc
Weight	10.36 lb.	4.9 kg.

FIGURE 10-105.   Dimensions and physical data SD-510HD. *Courtesy of Sanden International (USA) Inc.*

FIGURE 10-106. Removing clutch center bolt. *Courtesy of Sanden International (USA) Inc.*

FIGURE 10-108. Removing shaft key. *Courtesy of Sanden International (USA) Inc.*

into the threaded holes. Turn the center bolt clockwise with a ¾-inch socket until the front plate is loosened. (See Figure 10-107.)

NOTE: Steps 1 and 2 must be performed before servicing either the shaft seal or the clutch assembly.

3. Remove the shaft key by lightly tapping it loose with a slot screwdriver and a hammer (see Figure 10-108).

4. Remove the internal bearing snap ring using pinch-type snap ring pliers (see Figure 10-109).

5. Remove the external front housing snap ring using spread-type snap ring pliers (see Figure 10-110).

6. Remove the rotor assembly. Insert the lip of the jaws into the snap ring groove (snap ring removed in step 4). Place rotor puller shaft protector (puller set) over the exposed shaft

FIGURE 10-107. Using clutch front plate puller. *Courtesy of Sanden International (USA) Inc.*

FIGURE 10-109. Removing snap ring. *Courtesy of Sanden International (USA) Inc.*

FIGURE 10-110. Removing front housing snap ring. *Courtesy of Sanden International (USA) Inc.*

FIGURE 10-112. Aligning thumb bolts to puller jaws. *Courtesy of Sanden International (USA) Inc.*

(see Figure 10-111). Align thumb head bolts to puller jaws and finger-tighten (see Figure 10-112). Turn puller center bolt clockwise using ¾-inch socket until rotor pulley is free (see Figures 10-113 and 10-114).

7. Remove the field coil. Loosen the coil lead wire from the clip on top of the compressor front housing (see Figure 10-115). (Earlier models do not have this clip.)

FIGURE 10-113. Tightening center puller bolt. *Courtesy of Sanden International (USA) Inc.*

FIGURE 10-111. Using rotor shaft protector. *Courtesy of Sanden International (USA) Inc.*

FIGURE 10-114. Removing rotor pulley. *Courtesy of Sanden International (USA) Inc.*

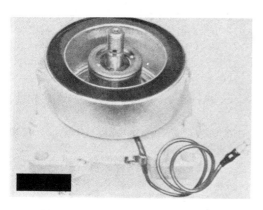

FIGURE 10-115.   Removing field coil. *Courtesy of Sanden International (USA) Inc.*

NOTE: 1979 and later models use a snap ring retainer for the field coil. For 1978 and prior model 508's, remove the fixing screws ($\#10 \times 14$).

8. Using spread-type snap ring pliers, remove snap ring and field coil (see Figure 10-116).

When installing a clutch, use the following steps:

1. Install the field coil (reverse the procedure outlined in step 7 above.) The coil flange protrusion must match the hole in the front housing to prevent coil movement and correctly locate the lead wire.

2. Replace rotor pulley. Support the compressor on the four mounting ears at the compressor rear. If using a vice, clamp only the mounting ear, never on the compressor body (see Figure 10-117). Align the rotor assembly squarely on the front housing hub. Place the ring part of the rotor installer set into the bearing cavity; making certain that the outer edge rests firmly on the rotor bearing outer race. Place the tool set driver into the ring (see Figure 10-118). With a hammer, tap the end of the driver while guiding the rotor to prevent binding. Tap until the rotor bottoms against the compressor front housing hub. Listen for a distinct change of sound during the tapping process. (See Figure 10-119.)

3. Reinstall the internal bearing snap ring with pinch-type pliers.

FIGURE 10-116.   Removing field coil snap ring. *Courtesy of Sanden International (USA) Inc.*

FIGURE 10-117.   Replacing rotor assembly. *Courtesy of Sanden International (USA) Inc.*

FIGURE 10-118. Using rotor installer set.
Courtesy of Sanden International (USA) Inc.

4. Reinstall external front housing snap ring with spread-type pliers.

5. Replace the front plate assembly. First check to see that the original shims are in place on the compressor shaft. Replace the compressor shaft key and align the front plate keyway

to the compressor shaft key. Using a shaft protector, tap the front plate to the shaft until it has bottomed to the clutch shims. Note the distinct sound change. (See Figure 10-120.)

6. Replace shaft hex nut and torque to 25 to 30 ft. lbs.

7. Check the air gap with a feeler gauge (#32437) to 0.016 to 0.031 inch. If the air gap is not consistent around the circumference, lightly pry up at the minimum variations. Lightly tap down at the points of maximum variation. (See Figure 10-121.)

NOTE: The air gap is determined by the spacer shims. When reinstalling or installing a new clutch assembly, try the original shims first. When installing a new clutch onto a compressor that previously did not have a clutch, use 0.040, 0.020, and 0.005 shims from the clutch accessory sack. If the air gap does not meet the specification in step 7, add or subtract shims, repeating steps 5 and 6.

Shaft Seal Service: Use the following steps for shaft seal removal:

FIGURE 10-119. Driving rotor into place.
Courtesy of Sanden International (USA) Inc.

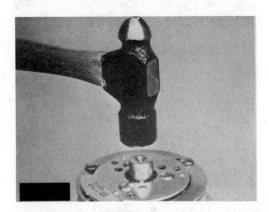

FIGURE 10-120. Using shaft protector. *Courtesy of Sanden International (USA) Inc.*

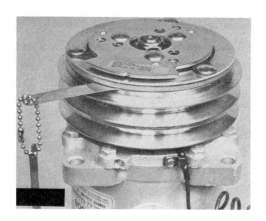

FIGURE 10-121. Checking air gap of clutch rotor. *Courtesy of Sanden International (USA) Inc.*

FIGURE 10-122. Installing retainer ring. *Courtesy of Sanden International (USA) Inc.*

1. Repeat steps 1 and 2 in the Clutch Removal section.

2. Refer to Figures 10-106 and 10-107.

   NOTE: Shaft seal replacement should be done on the work bench. Never use any old parts of the shaft seal assembly—renew the complete assembly. A felt ring and retainer for oil absorption were introduced in the production model year 1978.

3. Using either of the snap ring tools, insert the tool points into the two holes of the felt ring metal retainer and lift out the felt ring (see Figure 10-122).

4. Remove the clutch shims. Use the O-ring hook and a small screwdriver to prevent the shim from binding on the shaft. (See Figure 10-123.)

5. Remove the shaft seal seat retaining snap ring with pinch-type pliers (see Figure 10-124).

6. Remove the shaft seal seat, using tongs (see Figure 10-125). (For SD-

505 and 507 compressors, use tool #32473.)

7. Use the O-ring hook to remove the shaft seal O-ring. Be careful not to scratch the groove. (See Figure 10-126.)

8. Insert the seal remover and installer tool against the seal assembly. Press

FIGURE 10-123. Removing clutch shims. *Courtesy of Sanden International (USA) Inc.*

FIGURE 10-124. Removing shaft seal retaining ring. *Courtesy of Sanden International (USA) Inc.*

FIGURE 10-126. Removing the shaft seal O-ring. *Courtesy of Sanden International (USA) Inc.*

down against the seal spring and twist the tool until it engages in the slots of the seal cage. Lift out the seal assembly. (See Figure 10-127.)

When replacing a shaft seal, use the following steps:

1. Clean the seal cavity thoroughly with R-11 or R-12. First blow out with

dry pressurized vapor, then clean thoroughly with a lint-free or synthetic cloth and clean refrigerant oil. Blow out with dry pressurized vapor again and make certain that all foreign substances are completely removed.

2. Insert the seal sleeve protector over the compressor shaft (see Figure 10-128).

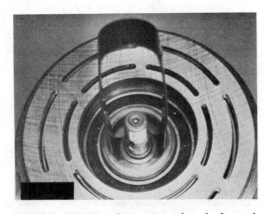

FIGURE 10-125. Removing the shaft seal seat. *Courtesy of Sanden International (USA) Inc.*

FIGURE 10-127. Inserting seal assembly. *Courtesy of Sanden International (USA) Inc.*

FIGURE 10-128.   Inserting seal sleeve protector. *Courtesy of Sanden International (USA) Inc.*

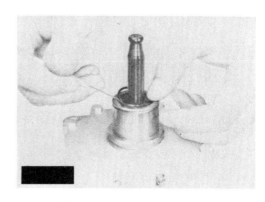

FIGURE 10-130.   Installing new O-ring. *Courtesy of Sanden International (USA) Inc.*

3. Do not touch the new seal lapping surfaces. Dip the mating surfaces in clean refrigeration oil before proceeding.

4. Engage the slots of the seal remover and installer to the new seal cage and insert the seal assembly firmly into place in the compressor seal cavity. Twist the tool in the opposite direction to disengage the removal

tool from the seal cage. (See Figure 10-129.)

5. Coat the new O-ring with clean refrigerant oil. Place carefully in the seal groove with the O-ring hook. Do not scratch the surface. (See Figure 10-130.)

6. Coat the seal retainer with clean refrigerant oil. Use tongs to install. Press lightly against the seal. (See Figure 10-131.)

FIGURE 10-129.   Using seal remover and installer. *Courtesy of Sanden International (USA) Inc.*

FIGURE 10-131.   Installing seal retainer. *Courtesy of Sanden International (USA) Inc.*

7. Reinstall the snap ring. The beveled edge lies outward (away) from the compressor. The flat side lies toward the compressor. It may be necessary to lightly tap the snap ring to securely position it in its groove. (See Figure 10-132.)

8. Tap the new felt ring into place. (See Figure 10-133.)

9. Reinstall the clutch front plate.

Cylinder Head and Valve Plate Service. Use the following steps for cylinder head and valve plate removal:

1. Inspect the cylinder head for fitting or thread damage; discard if damaged. Inspect the two service ports on back of the cylinder head. The valve core can be removed by using the valve core tool. (See Figure 10-134.)

2. The complete service port can be removed with a 14mm wrench. Inspect the service port O-ring (same as the oil filler plug O-ring). Replace if damaged. (See Figure 10-135.)

FIGURE 10-133. Installing felt ring. *Courtesy of Sanden International (USA) Inc.*

3. Remove the five cylinder head cap screws using a 13mm socket (see Figure 10-136).

4. Use a small hammer and the gasket scraper to tap the outer edge of the cylinder head until it frees from the valve plate. Inspect for damage. (The cylinder head gasket normally sticks to the valve plate.) (See Figure 10-137.)

5. Position the gasket scraper between the outside edge of the valve plate and the cylinder block and lightly tap the valve plate loose. Inspect the reed valves and discharge retainer. Discard assembly if any portion is damaged. (See Figure 10-138.)

FIGURE 10-132. Installing snap ring. *Courtesy of Sanden International (USA) Inc.*

FIGURE 10-134. Removing valve core. *Courtesy of Sanden International (USA) Inc.*

FIGURE 10-135. Removing service port.
Courtesy of Sanden International (USA) Inc.

FIGURE 10-138. Removing valve plate.
Courtesy of Sanden International (USA) Inc.

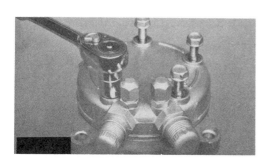

FIGURE 10-136. Removing cylinder head bolts. *Courtesy of Sanden International (USA) Inc.*

6. If the valve plate and/or cylinder head are to be reused, carefully remove the gasket materials using the gasket scraper. Do not damage the cylinder block or the valve plate surfaces. (See Figure 10-139.)

NOTE: The 1979 cylinder head is redesigned with locating pin holes. The cylinder heads will fit prior model compressors, but prior cylinder heads will not fit the later models. The 1979 gasket sets fit all SD-5 compressors, as well as prior models; however, earlier model gasket

FIGURE 10-137. Removing cylinder head.
Courtesy of Sanden International (USA) Inc.

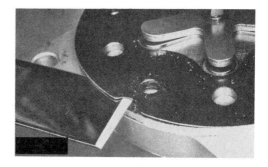

FIGURE 10-139. Removing gasket material.
Courtesy of Sanden International (USA) Inc.

Fig. Ref.	Description	505	507	508	HD-508	HD-510	Part Number
1	Snap Ring-Seal Seat		X	X	X	X	385-0880
1	Snap Ring-Seal Seat	X					9051-0880
2	Seal Kit with felt Ring Std.		X	X	X		385-9830
2	Seal Kit with felt Ring Std.	X					9051-9830
2	Seal Kit with felt Ring Viton					X	472-9830
3	O-Ring for Oil filler plug and Service Ports	X	X	X	X	X	385-0520
4	Oil Filler Plug	X	X	X	X	X	385-0511
5	Gasket Kit Cylinder Head and Valve Plate	X	X	X	X	X	385-9611
6	Valve Plate Assembly w/Gaskets	X	X	X	X	X	385-9623
7	Protective Cap for Suction Port	X	X	X	X	X	384-6330
8	Protective Cap for Discharge Port	X	X	X	X	X	384-6340
	Protective Cap 1"x14 Tube "O" (Not shown)				X		8363-6330
9	Cylinder Head-Flare (Vertical connections) w/Gasket	X	X				351-9631
10	Cylinder Head-Flare (Vertical connections) w/Gasket			X		X	384-9631
	Cylinder Head-(1"x14 Vertical Tube-O w/Gasket) (Not Shown)				X		8476-9631
11	Screw-Flare Cylinder Head	X	X				351-0470
12	Screw-Flare Cylinder Head			X	X	X	384-0471
13	Service Port	X	X	X	X	X	384-0590
14	Service Port Cap	X	X	X	X	X	384-0600
15	Shaft Key		X	X	X	X	385-0122
15	Shaft Key	X					9051-0120
	Compressor Only w/o Clutch	X					0563
	Compressor Only w/o Clutch		X				8357
	Compressor Only w/o Clutch			X			8366
	Compressor Only w/o Clutch					X	1033
	Compressor Only w/o Clutch				X		4763

FIGURE 10-140. Parts list. *Courtesy of Sanden International (USA) Inc.*

sets do not fit the 1979 and later model compressors. See Figure 10-140 for the correct applications and interchangeability; see Figure 10-141 to determine the year model. When installing the cylinder head or valve plate, use the new gaskets in the parts kits.

Use the following steps when replacing the cylinder head only:

1. Reinspect the valve plate for damage and removal of all old gasket material. Coat the valve plate top with clean refrigerant oil. Position the new gasket.

   NOTE: On 1979 models and later, position the gasket over the valve plate locating pins. On all models, align the gasket holes to the oil equalizer and orifice opening.

2. The cylinder head fittings must be pointing up or in line with the oil filler plug. On 1979 models and later; the valve locating pins must be securely in the location holes in the cylinder head. (See Figure 10-142.)

3. Insert the cylinder head cap screws thumb tight. *Very important:* Torque to 22–25 ft. lbs. using a star configuration. (See Figure 10-143.)

Use the following steps when replacing the cylinder head and valve plate:

1. Coat the new valve plate gasket with clean refrigerant oil.

2. Install the valve plate gasket. On 1979 models and later, align the valve plate gasket to the locating pin holes and the oil orifice in the cylinder block. (For easy reference, the gaskets have a notch in the bottom outside edge.)

3. Install the valve plate. On 1979 models and later, with the discharge valve, retainer, and nut pointing away from the cylinder block, align the valve plate locating pin holes in the block and position the valve plate. (See Figure 10-144.)

4. Install the cylinder head (see Figures 10-142 and 10-143).

NOTE: Truck or special applications using refrigerant hoses in excess of 15 total feet for discharge, liquid, and suction need additional oil in the compressor. For these applications, add one fluid ounce of oil for each additional seven feet of refrigerant hose and be sure hose length does not exceed 50 feet.

Compressor Replacement: When replacing a Sankyo compressor containing uncontaminated oil with a new Sankyo compressor, use the following steps:

1. Drain the oil from the compressor.

2. Drain and measure the oil from the old compressor.

3. Measure new oil equal to the amount drained from the old compressor. Add one fluid ounce of new oil to this amount and use it to refill the new compressor.

Should it become necessary to replace any other type compressor with a Sankyo compressor, use the appropriate steps given in the Oil Check Procedures section. Due to the high speed of SD-5 compressors, satisfactory operation depends on sufficient lubrication. However, too much oil will decrease cooling efficiency.

When installing a new compressor, give special attention to the following:

Label (508 shown)

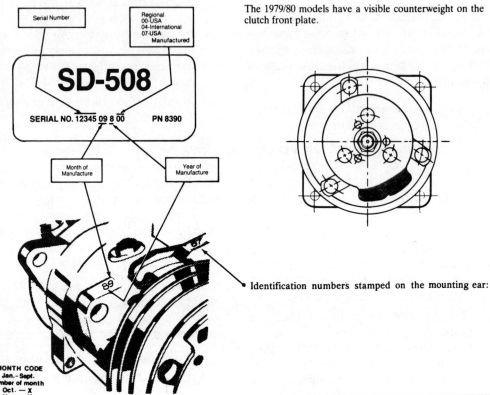

The 1979/80 models have a visible counterweight on the clutch front plate.

Front, left mounting ear viewed as facing clutch.

NOTE: The month and year date code are reversed order as in the label.

Identification numbers stamped on the mounting ear:

Compressor Model	Number
SD-505 (1980 Year Model)	51
SD-507 (1979/80 Year Model)	72
SD-507 (1978 and Prior Year Models)	71 or 7
SD-508 (1979/80 Year Model)	87
SD-508 (1978 and Prior Year Models)	84 (or lower numbers)
SD-510-HD (1980 Year Model)	01

NOTE: Identification numbers 87, 84, 71, 72, 7, 01, and 51 signify standard production specification.

OTHER (Clutch Field Coil)

12VDC Field Coil—Black Lead Wire
24VDC Field Coil—Green Lead Wire

FIGURE 10-141. Compressor identification. *Courtesy of Sanden International (USA) Inc.*

FIGURE 10-142. Installing cylinder head.
Courtesy of Sanden International (USA) Inc.

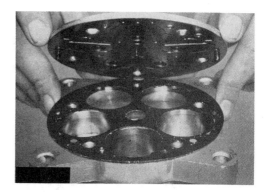

FIGURE 10-144.   Installing valve plate. *Courtesy of Sanden International (USA) Inc.*

1. Correct pulley alignment.
2. Accurate fit of mounting bracket surfaces to the engine and compressor mounting ears.
3. Correct torque of all securing bolts and nuts.
4. Correct tension of the drive belt.

IMPORTANT: Never operate the compressor at fast speed or for a prolonged period of time with an insufficient refrigerant charge.

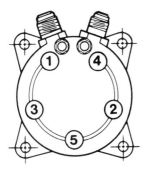

FIGURE 10-143.   Head bolt torque sequence.
Courtesy of Sanden International (USA) Inc.

Flush Procedure: It is advisable to flush the system when replacing a compressor or when a system has been contaminated.

Purging with R-12 vapor or other dry vapor pressure does not provide adequate cleansing—only recommended flushing materials should be used. Some satisfactory materials are available which combine refrigerants, such as R-11 as a liquid cleansing agent with R-12 vapor propellant. The following procedure is a method of using R-11.

NOTE: When flushing with R-11, do not allow it to enter the compressor.

1. Disconnect both hoses at the compressor.
2. Remove and discard the receiver-drier.
3. Connect the R-11 container at the discharge hose connection and allow approximately one pound of R-11 to enter the discharge side of the condenser.
4. Connect a dry vapor container at the same point, preferably using a dry

nitrogen container with the pressure set between 100 and 250 psig. Allow the pressurized vapor to enter until all R-11 is purged out the inlet to the receiver-drier hose connection.

5. Cap both connections.

6. Remove the expansion valve and clean.

7. Using the same procedure as above, flush and purge the liquid hose from the receiver-drier to the expansion valve and suction hose and the evaporator.

NOTE: A flush tool is useful for inserting the R-11 liquid and dry vapor propellant into the hose connections.

REVIEW QUESTIONS

1. What is one of the most important things to be observed when working on a refrigeration system?

2. Why should a system always be evacuated after it has been opened and repairs made?

3. Why should the air conditioning system be checked as soon as possible after an accident?

4. What is the purpose of an expansion tube?

5. Where is the expansion tube placed in the refrigeration system?

6. What is the proper check-out procedure to use when checking for a seized compressor?

7. What is the most economical procedure to use when a GM compressor needs rebuilding?

8. What should be done with the work area, tools, and parts when replacing a compressor shaft seal?

9. Why should the oil be drained and measured when a compressor has been removed from the system?

10. What should be done to the system when foreign material has been found inside it?

11. Why should the compressor shaft never be jarred?

12. When should the compressor shaft seal be replaced?

13. What should be observed about the seal face when replacing a compressor shaft seal?

14. Must the refrigerant be purged from the system when repairing or replacing the superheat switch?

15. What should be done to the thermal fuse on a GM unit when evacuating, charging, or making an analysis of the system?

16. Is it good practice to pry on the compressor shell when adjusting the compressor drive belt?

17. When replacing a shaft seal, is it considered good practice to use some of the old parts in place of new ones?

18. What determines the amount of oil that should be added to a replacement compressor?

19. How can the suction port of a compressor be determined?

20. Should the complete EEVIR unit be removed from the car for servicing?

21. What other component should be replaced when replacing the expansion valve or the POA valve capsule?

22. What precautions should be observed when replacing the VIR assembly?

23. What should be done before removing the expansion valve retaining screw in the VIR unit?

24. Is the Liquid Bleed Line Valve Core identical to the other valve cores used in the GM systems?

25. What type of magnetic clutch is used on Chrysler air conditioning units?

26. What should be done to a new seal before placing it in the compressor cavity?

27. Is the ETR valve used on Chrysler units electrically or pressure operated?

28. What precaution should be observed when replacing a rotating coil type of magnetic clutch?

29. What is the only recommended field repair for Nippondenso, Chrysler, and Ford compressors?

30. What type of lubricating system does the Sankyo SD-508 compressor use?

The heating systems used in automotive units are just as varied as the types of air-conditioning units used. To make a detailed description of every single unit would take many volumes of information, which would not be practical in a manual of this type. Therefore, we will limit our discussion to the general types used in American Motors, Chrysler Corporation, and Ford Motor Company automobiles.

AMERICAN MOTORS UNIT DESCRIPTION

This manufacturer uses a blend-air type of heater on all their models. This type of heating unit uses a full flow of engine coolant through the heating core at all times. The temperature of the air entering the passenger compartment is controlled by changing the amount of air that will flow through the heater core in relation to the amount of air that bypasses the core. The air that passes through the core is mixed with the air that bypasses the core and is therefore cooled to the desired temperature (see Figure 11-1).

Fresh Air Ventilation. Ventilation with fresh air is accomplished by the use of a two-cable-operated fresh air vent system located in the front of the passenger compartment. Each vent has its own control and is operated independently of the other vent.

Heater Operation. The control panel located in the dash of the car consists of a temperature control lever, a mode control lever, and a blower speed switch (see Figure 11-2).

The air control lever must be positioned in the HEAT position for the air to enter the passenger compartment through the heater duct system. When it is

——— 11 ———

Automotive Heating Systems

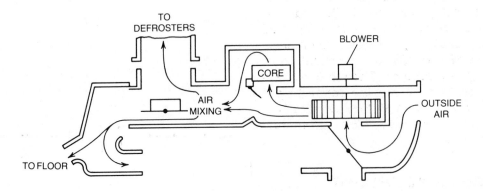

FIGURE 11-1. **Mixing bypass air with heated air.**

located in the HI–LO position, air is allowed to flow through both the floor ducts and the windshield ducts. When a larger volume of air is desired, the blower may be operated in one of the three blower speed positions.

Defroster Operation. When defrosting of the windshield is required, warmer air

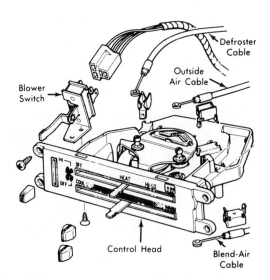

FIGURE 11-2. **Heater control head.** *Courtesy of American Motors Corp.*

can be applied to the windshield by moving the temperature control lever to the full heating position. The defrosting action may be sped up by operating the blower in one of the three speeds indicated on the switch.

The defrosting action is accomplished by placing the air control lever in the DEF position. In this manner, the defrost door is positioned so as to direct the heated air through the defroster duct system and through the defroster outlets. If the air control lever is placed in the HI–LO position, the air will be directed through both the defroster outlets and the floor outlets.

Adjusting the Blend Air Damper Door Cable. The later-model units are equipped with a self-adjusting clip. This clip is located on the blend air door crank arm. It is accessible at the rear of the package tray (if the car has one) and is adjacent to the right air outlet.

NOTE: Make certain that the cable is installed with the colored tape centered in the clamp that is attached to the housing.

Use the following steps when making adjustments on the air damper door cable:

1. While holding the temperature control lever in the WARM position, place the blend air door at the extreme right end of its travel (the full heat position).

2. Move the self-adjusting clip along the control cable wire about ½ in. This operation is moving the crank arm toward the control panel.

3. Next, move the temperature control lever from the WARM to the COLD position. Allow the control cable to slip through the self-adjusting clip to the correct location.

4. Check the operation of the control cable.

Adjusting the Heater Air and Defroster Damper Door Cable. The air control lever controls the heater air and defroster door operation. It uses a single cable, which is equipped with a self-adjusting clip. This clip is located on the cable wire at the heater–defroster door crank arm. It is accessible just above the left-hand floor heater air outlet.

NOTE: Make certain that the cable is installed with the colored tape centered in the clamp that is attached to the housing.

Use the following steps when making this adjustment:

1. Place the air control lever in the OFF position. Move the heater–defroster door crank arm to the full heat position.

2. Slide the self-adjusting clip along the control cable wire ½ in. while moving

the crank arm toward the cable clamp.

3. Place the air control lever in the DEF position. Allow the cable wire to pass through the self-adjusting clip to the correct location.

4. Check the operation of the lever and the door.

Adjusting the Outside Air Door Cable. Operation of the outside air door is obtained by using the air control lever, which uses a single cable and a self-adjusting clip. The clip is located at the outside air door crank arm and is accessible by removing the glove box from the dash.

NOTE: Make certain that the cable is installed with the colored tape centered in the clamp that is attached to the housing.

When making adjustments on this cable, use the following steps:

1. Place the control lever in the OFF position. Move the crank arm to the extreme left-hand position. Slide the self-adjusting clip away from the cable clamp about ½ in.

2. Place the control lever in the HEAT position. Allow the cable wire to slip through the self-adjusting clip.

3. Check the operation of the outside air door cable.

Blower Motor and Fan Replacement. The blower motor and fan are accessible and may be removed through the engine compartment. Use the following procedure when replacing the blower motor and fan assembly:

1. Disconnect the wires from the blower motor and remove the holding nuts. Remove the blower motor and fan assembly from the housing. Remove the blower wheel from the motor shaft and remove the motor attaching nuts.

2. Install the blower wheel on the shaft of the new motor leaving a clearance of 0.350 in. between the fan and the mounting plate for maximum air output. The retainer clip ears must be positioned over the flat surface on the motor shaft (see Figures 11-3 and 11-4).

Control Head Replacement. Use the following procedure when replacing the control head:

1. Disconnect the negative battery cable from the battery. Remove the screws holding the center panel on the instrument panel, which are located inside the glove box.

2. Remove the screws and the nut holding the ash tray, the radio knobs, and the attaching nuts. Remove the center housing. Remove the screws

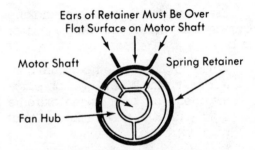

FIGURE 11-4. Blower fan retainer replacement. *Courtesy of American Motors Corp.*

holding the control head. Disconnect the cables from the control levers and remove the control head. When reinstalling the control head, make certain that the colored tape on the control cables is in the center of the clips fastened to the control head.

Heater Core and Blower Housing Replacement. Use the following steps when replacing the heater core and blower housing:

1. Disconnect the negative battery cable. Drain about 2 quarts of coolant from the car's cooling system. Disconnect the heater hoses from the heater core and plug the core tubes. Remove the blower motor and fan assembly. Remove the housing attaching nuts located in the engine compartment close to the blower motor. Remove the package tray (if equipped) and disconnect the wire at the blower motor resistor.

2. Snap open the cover on the right side of the plenum chamber. Remove the wiring harness and tape it to the plenum chamber. Disconnect the heater, defroster, and the blend-air cables from the housing. Remove the

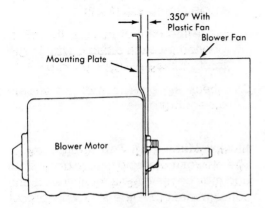

FIGURE 11-3. Blower mounting plate clearance. *Courtesy of American Motors Corp.*

door sill plate and the right-side cowling trim panel. Remove the right-side windshield pillar molding, the instrument panel upper fastening screws, and the screw attaching the instrument panel to the right-hand door post.

3. Remove the screws holding the housing and pull the right side of the instrument panel slightly forward while removing the housing. Remove the cover and screws holding the heater core to the housing. Remove the core from the housing. To install the new unit, reverse the preceding procedure. Make certain that the heater core seals are in their proper position to prevent any air leakage around the outside of the heater core.

Troubleshooting and System Diagnosis. Information on troubleshooting or making system diagnosis on these units is given in Table 11-1.

Heater Wiring Diagram. Refer to the wiring diagram in Figure 11-5 when

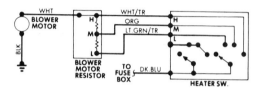

FIGURE 11-5.   Heater wiring diagram. *Courtesy of American Motors Corp.*

making electrical connections on these units.

CHRYSLER CORPORATION HEATING UNITS

All Chrysler Corporation units use the blend-air-type heating unit. The outside air enters the heating unit through the cowling grill. It then passes through the plenum chamber, and then into the heater core. The temperature control door, located in the plenum chamber, directs the entering air in one of two directions: through the heater core, or past the heater core. The amount of air mixing, or blending, is determined by the

TABLE 11.1   Troubleshooting and Diagnosis

Condition and Possible Cause	Condition and Possible Cause

Little or no air from heater floor outlets
    Misadjusted heater air door cable
    Obstructed heater housing or ducts
    Clogged heater core fins
    Leaking air duct seals
	Heat output when controls are off
	    Outside air door cable misadjusted
	    Outside air door binding in housing

Little or no air from defroster outlets
    Defroster duct misaligned
    Defroster cable incorrectly adjusted
    Leaking air duct seals
	Not enough heat with controls fully on
	    Low coolant or plugged heater core
	    Incorrect thermostat
	    Incorrect adjustment of cables
	    Heater system air leaks

(Courtesy of American Motors Corp.)

setting of the temperature control lever located on the control panel. The heater–defroster lever controls the direction of the blended air. A blower switch is also located on the control panel.

Control Systems: Cordoba, Diplomat, Gran Fury, Mirada, and New Yorker. Push-button controls are used on these models to select routing of the vacuum to all the operating doors used in the system, except the blend air door (see Figure 11-6). The heater valve and the blend air door are operated by the temperature lever, without use of the vacuum push buttons on the control panel. The blower motor does not oper-

ate when the OFF push button is pushed in (see Table 11-2).

Control Systems: Aries, Horizon, LeBaron, Omni, Reliant, and 400. On these models, lever and cable controls are used to operate the heating unit. One cable is used to operate the heater mode door, while another is used to operate the blend air door.

Heater Cable Adjustment. The temperature and mode control cables are fastened to the heater control by color-coded, T-shaped, snap-in flags. The red flag denotes the temperature cable and the yellow, larger flag denotes the mode control cable. The control cables are

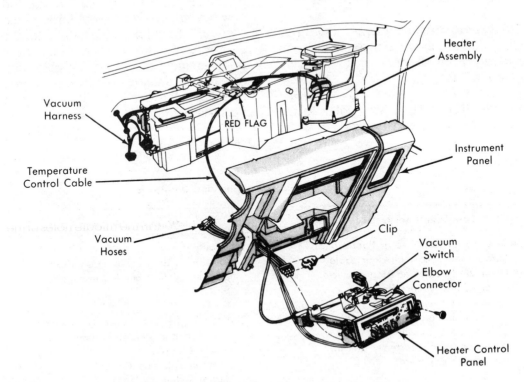

FIGURE 11-6. Heater assembly and control cable routing (Cordoba, Diplomat, Gran Fury, Mirada, and New Yorker). *Courtesy of Chrysler Corp.*

TABLE 11-2. Vacuum Control Chart

Mode	Off	Bilevel	Heat	Defrost
Inlet air door to	Inside	Outside	Outside	Outside
Heat Hi-Lo Door to	Bilevel	Bilevel	Heat	Heat
Heat-Defrost Door to	Heat	Heat	Heat	Defrost
Water valve	*	*	*	*
Blower	Off	On**	On**	On**

Courtesy of Chrysler Corp.

*Off when temperature lever is in cool position.

**4 Speeds

fastened to the heating unit assembly by use of a ribbed, snap-in flag. The rib gives the necessary installation orientation and retention. The flag may be removed from the cable only after the tab has been depressed into the proper receiver.

Heater Cable Adjustment: Cordoba, Diplomat, Gran Fury, Mirada, and New Yorker

NOTE: The top panel cover, center air duct, and the heater control panel must be removed in order to make any adjustments on the temperature control cable.

To adjust the temperature cable on these models, use the following procedures:

1. Position the self-adjusting clip on the core wire 2 in. from the loop on the heater assembly end of the wire. Pry the clip into the locked position (see Figure 11-7). Be certain that the cable is routed through the plastic cable clamp on the brake support bracket and over the steering column and then to the control panel (see Figure 11-8).

2. The flag on the cable is now connected to the receiver on the heater assembly, and the cable is fastened to the control panel. Install the control panel on the instrument panel. Position the temperature control lever all the way to the right to adjust the temperature control cable.

3. Install the center air duct and the top panel cover on the unit.

Heater Cable Adjustment: Aries, Horizon, LeBaron, Omni, Reliant, and 400. To adjust the temperature cable on these models, use the following procedures:

1. Twist the self-adjusting clip into position at a point 2 in. from the heater end of the cable core wire. Route the cable through the middle holes of the

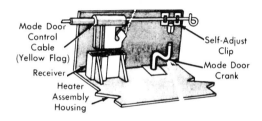

Mode Door Control Cable (Yellow Flag)

Receiver

Heater Assembly Housing

Self-Adjust Clip

Mode Door Crank

FIGURE 11-7.   Control cable mounting. *Courtesy of Chrysler Corp.*

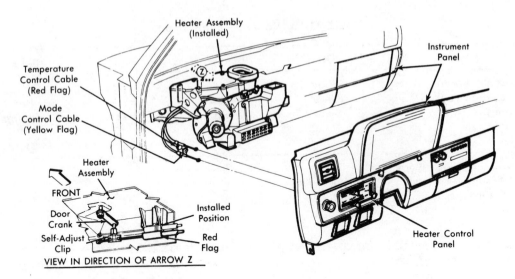

FIGURE 11-8. **Heater assembly and control cable routing (Horizon and Omni).** *Courtesy of Chrysler Corp.*

brake support bracket, then in front of and around the main wiring harness.

2. Line the door crank pin up with the clip, and at the same time seat the cable flag into the retainer. Place the clip over the crank pin (see Figure 11-9).

3. Locate the temperature control lever in the COOL position. Fasten the

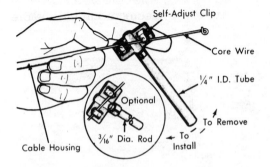

FIGURE 11-9. **Self-adjust clip removal and installation.** *Courtesy of Chrysler Corp.*

cable core wire to the control lever pin. Snap the cable housing into the retaining clip.

4. If the control panel has been removed, replace it at this time.

5. Adjust the cable by placing the control lever in the WARM position. Make certain that it touches the right edge of the bezel slot.

Mode Door Cable Adjustment. Use the following procedures when adjusting the mode door cable:

1. Twist the self-adjusting clip into position at a point 2 in. from the small loop at the heater end of the core wire (see Figure 11-9). Route the cable through the small holes in the brake support bracket, then in front of and around the main wiring harness (see Figure 11-10).

2. Line up the crank door pin with the clip. At the same time, seat the cable

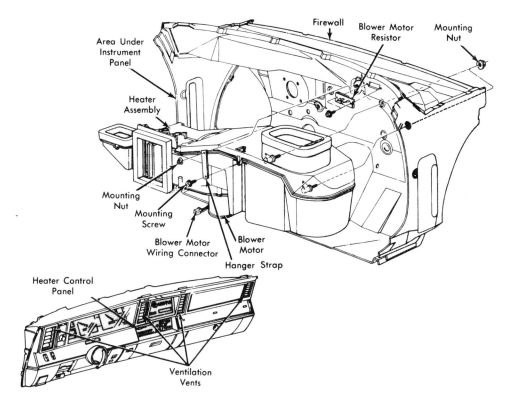

FIGURE 11-10. Heater assembly (Aries, LeBaron, Reliant, and 400).
Courtesy of Chrysler Corp.

flag in the retainer and place the clip over the crank pin.

3. Move the mode control lever to the OFF position. Connect the cable core wire to the control lever pin. Snap the cable housing into the retaining clip.

4. If the control panel was removed, replace it at this time.

5. Adjust the cable by placing the control lever in the DEFROST position. Make certain that it touches the right edge of the bezel slot.

Testing the Vacuum Control System: Cordoba, Diplomat, Gran Fury, Mirada,

and New Yorker. A proper test of the push-button-operated control will determine whether or not there is proper connection and functioning of the vacuum and the electrical circuits. Before attempting to make this test, make certain that the main vacuum source hose is tight on the engine intake manifold connection. When there is a low vacuum source, it is possible that the system will function properly at low engine speeds, and malfunction when the engine is operating at a higher speed. To make the following tests, regulate the vacuum source to a steady 8 in. of mercury (Hg); then test as follows:

NOTE: When the vacuum lines are to be serviced or rerouted, use only nylon tape. The adhesive used on vinyl electrical tape will cause the vacuum lines to deteriorate.

1. Disconnect the vacuum source from the engine. Connect a vacuum tester to the hose leading to the control switch. Push the HEAT button to obtain a reading on the vacuum gauge. The vacuum gauge reading should drop until the actuator has completed its operation. The vacuum reading should be 8 in. of mercury (Hg) at the start and should drop to about 7¼ in. while the actuator is operating, and then return to 8 in. The maximum vacuum loss is ¾ in. (Hg). The vacuum storage tank should be bypassed during this test.

2. Repeat the test by pushing the OFF, HI-LO, DEFROST, and HEAT buttons. If there is more than ¾-in. loss, recheck the tester for an 8-in. reading; then check the fit of the number 7 hole hose connector plug on the heater control switch.

    NOTE: Do not use any type of lubricant on the switch holes or ports in the plug because of possible damage to the vacuum valve located inside the switch. To aid in positioning the plug on the switch ports, use a drop or two of clean water on the connector plug holes.

3. If the vacuum drop is now within the prescribed limits, proceed to make the overall performance test. Should the vacuum drop still bypass the ¾-in. limit, remove the port 7 connector from the switch and seal port 3 with your finger to block the vacuum source hose. Insert the vacuum source

alternately into each of the connector holes, except number 3. If the vacuum gauge reading should return to 8 in. after each of the actuators has operated, the control is leaking and must be replaced before the unit will function as it was designed.

4. Should there be an excessive vacuum drop at one or more of the connection holes in the connector block, isolate the faulty hose or the faulty actuator. Even though a vacuum drop of ¾ in. or more would not significantly affect operation of the engine, it could possibly prevent the proper operation of the heating system at high-speed operation or during engine acceleration.

5. Repair any leaks found in the vacuum lines by removing the leaking section and replacing it with either a new hose or some other suitable replacement hose or fitting.

Replacement of the Heater Core: Cordoba and Mirada. When replacing the heater core on these models, use the following procedures:

1. Disconnect the battery cable and drain the engine coolant from the radiator. Disconnect the water hoses from the heater core and plug the tubes to prevent water leaking into the interior of the car. Next, disconnect the vacuum lines from the water valve and the manifold T. Push the rubber grommet and the vacuum lines through the dash panel. Remove the four nuts that are holding the heater to the dash panel.

2. Slide the seat to the rear as far as possible and remove the console, if the car is so equipped. Next, remove

the glove box assembly, the ash tray, and housing assembly. Remove the lower right trim panel, the right cowling trim pad, and the top panel cover.

3. Disconnect the blower motor feed and ground wires. Remove the center air-distribution duct. Next disconnect the vacuum harness from the extension harness connector.

4. Depress the tab holding the flag on the temperature control cable and remove it from the receiver holding it on the heater housing. Remove the heater air-distribution housing and pull the assembly back and rotate it to the right to clear the discharge air plenum mounting brace. Remove the complete assembly.

5. Place the heater assembly on a workbench and remove the top cover. Remove the core to housing retaining screw. Remove the heater core from the housing. When replacing the core, reverse the above procedure.

Replacement of the Heater Core: Diplomat, Gran Fury, and New Yorker. When replacing the heater core on these models, use the following procedures:

1. Disconnect the battery cable and drain the radiator coolant. Disconnect the water hoses from the heater core and plug the tubes to prevent water leaking into the interior of the car. Disconnect the vacuum lines from the water valve and the manifold T. Push the rubber grommet and the vacuum lines through the dash panel. Remove all four of the nuts that are holding the heater to the dash panel.

2. Slide the seat as far to the rear as is possible and remove the console, if

so equipped. Remove the cluster bezel assembly, the instrument panel upper cover, the steering column cover, and the right intermediate-side cowling trim panel.

3. Next, remove the lower instrument panel; then remove the reinforcement between the lower and the center instrument panel. Disconnect the locking tab and remove the right center air-distribution duct.

4. Disconnect the blower motor feed and ground wires.

5. Remove the heat distribution housing. Depress the tab holding the flag on the temperature control cable, and remove the cable from the receiver on the heater core housing. While supporting the heater assembly, remove the discharge air plenum mounting brace. Pull the heater assembly back and rotate it to the right. Remove the heater assembly from under the dash.

6. Place the heater assembly on a workbench and remove the top cover. Remove the core to housing retaining screw and remove the core from the housing. To install the heater assembly, reverse the above procedure.

Replacing the Heater Core: Aries, LeBaron, Reliant, and 400. When replacing the heater core on these models, use the following procedures:

1. Disconnect the battery negative terminal and drain the engine coolant from the radiator. Disconnect the blower motor wiring connector. Reaching under the heater assembly, depress the tabs on the mode door and the temperature control cables. Pull the flags from their receivers.

Remove the self-adjusting clip from the door crank arms.

2. Disconnect the heater water hoses on the engine side of the fire wall. Plug the water hoses and the core tubes to prevent water leaking from these points. Remove the glove box assembly. Remove the hanger strap to heater assembly screw by reaching through the glove box opening. Remove the two heater assembly attaching nuts from inside the engine compartment.

3. Pull the instrument panel outward just enough to allow the heater assembly to be removed. Remove the heater assembly. To install the heater assembly, reverse the above procedure.

Heater Core Replacement: Horizon and Omni. When replacing the heater core on these models, use the following procedures:

1. Disconnect the battery negative cable and drain the engine coolant from the radiator. Disconnect the blower motor wiring connector. Remove the ash tray and holder assembly.

2. Depress the tabs on the temperature control cable flag. Remove the cable from the receiver on the heater assembly. Remove the glove box assembly. Disconnect the heater water hoses, and plug the hoses and the core tubes to prevent water leaking into the interior of the car.

3. Remove the two nuts holding the heater assembly to the firewall from inside the engine compartment. Remove the wire connector from the blower motor and resistor block. Disconnect the heater assembly brace.

4. Remove the heater support bracket nut. Disconnect the strap from the stud in the discharge air plenum. Lower the heater assembly from under the dash just enough to reach the mode door control cable. Depress the tab on the flag and pull the mode door control cable out of its receiver on the heater assembly.

5. Move the heater assembly toward the right side of the car. Then lower the assembly from under the instrument panel. To install the heater assembly, reverse the above procedures.

Blower Motor Replacement: Cordoba, Diplomat, Gran Fury, Mirada, and New Yorker. When replacing the blower motor on these models, use the following procedures:

1. Disconnect the battery negative terminal. Disconnect the blower motor feed and ground wires.

2. Remove the screws holding the blower motor to the heater assembly. Remove the blower motor. To install the blower motor, reverse the above procedures.

Blower Motor Replacement: Aries, Horizon, LeBaron, Omni, Reliant, and 400. When replacing the blower motor on these models, use the following procedures:

1. Disconnect the battery negative terminal. Disconnect the blower motor wiring connector.

2. When Horizon and Omni models are considered, remove the left heater air outlet duct mounting screws and remove the duct.

3. On all these models, remove the five screws holding the blower motor to the heater assembly. Remove the blower motor and fan assembly. When removing the fan wheel from the motor shaft, remove the retaining clamp from the motor shaft and remove the fan wheel.

4. On Aries, LeBaron, Reliant, and 400 models, remove the two nuts holding the plate to the blower motor and remove the plate. To assemble and install the blower motor assembly, reverse the above procedures.

Control Head Replacement: Cordoba, Diplomat, Gran Fury, Mirada, and New Yorker.

When replacing the control head on these models, use the following procedure:

Disconnect the negative battery terminal. Remove the screws from the center bezel and remove the bezel. Remove the control head screws and pull the control head forward. Disconnect the cables, vacuum lines, and the electrical wiring. Remove the control head. To install the control head, reverse the above procedures and adjust the cables (see Figure 11-11).

Control Head Replacement: Horizon and Omni.

When replacing the control head on these models, use the following procedures:

Disconnect the negative battery terminal. While reaching under the left side of the instrument panel, press the head light knob release button while pulling the knob outward. Remove the four screws and the left bezel. Remove the control mounting screws and pull the control head

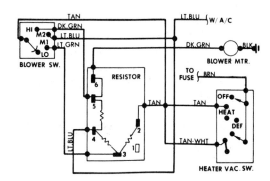

FIGURE 11-11. Heater wiring diagram (Cordoba, Diplomat, Gran Fury, Mirada, and New Yorker). *Courtesy of Chrysler Corp.*

out. Disconnect the cables and wiring and remove the head. To install the control head, reverse the above procedures and adjust the control cables (see Figure 11-12).

Control Head Replacement: Aries, LeBaron, Reliant and 400.

When replacing the control head on these models, use the following procedures:

Remove the negative battery terminal. Remove the two screws holding the heater control bezel to the heater control. Remove the bezel by rolling it out and lifting upward to free the bezel locking tabs. Remove the two heater control screws and slide the control outward enough so that the

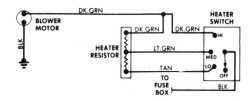

FIGURE 11-12. Heater wiring diagram (Aries, Horizon, LeBaron, Omni, Reliant, and 400). *Courtesy of Chrysler Corp.*

control cables and the electrical connector can be disconnected. Remove the heater control from the panel. To install the heater control, reverse the above procedures (see Figure 11-13).

Troubleshooting and Diagnosis. Use Table 11-3 when troubleshooting these systems.

FORD MOTOR COMPANY HEATING UNITS

All the heating systems used on Ford Motor Company cars are of the blend-air type. In these units, outside air is drawn into the blower housing and is directed either through or around the heater core, and is mixed in the discharge air plenum and then discharged through the de-

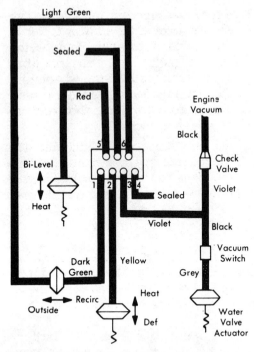

FIGURE 11-13.   Heater vacuum circuits (push-button controls). *Courtesy of Chrysler Corp.*

TABLE 11-3.   Troubleshooting and Diagnosis

Conditions and Possible Causes	Conditions and Possible Causes
Insufficient Heat	Blower Inoperative
Obstructed outlets	Fuse blown
Temperature door binding	Motor stalled
Temperature door misadjusted	Ground wire faulty
Kinked or unattached temperature control cable	Motor continuity problem
Mode door binding or improperly adjusted	Resistor continuity problem
Mode door cable unattached (Aries, Horizon, LeBaron, Omni, and Reliant models)	Blower switch problems
Defective mode door actuator (Cordoba, Diplomat, Gran Fury, Mirada, and New Yorker models)	
Defective push-button switch (Cordoba, Diplomat, Gran Fury, Mirada, and New Yorker models)	Blower operates on high only
Kinked or plugged heater hoses	Fuse blown
Heater core plugged	Short in wiring
Defective water valve	Resistor block defective
Engine temperature low	Blower switch defective

Courtesy of Chrysler Corp.

froster outlets, vent registers, or the floor outlet ducts.

The temperature of the discharge air is determined by a temperature blend door, which is controlled by a lever located on the control panel. The positioning of the blend door determines what percentage of outside air passes through the heater core and what percentage bypasses the heater core and is then mixed in the discharge air plenum. The discharge air delivery is directed by the various doors to maintain the desired mode of operation. These doors may be operated by either a cable or a vacuum-

controlled motor. However, the cables and motors are controlled, in all cases, by either a functional lever or a temperature lever located on the control panel (see Figure 11-14).

Heating System Components: Ford and Mercury. The heater control assembly on these cars is made up of a functional lever, a temperature lever, a vacuum selector valve, and a blower switch. On models having a rear window defogger, the switch is included in the control assembly. Outside air ventilation is obtained by setting the temperature lever

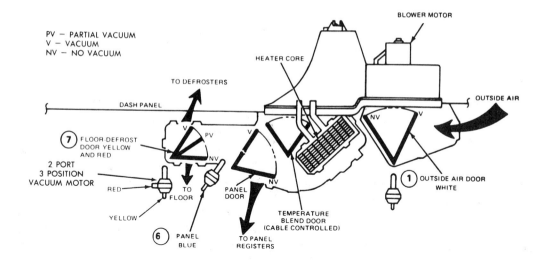

Ford and Mercury Heater System Vacuum Motor Test Chart				
FUNCTION CONTROL LEVER POSITION	VACUUM MOTORS APPLIED WITH VACUUM			
		PANEL	FLOOR	
	OUTSIDE	FULL	FULL	PARTIAL
OFF	1	—	7	7
VENT	—	6b	7	7
FLOOR	—	—	7	7
MIX	—	—	—	7
DEFROST	—	—	—	—
VACUUM LINE COLOR CODE	WHITE	BLUE	RED	YELLOW

— No Vacuum

FIGURE 11-14. Heater and air flow function (Ford and Mercury). *Courtesy Ford Motor Co.*

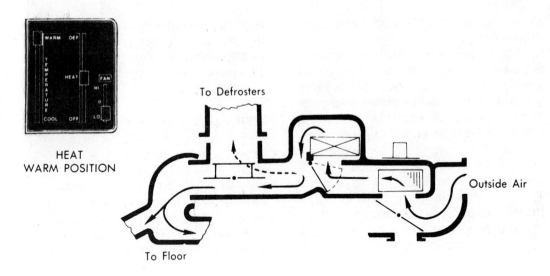

To Defrosters

Outside Air

To Floor

HEAT
WARM POSITION

FIGURE 11-15. Heater air flow and function (Capri, Cougar, Escort, Fairmont, Granada, Lynx, Mustang, and Zephyr). *Courtesy of Ford Motor Co.*

to the COOL position and the functional lever at the VENT position. The blower speed may be selected or it may be left off.

Heating System Components: Thunderbird and XR7. On these models the temperature control lever is connected by a cable to the temperature blend door. The functional lever operates the system on–off switch and is connected by a vacuum hose to all mode doors. The blower motor speed is controlled by a four-position blower switch.

Heating System Components: Capri, Cougar, Escort, EXP, Fairmont, Granada, LN7, Lynx, Mustang, and Zephyr. On these models, the control panel consists of a temperature lever, a functional lever, and a three-position blower switch. The temperature control lever is con-

nected to the temperature blend door by a cable. The functional lever is connected to the heat–defrost door by a cable and operates the system on–off switch. The three-speed blower switch controls the blower speed (see Figure 11-15).

Heater Control Operation: Ford and Mercury. When checking the operation of one of these units, refer to Figures 11-16, 11-17, or 11-18 depending on which car is in question. The discharge air temperature from these units is controlled by a temperature control lever, which determines the position of the blend air door in the heating system. The functional control lever interrupts the electrical power to the blower motor when placed in the off position. It also controls the direction of the air flow through the system by placing the actuating doors and valves in the different positions. The

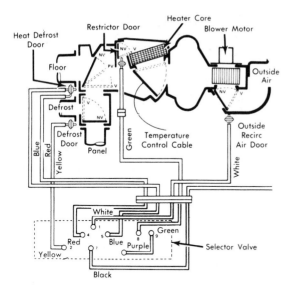

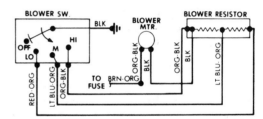

FIGURE 11-18. Heater system wiring diagram (All except Ford, Mercury, Thunderbird, and XR7). *Courtesy of Ford Motor Co.*

FIGURE 11-16. Heater function vacuum diagram (Thunderbird and XR7). *Courtesy of Ford Motor Co.*

modes of operation for these units are as follows:

Off Mode. The blower motor is turned off, and the outside air door is fully closed and has full vacuum applied to its controls. The panel doors are in the no-vacuum position, which allows air to flow

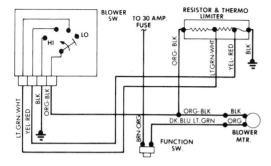

FIGURE 11-17. Heater system wiring diagram (Ford, Mercury, Thunderbird, and XR7). *Courtesy of Ford Motor Co.*

to the registers. The floor-defrost door is in the vacuum position, which allows air to flow freely to the floor vent.

VENT Mode. The blower motor is turned on. The outside air doors are fully open. The partial and full panel doors are in the vacuum position and are distributing air to the panel registers. The floor-defrost door is in the vacuum position, allowing small amounts of air to be directed to the floor air outlets.

FLOOR Mode. The flow of air is directed to the floor outlets, while a small amount is being directed to the defroster. There is no vacuum on the panel door, and the air flow is stopped in this direction.

MIX Mode. This position is similar to the VENT position with the following exception: The air flow is divided between the floor outlets and the defroster outlets.

DEFROST Mode. The panel and floor-defrost doors have no vacuum applied and all the incoming air is directed to the defroster outlets. A small amount is being directed toward the floor in the form of bleed air.

Heating Unit Control Operation: All except Ford and Mercury. The modes of operation for these units are as follows:

OFF Mode. The blower motor is turned off. The heat–defrost door is in the closed position, and there is no flow of air through the system. When the functional control lever is moved approximately ½ in. from the OFF position, the electrical circuit to the blower motor is closed, and the blower motor will run at the speed setting of the blower switch.

HEAT Mode. The heat–defrost door changes position to cause the air to be discharged to the floor area.

DEFROST Mode. The heat–defrost door is positioned so as to cause the air to be directed to the defroster nozzles. The flow of air may be divided between the defrost nozzles and the heater outlets by placing the functional control lever in the desired position.

Control Cable Adjustments: All Models. To adjust the control cables, use the following procedures:

1. The temperature control cable and the functional control cable self-adjust when the levers are moved all the way to the end of their slots. The only adjustment required is when a new cable has been installed. Preset the cable adjustment by inserting a small screwdriver in the loop on the crank arm end of the cable before self-adjusting the cable. Then slide the self-adjusting clip so that it is 1 in. from the loop (see Figure 11-19).

2. When the cable has been installed, move the lever to either the WARM or the DEF position to position the self-

adjusting clip. Check the unit for proper operation, and make any adjustments required.

Heater Core Replacement: Ford and Mercury. When replacing the heater core on these models, use the following procedures:

1. Disconnect the battery negative terminal. Drain the engine coolant from the radiator. Remove the heater water hoses from the heater core tubes. Plug the tubes and the hoses to prevent water leaking into the interior of the car. Remove the vacuum hose from the source of vacuum. Push the grommet and water hose into the passenger compartment.

2. Remove the temperature control cable housing from the top of the plenum. Remove the cable from the blend air door crank arm. Remove the vacuum jumper harness at the multiple connector. Remove the white vacuum hose from the outside air door vacuum motor.

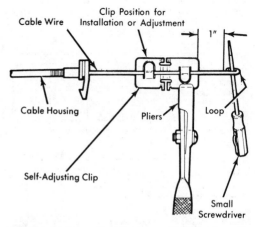

FIGURE 11-19. Positioning self-adjusting clip on cable. *Courtesy of Ford Motor Co.*

3. Remove the bolt below the windshield wiper motor that is holding the left end of the air plenum to the dash (see Figure 11-20). Remove the nut holding the upper left corner of the heater case to the dash.

4. Remove the glove compartment and the right-side cowling trim panel. Remove the bolt holding the lower-right end of the instrument panel to the side cowling. Remove the instrument panel pad.

5. Remove the clip holding the center register duct bracket to the plenum; rotate the clip up and to the right.

Remove the screws holding the rear side of the floor air duct to the plenum, and, if necessary, remove the two screws holding the partial panel door vacuum motor to the mounting bracket to gain access to the right-hand screw. Remove the nuts from along the lower flange of the discharge air plenum.

6. Carefully move the plenum to the rear to allow the heater core tubes and the stud at the top of the plenum to clear the holes in the dash panel. Rotate the top of the plenum downward, forward, and out from under

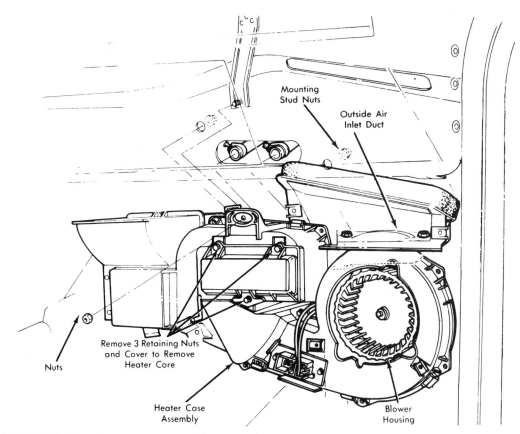

FIGURE 11-20.   Heater case assembly removal. *Courtesy of Ford Motor Co.*

the instrument panel. Carefully pull the lower edge of the instrument panel to the rear while rolling the plenum from behind it. Remove the plenum from the car.

7. Place the heating unit on a workbench, remove the retaining screws from the core cover, and remove the cover. Remove the retaining screw from the tube bracket and pull the heater core from the case and plenum assembly. Reverse these procedures to install the heater core back into the case and plenum assembly. Make certain that the seal is properly positioned.

8. To install the heating unit into the car, reverse the above procedures. Adjust the control cables as outlined under the proper heading above.

Heater Core Replacement: Capri, Cougar, Escort, EXP, Fairmont, Granada, LN7, Lynx, Mustang, and Zephyr. When replacing the heater core on these models, use the following procedures:

1. Disconnect the negative battery terminal, drain the engine coolant from the radiator, and disconnect the heater water hoses; plug the hoses and the core tubes to prevent water leaking into the interior of the car. Remove the glove box liner and the instrument panel to cowling brace.

2. Place the temperature control lever in the WARM position. Remove the heater core cover screws. Remove the heater case mounting stud nuts located in the engine compartment.

3. Push the heater core tubes and the seal to the rear into the passenger compartment. Remove the heater core through the glove box area.

4. To install the heater core, reverse the removal procedures for the appropriate model being repaired.

Heater Core Replacement: Thunderbird and XR7. When replacing the heater core in these models, use the following procedures:

1. Disconnect the battery negative terminal. Drain the engine coolant from the radiator and remove the water hoses from the core tubes. Plug the tubes to prevent water leaking into the interior of the car. Remove the instrument panel. Remove the screw holding the air inlet duct and the blower housing assembly to the cowling top panel.

2. Disconnect the vacuum supply hose from the vacuum check valve. Disconnect the ground wire from the blower motor and the wire harness from the resistor and blower motor. Remove the nuts holding the heater assembly to the dash panel, which are located in the engine compartment.

3. Remove the screw holding the heater assembly support bracket to the cowling top panel, located inside the car. Remove the nuts from the brackets at the left end and beneath the heater assembly. Pull the heater assembly away from the dash panel and remove the heater assembly.

4. To install a new heater core, remove the heater assembly just enough to have access to the heater core access cover located on top of the heater assembly. Remove the retaining screws from the access cover and remove the heater core from the

case. To install the heater core, reverse this procedure.

5. To install the heater assembly into the car, reverse the procedures listed in steps 1 through 3.

Blower Motor Replacement: Ford and Mercury. When replacing the blower motor on these models, use the following procedures:

1. Disconnect the negative battery terminal at the battery. Disconnect the ground wire from the blower motor and the engine. Disconnect the blower motor lead connector from the wiring harness hard shell connector. Remove the blower motor cooling tube from the blower motor.

2. Remove the screws from the blower mounting plate. Turn the blower motor and wheel assembly so that the bottom edge of the mounting plate follows the wheel well splash panel contour. Lift the blower assembly up and out of the housing assembly.

3. To install the blower motor, reverse the above procedures. Check the unit for proper operation.

Blower Motor Replacement: Capri, Cougar, Fairmont, Granada, Mustang, and Zephyr. When replacing the blower motor on these models, use the following procedures:

1. Disconnect the negative terminal at the battery. Remove the right ventilator assembly. Remove the hub clamp spring from the blower wheel hub and slide the blower wheel off the motor shaft.

2. Remove the three motor flange holding screws located inside the blower housing. Pull the blower motor out of the housing and disconnect the wires from the motor.

3. To install the blower motor, reverse the above procedures.

Blower Motor Replacement: Escort, EXP, LN7, and Lynx. When replacing the blower motor in these models, use the following procedures:

1. Disconnect the negative battery terminal. Remove the air intake and blower housing assembly from the car. Remove the four mounting screws from the mounting plate. Remove the blower motor and wheel assembly from the housing. Do not remove the mounting plate from the blower motor.

2. To install the blower in the car, place the blower motor and wheel with the flat side of the flange near the blower outlet and reverse the above procedures.

Blower Motor Replacement: Thunderbird and XR7. When replacing the blower motor in these models, use the following procedures:

1. Disconnect the negative battery terminal. Remove the right ventilator assembly. Remove the clamp spring from the blower hub and pull the blower wheel from the shaft. Remove the three flange holding screws located inside the blower housing; remove the blower motor from the heater case. Disconnect the wires from the blower motor.

2. To install a blower motor in these models, reverse the above procedures.

Control Head Replacement: Ford and Mercury. When replacing the control head on these models, refer to the appropriate figure for the model under consideration (see Figures 11-21, 11-22, and 11-23).

1. Disconnect the negative battery terminal. Remove the radio knobs and open the ash tray. Remove the screws holding the center finish panel at the ash tray opening. Pull the lower edge of the finish panel outward and release the upper tabs of the finish panel from the instrument panel.

2. Remove the screws holding the control head to the instrument panel.

Remove the control assembly from the panel opening. Disconnect all wire connectors, vacuum harness, and the control cables from the control head. If necessary, remove the blower and defroster switch.

3. To install the control head on these models, reverse the above procedure. Note that on models equipped with a vacuum harness the retaining nut is pushed onto the post rather than screwed on.

Control Head Replacement: Thunderbird and XR7. When replacing the control head on these models, use the following procedures:

1. Disconnect the negative terminal at the battery. Remove the four screws holding the control assembly to the

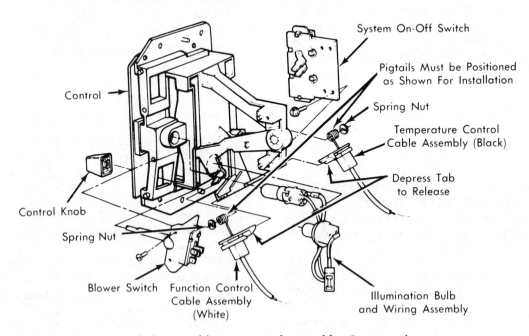

FIGURE 11-21. Exploded view of heater control assembly. *Courtesy of Ford Motor Co.*

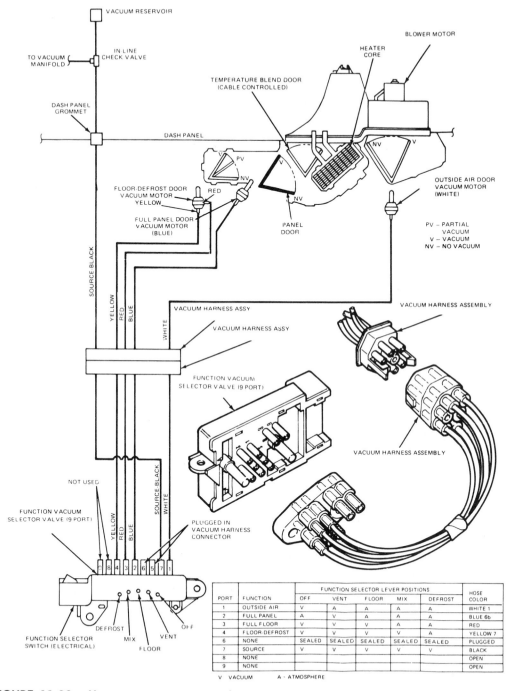

FIGURE 11-22. Heater system vacuum diagram (Ford and Mercury).
Courtesy of Ford Motor Co.

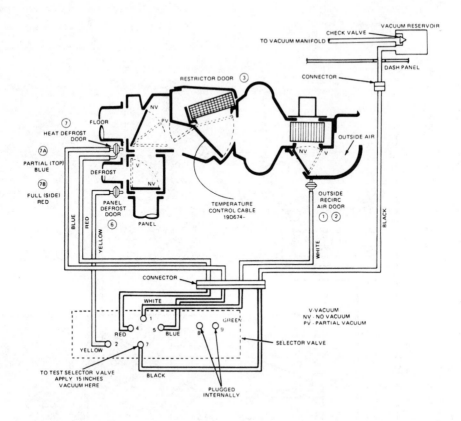

FUNCTION SELECTOR LEVER		DETENT POSITIONS					
PORT	FUNCTION	OFF	VENT	HI-LO	FLOOR	MIX	DEF
1	OUTSIDE-RECIRC	V	—	—	—	—	—
2	PANEL-DEF	V	V	V	—	—	—
3	SEALED	—	—	—	—	—	—
4	FULL FLOOR	V	—	—	V	—	—
5	PANEL-FLOOR	V	—	V	V	V	—
6	SEALED	—	—	—	—	—	—
7	SOURCE	V	V	V	V	V	V
8	OPEN	—	—	—	—	—	—
9	OPEN	—	—	—	—	—	—

FIGURE 11-23. Heater system vacuum diagram (all except Ford, Mercury, Thunderbird, and XR7). *Courtesy of Ford Motor Co.*

instrument panel. Remove the control head assembly from the instrument panel and disconnect all the wiring connectors, the vacuum harness, and the temperature control cable from the control assembly.

2. To install the control head on these models, reverse the above procedure.

Control Head Replacement: Capri, Cougar, Fairmont, Granada, Mustang, and Zephyr. When replacing the control head on these models, use the following procedures:

1. Disconnect the negative terminal from the battery. Remove the three screws holding the top edge of the instru-

ment cluster bezel, and remove the bezel to gain access to the control assembly. Remove the four screws holding the control assembly to the instrument panel. Pull the control head to the rear, away from the instrument panel. Remove the electrical wire harness connectors and the control housing attachments.

2. Disconnect the temperature and function control assemblies from the heater case assembly. Disconnect the blower speed switch and the control illumination wire harness wire connectors. Remove the control assembly with the control cables attached.

3. Remove the push nut holding the function cable end loop of the function control lever. Depress the white locking tang on the end of the function control housing, thus disengaging the function control cable and housing from the function lever tang and from the control assembly.

4. Remove the push nut holding the temperature cable end loop of the temperature control lever. Depress the black locking tang on the end of the temperature control cable housing assembly. Disengage the function control cable and housing assembly from the temperature lever tang and frame of the control assembly.

Control Head Replacement: Escort, EXP, LN7, and Lynx. When replacing the control head on these models, use the following procedures:

1. Disconnect the negative battery terminal at the battery. Remove the two screws holding the center panel to the instrument panel and unsnap the finish panel. Remove the four screws holding the control assembly to the instrument panel. Place the control assembly function lever in the OFF position. Place the temperature control lever in the COOL position. Disconnect the control clip from the door crank.

2. Disconnect the control cable housing from the cable bracket. Pull the control assembly out of the instrument panel and disconnect the wire connector from the blower switch. Remove the spring nuts connecting the control cables to the lever arms. Place the function lever in the DEFROST position and the temperature lever in the WARM position. Disconnect the control end loop from the control lever. Disconnect the control cable housing from the mounting bracket.

3. To install a control head on these models, reverse the removal procedure above.

Troubleshooting and Diagnosis. When troubleshooting and diagnosing troubles in Ford Motor Company cars, refer to Table 11-4.

TABLE 11-4. Troubleshooting and Diagnosis

Condition and Possible Cause	Condition and Possible Cause

Insufficient, erratic, or no heat or defrost
    Low radiator coolant
    Engine overheating
    Loose fan belt
    Thermostat
    Heater core plugged
    Loose or misaligned cables
    Vacuum hoses collapse, kinked, or crossed
    Air flow control doors sticking or binding
    Vacuum motor or hose leaks
    Defective or kinked water hoses
    Blocked air inlet
    Vent open
	Air from defroster in any control position
	    Severe vacuum system leak
	
	Cowl vent system leaks air
	    Vent door not fully closed

Too much heat
    Loose or misadjusted cables
    Temperature control door stuck fully open
	Blower does not operate properly
	    Blower motor
	    Blower resistor defective
	    Blower wire harness
	    Blower switch
	    Selector valve switch

Air flow changes direction when vehicle is accelerated
    Vacuum system leak
	Blower Motor Inoperative
	    Blown fuse
	    Open circuit

Courtesy of Ford Motor Co.

REVIEW QUESTIONS

1. What type of heating unit is used in American Motors cars?

2. In American Motors cars, in what position must the air control lever be placed for air to flow through both the floor ducts and the windshield ducts?

3. On an American Motors unit, which control lever controls the heater air and defroster door operation?

4. When adjusting the heater air and defroster damper door cable on an American Motors unit, what precaution should be taken?

5. What type of clip is used on the American Motors outside air door cable?

6. Where does the outside air enter the heating unit on Chrysler cars?

7. On Chrysler units, what operates the heater valve and the blend air door?

8. On Chrysler units, what do the red and yellow flags indicate?

9. What should be done to the battery before removing any of the automotive heating unit components?

10. On Ford Motor Company units, what determines the temperature of the discharge air?

Index